INTERNATIONAL LAW IN PUBLIC DEBATE

Public debates in the language of international law have occurred across the twentieth and twenty-first centuries and have produced a popular form of international law that matters for international practice. This book analyses the people who used international law and how they used it in debates over Australia's participation in the 2003 Iraq War, the Vietnam War and the First World War. It examines texts such as newspapers, parliamentary debates, public protests and other expressions of public opinion. It argues that these interventions produced a form of international law that shares a vocabulary and grammar with the expert forms of that language and distinct competences in order to be persuasive. This longer history also illustrates a move from the use of international legal language as part of collective justifications to the use of international law as an autonomous justification for state action.

MADELAINE CHIAM is a senior lecturer at La Trobe University Law School. She is also a founding member of the La Trobe International Legal Studies Research Group.

INTERNATIONAL LAW IN PUBLIC DEBATE

MADELAINE CHIAM
La Trobe University

CAMBRIDGE
UNIVERSITY PRESS

University Printing House, Cambridge CB2 8BS, United Kingdom

One Liberty Plaza, 20th Floor, New York, NY 10006, USA

477 Williamstown Road, Port Melbourne, VIC 3207, Australia

314–321, 3rd Floor, Plot 3, Splendor Forum, Jasola District Centre, New Delhi – 110025, India

79 Anson Road, #06-04/06, Singapore 079906

Cambridge University Press is part of the University of Cambridge.

It furthers the University's mission by disseminating knowledge in the pursuit of education, learning, and research at the highest international levels of excellence.

www.cambridge.org
Information on this title: www.cambridge.org/9781108499293
DOI: 10.1017/9781108588584

© Madelaine Chiam 2021

This publication is in copyright. Subject to statutory exception and to the provisions of relevant collective licensing agreements, no reproduction of any part may take place without the written permission of Cambridge University Press.

First published 2021

A catalogue record for this publication is available from the British Library.

ISBN 978-1-108-49929-3 Hardback

Cambridge University Press has no responsibility for the persistence or accuracy of URLs for external or third-party internet websites referred to in this publication and does not guarantee that any content on such websites is, or will remain, accurate or appropriate.

CONTENTS

Foreword	*page* ix
Acknowledgements	xii

1 International Law in Public Debate   1

  1.1 Two Stories   3
    1.1.1 The United Kingdom Iraq Inquiry Report, 2016   3
    1.1.2 The World Tribunal on Iraq, 2005   7
    1.1.3 What the Stories Tell Us   9

  1.2 Overview of the Book   11
    1.2.1 Choosing Australia and Choosing Wars   11
    1.2.2 The Argument   14

2 A 'Popular' International Law   18

  2.1 Producing Legality through 'Popular' Law   19

  2.2 Public Debate and Law as Language   22
    2.2.1 Public Debate and Its Texts   22
    2.2.2 International Law as Language   25
    2.2.3 Speakers and Analytical Tools   30

  2.3 Some Final Notes on Historical Method   36

3 Public Debate in 2003: The Iraq War   41

  3.1 Introduction   41

  3.2 Timing and Sources   42

  3.3 The Context   44
    3.3.1 The Howard Government's Australia   44
    3.3.2 Alignment with the Bush Administration   47

  3.3.3 Australia, the Security Council and the Final Push to War 51

 3.4 The Public Debate 56
  3.4.1 International Legal Language and Legality 57
  3.4.2 International Law as Self-Defence, Humanitarianism and the Just War 71
  3.4.3 International Law as Alliance 81

 3.5 Conclusion 84

4 Public Debate in 1965–66: The Vietnam War 89

 4.1 Introduction 89
 4.2 Timing and Sources 91
 4.3 The Contexts 94
 4.4 The Public Debate 107
  4.4.1 International Legal Language and Legality 108
  4.4.2 International Law as a Standard of Morality 121
  4.4.3 International Law as Alliance 128
 4.5 Conclusion 130

5 Public Debate in 1916: The First World War 134

 5.1 Introduction 134
 5.2 Timing and Sources 137
 5.3 The Context 138
 5.4 The Public Debate 148
  5.4.1 The Legal Quibble 149
  5.4.2 White Australia, Civil Liberties and Empire 152
  5.4.3 Equality of Sacrifice: A Different Internationalism 165
 5.5 Conclusion 170

6 Conclusion 174

 6.1 A Popular International Law 174
  6.1.1 Who Spoke International Legal Language? 174

	6.1.2	What Were the Characteristics of This Popular International Law?	177
	6.1.3	Generalising from the Particular	180
6.2	Some Final Observations		180

Bibliography 185
Index 212

FOREWORD

In one of his final poems, *The Solution,* Bertolt Brecht describes people who have lost the confidence of the government: "Would it not be easier" he writes, "...in that case for the government to dissolve the people..." (*Poems, 1913-1956,* 440). This idea of un-electing or disenfranchising people has regularly tempted some liberals in their off-the-record moments (especially in times of populism) and goes back, at least, to Plato and his rule of the philosopher kings.

Public international law and diplomacy is a kind of rule of the elites – a *raison de clercs*, if you will – a profession and service conducted by hyper-qualified individuals who speak a particular and, perhaps deliberately exclusionary, language with its show-off Latin phrases (*jus cogens, erga omnes*) and obscure modes of logic and thought. One very familiar item in the repertoire of international legal tics is a tendency to complain about (or celebrate) the ways in which international lawyers are misunderstood in the media ("how can you even respond to idiotic questions like that?") or around dinner tables ("they missed the point as usual") or at inter-disciplinary conferences ("they took me to be saying x, I was saying *exactly* the opposite") or by the political class ("hasn't the leader of the Dockers' Union ever heard of *rebus sic stantibus?*").

Madelaine Chiam's very fine study is an astringent corrective to all of this and to the associated commonplace that international law is what international lawyers do and say. Instead, *International Law in Public Debate* wants to enfranchise the people and give them, or give due weight to, their voice in international legal affairs. It is often supposed that this voice was first heard around the time of the Iraq War when everyone became an amateur international lawyer and legal opinions fell from the sky like confetti. Suddenly, international law was front-page news. This not only meant that international lawyers were greatly in demand (at first, this was thought to be a good thing) but it also meant that the untrained masses felt able to chip in as pseudo-scholars (a bad thing). In 2020, everyone is now an epidemiologist but, in 2003, the average person was an international legal theorist. The most common response to this from the international legal guild was twofold: it tended to treat these plebeian intrusions as bafflingly novel and it set about defending its shrinking patch of expert terrain.

Dr Chiam is having none of this (though she does argue that, in the case of Iraq, there were novel aspects to the way in which international legal arguments were marshalled and understood as autonomous zones of reasoning). In her book, she wants to take seriously the speech claims of those outside the profession and, just as importantly, she seeks to expose a long history of what might be termed international law's popular jurisprudence. Who speaks and who has spoken? These are the salient questions of this study.

She answers these questions across several case studies opening with a survey of legal argumentation around the Iraq War including in the UK's Chilcot Report, which, in voluminous detail, refused the invitation to pronounce on the legality of the war, and at the World Tribunal on Iraq convened in Turkey and the United States. In each case, the perennial question of authorisation to speak looms large, a question that leads Dr Chiam, in a diverting encounter with the ancients, back to Thucydides and Herodotus (she favours the latter's more plural – perhaps demotic – view of the historical material). But *International Law in Public Debate* is not sited in classical Greece or contemporary London, New York or Istanbul. This is, instead, an Australian account of international legal speech, an account of speech from the semi-periphery, or as Dr Chiam puts it, in "an unusual location".

And so, there are chapters devoted to international legal controversies during the Iraq War, around the time of the Vietnam conflict and arising out of the Great War. These chapters provide a thickly textured and illuminating foundation for the central conceptual claims about the polyphony of lawful voices and texts, the relationship between law as an autonomous source of authority (Iraq) and law as an ingredient in a broader strategy of persuasion and justification, and the need to place legal argument in its proper socio-political context.

At its best, though, a book is much more than just its central theses (however persuasive, as in this case, these arguments are) and Dr Chiam's study is gloriously enlivened by its unexpected details and its colourful digressions ranging from the television debate in late March 2003 between ABC News presenter Kerry O'Brien (armed with the opinions of Oxford and Cambridge international lawyers) and John Howard, the Australian Prime Minister (clutching the legal advice of his own government lawyers and doubting the experience of the Oxbridge professors; "I'm sure they are very learned", he says at one point), to the exchange of letters between a group of bishops and an earlier Prime Minister, Robert Menzies, over the legality of the Vietnam War (later to be published as a pamphlet by his government) to the raucous, cabbage-throwing, town hall meetings around Australia in the second half of 1916 where the rights and wrongs of the Great War were being debated.

As I write this, a fresh storm has broken over the Johnson Government's statement that it will be willing to break international law in a "specific and limited way" as part of its bargaining with the European Union over the Irish Question. Lawyers have had their say, of course, but again, I have been reminded of Dr Chiam's important argument that international law is also public speech. This book – a book I am delighted to see published – gives us the intellectual equipment to think through these moments (and they will recur) with a keener awareness of the stakes involved, and a richer appreciation of their location in a history of such moments.

Gerry Simpson
London, 1 October 2020

ACKNOWLEDGEMENTS

It has taken ten years to write this book. In that time, my children have grown into teenagers, my husband has had four different jobs, we have moved house, acquired a mortgage, nurtured guinea pigs, a dog and a cat, and destroyed a shamefully large number of tomato plants. And, as with any decade-long project, there are many people to thank. I hope that all of the people mentioned in these pages know how fortunate I feel to have them as a part of my life. And that anyone I have forgotten forgives me.

This book began as my doctoral thesis at the Melbourne Law School (MLS), which was an energetic and stimulating place to undertake such a project. Gerry Simpson was a demanding and inspiring supervisor, fitting into our sometimes fifteen-minute conversations enough nuggets of feedback to keep me going for weeks. And he made me laugh – a most underrated quality in PhD supervisors. I thank Gerry for his wise counsel, his support and his always insightful comments. As a co-supervisor, Ann Genovese was unfailingly patient and attentive, and I thank her for her careful and committed approach to my project. Hilary Charlesworth became my third PhD supervisor after Gerry moved to the London School of Economics, and I thank Hilary for the joy and privilege of working with her again.

My professional life would be greatly impoverished without the conversations, friendship, support, fearlessness and critical eyes of the many scholars whom I am lucky to have as comrades. For enriching my PhD experience at MLS in formal and informal ways, I give heartfelt thanks to Jason Bosland, Maria Elander, Michelle Foster, Barbara Keys, Jonathan Kolieb, Rain Liivoja, Dylan Lino, Simon McKenzie, Caitlin Mahar, Anne Orford, Bruce Oswald, Sundhya Pahuja, James Parker, Sasha Radin, Sophie Rigney, Cait Storr, Adrienne Stone and John Tobin. I have been working at the wonderful La Trobe Law School since 2017 and for their support through the process of putting this book together I thank Tom Andrews, Lola Akin Ojelabi, Julia Dehm, Maria Elander (again), Laura Griffin, Emma Henderson, Fiona Kelly, Anita Mackay, Francine

ACKNOWLEDGEMENTS   xiii

Rochford, Kerstin Steiner, Savitri Taylor and Marc Trabsky. I stumbled into engagement with the Harvard Law School Institute for Global Law and Policy (IGLP) in 2013, and the experience has been transformational. For the opportunities they have given me through IGLP, I thank David Kennedy and Kristen Verdeaux. And for their different contributions to my thinking via our many IGLP-related encounters, I thank Antony Anghie, Matt Craven, Deval Desai, Karen Engle, Luis Eslava, Michael Fakhri, Christopher Gevers, Kate Grady, Vanja Hamzic, Richard Joyce, Adil Hasan Khan, Tor Krever, Vidya Kumar, Frederic Megret, Zina Miller, Vasuki Nesiah, Zoran Oklopcic, Rose Parfitt, Genevieve Painter, Charlie Peevers, Jothie Rajah and Kerry Rittich.

Three people in particular have been companions throughout the writing of this book. They were there at the start of my PhD, they remain 'there' in the electronic ways in which we now communicate, and they are wonderful friends and readers. For all that they have contributed to this book and to my everyday life, I thank Monique Cormier, Alison Duxbury and Anna Hood.

Dino Kritsiotis and Karen Knop examined the thesis on which this book is based, and three anonymous readers reviewed this book for Cambridge University Press. All of them wrote extraordinarily helpful reports for which I am grateful. I gained valuable feedback on the theory and method parts of this book from an 'Early Career Workshop' organised by Anne Orford's Laureate project at MLS. For their feedback in that Workshop, I thank Luis Bogliolo, Sara Dehm, Kathryn Greenman, Martti Koskenniemi, Anne Orford, Ntina Tzouvala, Fabia Vecoso and Pal Wrange. For reading and commenting so generously on different parts of this book, I thank Tom Andrews, Monique Cormier, Kirsty Duncanson, Alison Duxbury, Maria Elander, Christopher Gevers, Kate Grady, Laura Griffin, Anna Hood, Vidya Kumar, Charlie Peevers, Jon Piccini and Emma Russell.

I am grateful to the La Trobe University Social Research Assistance Platform for funding to help with the completion of this book and to Kate McIntosh and Wendy Monaghan for their work on indexing and editing. My primary source of PhD funding was an Australian Government Research Training Program Scholarship. I also received funding from the MLS Research Support Funds, the Asia Pacific Centre of Military Law, the Australian and New Zealand Society of International Law and the IGLP. I presented parts of Chapter 3 to Cold War International Law Workshops in Melbourne and London, funded in part by the Australian Research Council (Australia) and the Arts and Humanities Research

Council (UK). I thank the participants of all those events for their comments. Parts of Chapter 5 appear in similar form in 'Tom Barker's "To Arms!" Poster: Internationalism and Resistance in First World War Australia' (2017) *London Review of International Law* 125. Parts of Chapter 4 have been published in 'More than a "Parlour Game": International Law in Australian Public Debate, 1965–1966', Matthew Craven, Sundhya Pahuja and Gerry Simpson (eds), *International Law and the Cold* War (Cambridge University Press, 2020) 214–231.

For their unwavering support throughout the writing of this book and the PhD, I thank my family (who are too numerous to name). And for helping me to keep the book in perspective, I thank Melissa Abrahams and Lee Cath. My mother's generosity and child-minding skills allowed me to work on this project when I otherwise could not have. I thank her, Helen Walsh, for all she has done for me and ask her forgiveness for ten years of failing to answer when she asked me how the thesis/book was going.

This book would not exist without the patience, support and understanding of Jason Cormier, who deserves more thanks than any words can express. It would have been quicker and, presumably, easier to have written a book before I had children, but it would not have been *this* book. And for all the reasons that I have identified in these acknowledgements and more, I am happy to have (finally!) written *this* book. This is for Saskia, Francesca and Jason.

1

International Law in Public Debate

The 2003 Iraq War was a key moment for international law. As an event,[1] the War has generated reams of literature and remains a touchstone for many international legal analyses.[2] As part of public debate, the War is seen as the point at which international legal argument moved from the periphery to the centre of public and political consciousness.[3] At the height of the Iraq debates, Phillip Allott and Alan Dashwood wrote that '[t]he question of legality of the use of armed force against Iraq has assumed a surprising prominence'.[4] Allott and Dashwood lamented this state of affairs, suggesting that the international law on the use of force was too complex to be a subject of public debate. Such law was not, they wrote, 'a set of laws to be construed and applied like a Road Traffic

---

[1] Fleur Johns, Richard Joyce and Sundhya Pahuja (eds.), *Events: The Force of International Law* (Routledge, 2010).

[2] Sources here are too many to cite. For a small sample, see, for example, Richard Falk, *The Costs of War: International Law, the UN and World Order after Iraq* (Taylor & Francis, 2012); Charlotte Peevers, *The Politics of Justifying Force: The Suez Crisis, the Iraq War and International Law* (Oxford University Press, 2013); 'Agora: The Case of Iraq: International Law and Politics' (2011) 42 *Netherlands Yearbook of International Law* 69; Philippe Sands, *Lawless World: America and the Making and Breaking of Global Rules* (Allen Lane, 2005); Mark Mazower, *Governing the World: The History of an Idea* (Penguin Press, 2012).

[3] See, for example, Hilary Charlesworth, 'Saddam Hussein: My Part in His Downfall' (2005) 23 *Wisconsin International Law Journal* 127; Matthew Craven et al., 'We Are Teachers of International Law' (2004) 17 *Leiden Journal of International Law* 363; Gerry Simpson, 'Warriors, Humanitarians, Lawyers: The Howard Government and the Use of Force' (2008) 27 *Australian Yearbook of International Law* 143; Gerry Simpson, '"Stop Calling it Aggression": War as Crime' (2008) *Current Legal Problems* 191; John Strawson, 'Provoking International Law: War and Regime change in Iraq' in Fleur Johns, Richard Joyce and Sundhya Pahuja (eds.), *Events: The Force of International Law* (Routledge, 2010) 246. For critiques of the rise of international law in public debate, see, for example, David Kennedy, *Of War and Law* (Princeton University Press, 2006); Samuel Moyn, 'From Antiwar Politics to Antitorture Politics' in Austin Sarat, Lawrence Douglas and Martha Merrill (eds.), *Law and War* (Stanford University Press, 2014) 154.

[4] Phillip Allott and Alan Dashwood, 'Letter to the Editor', *The Times* (London, 19 March 2003) 23.

Act'.⁵ Later, Stephen Toope suggested that 'at no time in recent world history has international law ... been more debated by elites and even by the person in the street'.⁶ And Dapo Akande captured the surprise and relief of many (self-flagellating) international lawyers when he wrote during the UK Iraq War Inquiry that '[I]nternational law mattered!'.⁷

A careful look at events over the twentieth century suggests, however, that, rather than being a new phenomenon in 2003, there has been a long practice of using the language of international law within public debates. In this book, I argue that public debates in the language of international law have occurred across the twentieth and now twenty-first centuries and that the uses of international law in these debates have produced a popular form of international law that matters for international practice. I make this argument by analysing the people who used international law and how they used it in debates over Australia's participation in the 2003 Iraq War, the Vietnam War and the First World War. I examine a series of texts that constituted interventions in the debates from three main groups of people – politicians, trade unions and religious groups. I argue that these interventions produced a popular form of international law that shares a vocabulary and grammar with the expert forms of that language, and that speakers in public debates display distinct competences in the popular form in order to be persuasive.

Existing scholarship has generally examined international law in public debates for how it helps to explain other phenomena, in particular decision-making by governments.⁸ This book gives a different account of international law in public debates by investigating the uses of that language for what it can tell us about the development of international law itself. Viewing the 2003 Iraq War debates in a longer history suggests that those debates were different from earlier ones, but not because there was a shift from the absence to the presence of international law. Rather,

---

⁵ Ibid.

⁶ Stephen J Toope, 'Public Commitment to International Law: Canadian and British Media Perspectives on the Use of Force' in Christopher PM Waters (ed.), *British and Canadian Perspectives on International Law* (Brill, 2006) 17. See also Martti Koskenniemi, 'What Should International Lawyers Learn from Karl Marx?' (2004) 17 *Leiden Journal of International Law* 229, 244–46.

⁷ Dapo Akande, 'How and Why International Law Matters – Lessons from the UK's Iraq Inquiry', *EJIL: Talk! Blog of the European Journal of International Law* (Blog Post, 31 January 2010) www.ejiltalk.org/how-and-why-international-law-matters-lessons-from-the-uks-iraq-inquiry/.

⁸ See, for example, Peevers (n 2); Philip Liste, '"Public" International Law? Democracy and Discourses of Legal Reality' (2011) 42 *Netherlands Yearbook of International Law* 177.

the 2003 debates saw a change in the competences needed to be persuasive in those debates. Specifically, the 2003 debates illustrate a move from the use of international legal language as part of collective justifications to the use of international law as an autonomous justification for state actions. This move is a central characteristic of a popular international law that I begin to unravel in this book.

In this chapter, I present the first step in that unravelling by describing two events that arose out of the 2003 Iraq War: the release of the Report of the Iraq Inquiry in the United Kingdom ('Iraq Inquiry') and the outcomes of the World Tribunal on Iraq ('WTI'). These examples serve two purposes. First, they illustrate the three questions that this book has asked of public debates: who spoke – and who was considered to have authority to speak – international legal language? What forms of international legal language did speakers use? How did speakers characterise their uses of international law? Second, they provide context for the analysis in Chapters 3, 4 and 5. My curiosity about the role of international law in the 2003 Iraq War debates gave rise to the three questions I ask in this book, and it was with those questions that I examined the Vietnam War and First World War debates. The examples of the Iraq Inquiry and the WTI illustrate how international law continues to form part of public debate and they underpin the need to understand better how this form of international legal language works.

1.1 Two Stories

1.1.1 The United Kingdom Iraq Inquiry Report, 2016

On 6 July 2016, the Iraq Inquiry released its report into the UK's role in the 2003 invasion of Iraq.[9] The Report was the result of a seven-year investigation by a committee of Privy Counsellors, chaired by Sir John Chilcot, who analysed written evidence and oral testimony in relation to the circumstances surrounding the UK's decision to participate in the 2003 Iraq War. In his Statement introducing the Report, Chilcot noted that the Inquiry had 'not expressed a view on whether military action was legal' because the Inquiry was not 'a properly constituted and internationally recognised Court'.[10] The Report's lack of

---

[9] *The Report of the Iraq Inquiry: Report of a Committee of Privy Counsellors* (6 July 2016) (*The Report of the Iraq Inquiry*).
[10] The Iraq Inquiry, 'Statement by Sir John Chilcot', 6 July 2016, 4 ('Statement by Sir John Chilcot') https://webarchive.nationalarchives.gov.uk/20171123123519/http://www.iraqinquiry.org.uk/media/247010/2016-09-06-sir-john-chilcots-public-statement.pdf

a conclusion on the question of legality was consistent with the Inquiry's terms of reference.[11] Nevertheless, Chilcot's suggestion that such a conclusion was only open to a 'properly constituted' international court displayed a formalist view of international legality that was also exhibited in the construction of Chilcot's Statement and in the Report itself.

Chilcot's avoidance of a decision on legality was the second of the four major points in his Statement.[12] In the comments immediately surrounding his explanation on legality, Chilcot concluded that the UK's support for the invasion of Iraq had 'undermin[ed] the Security Council's authority', and that 'the circumstances in which it was decided that there was a legal basis for UK military action were far from satisfactory'.[13] Depending on how one counts it, the material used to support this non-conclusion occupied at least 350 pages of the Report itself.[14] Those 350 pages contained detailed accounts of the discussions within the UK government and between the UK and its Security Council counterparts on the drafting of Security Council Resolution 1441, the interpretation of which was so significant in the debate over the legality of the Iraq invasion.[15] About 170 of those 350 pages were devoted to a fine-grained account of the public and private processes surrounding the provision of legal advice on the proposed invasion to then Prime Minister Tony Blair, and the negotiations over a second Security Council resolution, which could have provided legal authorisation for invading Iraq.[16] The Report contains forensic detail – from Foreign Secretary Jack Straw asking whether it was possible for a Permanent Member of the Council to vote against a resolution without

---

[11] See Sir John Chilcot, 'Statement by Sir John Chilcot, Chairman of the Iraq Inquiry, at a News Conference, 30 July 2009', *The Iraq Inquiry* (Media Statement, 30 July 2009) www.iraqinquiry.org.uk/the-inquiry/news-archive/2009/2009-07-30-opening/statement-by-sir-john-chilcot-chairman-of-the-iraq-inquiry-at-a-news-conference-on-thursday-30-july-2009/.

[12] The other three points are the process through which the formal decision for invasion was made, the assessments of Iraq's weapons of mass destruction and the shortcomings in planning and preparation for the invasion: Statement by Sir John Chilcot (n 10) 2, 5 and 7.

[13] Statement by Sir John Chilcot (n 10) 4.

[14] I am counting here the following two sections of the actual report *The Report of the Iraq Inquiry* (n 9): section 3.5 'Development of UK Strategy and Options, September to November 2002: The Negotiation of Resolution 1441' and section 5 'Advice on the Legal Basis for Military Action, November 2002 to March 2003'. Depending on how one conceives of the legal case for war, more sections of the report could be included.

[15] 'Report of Iraq Inquiry' (n 9) Section 3.5.

[16] Ibid., Section 5.

that acting as a veto (the "short answer is 'no'");[17] to a description of Attorney-General Lord Goldsmith's meeting with Prime Ministerial officials on 27 February 2003 as one in which he 'advised that the safest legal course would be to secure a further Security Council resolution'.[18] Notwithstanding this level of detail about the law, Chilcot characterised the Report as having reserved judgment on the question of legality.

How can we reconcile Chilcot's claim not to be making a legal judgment with the Report's inclusion of so many pages of material directed at enabling the determination of exactly such a question? What is that marshalling of recollection, documentation and conclusion if not a contribution to the debate on the international legality of the Iraq War? Chilcot and the other Privy Counsellors characterised their description as a question of process; an account of the circumstances in which the decision about legality was taken ('not law'), which was somehow different from the decision itself ('law'). Others viewed their conclusions differently. Philippe Sands characterised the Report's reluctance as 'pull[ing] ... punches', arguing that the Inquiry had access to 'plenty of material ... which would have allowed it to express a view on the war's legality'.[19] John Prescott, UK Deputy Prime Minister at the time of the Iraq War, issued a public apology for his role and on the basis of the Report's conclusions admitted to 'now' believing that the War was illegal.[20] Some have seized on the potential of the Report's lack of conclusion on legality. John Bellinger, former legal adviser to the US government and one of the negotiators of Resolution 1441, read the Report's failure to 'criticize' Lord Goldsmith's eventual advice that an invasion would be legal as implicit acknowledgement of the plausibility, even correctness, of that position.[21] Oona Hathaway, on the other hand, saw the Report as further support for the existing and widely expressed repudiation of Lord Goldsmith's legal justification for the Iraq War.[22]

---

[17] Ibid., 90.
[18] Ibid., 81.
[19] Philippe Sands, 'A Grand and Disastrous Deceit' (2016) 38 *London Review of Books*, 9–11.
[20] John Prescott, 'John Prescott reveals his guilt at the "illegal" Iraq War will haunt him for the rest of his life' *Mirror* (online), 10 July 2016 www.mirror.co.uk/news/uk-news/john-prescott-reveals-guilt-illegal-8387319.
[21] John Bellinger, 'The Chilcot Inquiry and the Legal Basis for the Iraq War', *Lawfare* (Blog Post, 11 July 2016) www.lawfareblog.com/chilcot-inquiry-and-legal-basis-iraq-war.
[22] Oona Hathaway, 'What the Chilcot Report Teaches Us about National Security Lawyering', *Just Security* (Forum Post, 11 July 2016) www.justsecurity.org/31946/chilcot-report-teaches-national-security-lawyering/.

The Report displayed a highly formalist view of international law, where the circumstances surrounding the UK government's decision to go to war were characterised as politics, only the final determination on legality was law, and the distinction between them was concrete. Such a characterisation entrenches two related views about international law. First, that international legality is a status that can be definitively determined and, second, that any such determination can only be made by a 'properly constituted' international court. The Report's formalist account of international law has allowed for multiple interpretations of the legality question including, in the case of Hathaway and Bellinger, support for their opposing views on the Iraq War.

Perhaps it is not surprising that such a formalist characterisation of international law emerged from an inquiry into the 2003 Iraq War. It was, after all, this War that generated the view that international law had never 'been more debated by elites and even by the person in the street',[23] many of whom, with no professional expertise in international law, condemned the War as illegal. The formalism of the Report was likely one consequence of its status as an official history of the UK's involvement in the Iraq War.[24] It can also be read as a response to, and a retreat from, the idea that *anyone* – not just expert lawyers – can make an assessment of international legality. In the eyes of the Iraq Inquiry, only formally constituted institutions, and the individuals connected to them, are authorised speakers of international legal language. And the authoritative form of international law is that produced by and for such formally constituted institutions. Not everyone shared the Report's view of international law. The varied reactions of Prescott, Sands, Bellinger and Hathaway resisted the Report's formalism, and emphasised how its conclusions remain open to the multiple interpretations that are enabled by the indeterminacy of international law.[25]

---

[23] Toope (n 6) 17.
[24] On this point, see Charlotte Peevers, 'Media Spectacles of Legal Accountability in the Reporting of an Official History' (2018) 87 *The British Yearbook of International Law* 231.
[25] I use 'indeterminacy' here in two senses: (a) in the sense that words have multiple meanings and thus legal arguments can be made to support any position, and (b) in the sense developed by Martti Koskenniemi in which the structure of international legal argumentation is governed by a radical indeterminacy. See Martti Koskenniemi, *From Apology to Utopia: The Structure of International Legal Argument* (Cambridge University Press, reissue, 2005) (*From Apology to Utopia*).

1.1.2 The World Tribunal on Iraq, 2005

Eleven years before Chilcot and his colleagues issued their Report, a collection of civil society and anti-war activists made a different assessment of the Iraq War. Developed in the tradition of peoples' tribunals, the World Tribunal on Iraq (WTI) was a 'transnational platform where the war on Iraq could be publicly judged'.[26] The WTI consisted of a series of national hearings, the momentum for which developed through the mass anti-war movements around the world against the Iraq invasion.[27] The hearings culminated in a three-day event in Istanbul in June 2005 designed to bring together the material from the earlier hearings, listen to further evidence and issue conclusions.[28] In Istanbul, a 'panel of advocates', led by Richard Falk, presented fifty-four testimonies to a 'jury of conscience', led by Arundhati Roy and consisting of individuals with backgrounds in the arts, education and civil society, and only one lawyer.[29] These testimonies held the legality of the Iraq War to be a central concern, but they also covered other issues, including the effects of the War on the environment and public health, and the role of the mainstream media in propagating war.[30]

From its inception, the WTI had characterised itself as a project of protest against both the states that had led the Iraq invasion and the international system that had failed to stop them. In her speech at the opening of the Istanbul proceedings, Roy described the WTI as an act of resistance – 'a defense mounted against one of the most cowardly wars ever fought in history'.[31] The WTI, working in the name of 'humanity', made the question of legality central to its work. The Tribunal heard testimony from many individuals, including members of Iraqi civil society, and marshalled a significant volume of evidence into an 'International Law Appendix'.[32] The WTI concluded by issuing a declaration from the Jury of Conscience, read by Roy to the

---

[26] Ayça Çubukçu, *For the Love of Humanity: The World Tribunal on Iraq* (University of Pennsylvania Press, 2018) 4. For a comprehensive account of the WTI, see also Müge Gürsoy Sökmen (ed), *World Tribunal on Iraq; Making the Case Against War* (Olive Branch Press, 2008).

[27] Craig Borowiak, 'The World Tribunal on Iraq: Citizens' Tribunals and the Struggle for Accountability' (2008) 30 *New Political Science* 161.

[28] Falk (n 2) 177.

[29] Ibid., 178.

[30] Borowiak (n 27) 179.

[31] Arundhati Roy, 'Opening Statement on Behalf of the Jury of Conscience of the World Tribunal of Iraq' (Speech, World Tribunal on Iraq, Istanbul, 24 June 2005).

[32] Falk (n 2) 178–79.

participants on 27 June 2005.[33] Grounding its legitimacy in the 'collective conscience of humanity', the Declaration's 'Overview of Findings' opened with the statement that '[t]he invasion and occupation of Iraq was and is illegal'.[34] The Declaration laid sixteen 'charges' against the United States and the United Kingdom, six against the UN Security Council and a range of others against different governments, private corporations and the media.[35] The charges against the United States and the United Kingdom included 'waging the supreme crime of a war of aggression', 'targeting the civilian population of Iraq', 'redefining torture in violation of international law' and 'committing a crime against peace'.[36] The recommendations of the Jury included 'recognizing the right of the Iraqi people to resist the illegal occupation of their country', 'the immediate and unconditional withdrawal of the coalition forces' and 'an exhaustive investigation of those responsible for crimes of aggression and crimes against humanity', a list of individuals that included George W Bush and Tony Blair.[37] In total, the Declaration of the Jury of Conscience used the word 'illegal' (or derivations of it) fifteen times. Falk's view, as leader of the advocates, was that the determinations of the Jury were 'fully consistent with leading academic discussions that reach comparable conclusions'.[38]

But in a project of protest against the international legal system itself, the question of legality was a fraught one. The WTI foregrounded the tension between critiquing the international legal system and using that same system to speak law back to power. Ayça Çubukçu has described the WTI participants as acknowledging though not resolving the 'lived tensions between *legalist* and *political* imaginaries that animate rival visions of global peace and justice'.[39] But it was legal imaginaries that dominated the Jury Declaration's argument that 'the impunity [of the US and its allies] has created a serious international crisis that questions the import and significance of international law, of human rights covenants and of ... international institutions',[40] and the Jury's aim to use that system both to construct the charges of illegality and to address them.

[33] Jury of Conscience, 'Declaration of Jury of Conscience World Tribunal on Iraq: Istanbul 23–27 June 2005' (2005) 81 *Feminist Review* 95.
[34] Ibid., 96.
[35] Ibid., 97–100.
[36] Ibid., 97–99.
[37] Ibid., 101.
[38] Falk (n 2) 179.
[39] Çubukçu (n 26) 16 (emphasis in original).
[40] Jury of Conscience (n 33) 96.

The legal imaginary is apparent too in Richard Falk's reflections on the WTI, where he describes the Jury as an 'organ of conscience that made no pretense to be an expert legal body' but that also sought to 'lift its views above morality and politics [by paying] great attention ... [to] arguments relating to the legality of the Iraq War'.[41]

Although not formally constituted by a state nor having any international legal status, the WTI did not hesitate to draw conclusions that international law had been violated by the Iraq invasion. For the WTI participants, international law was many things; it was a legal standard, of course, but it was more. The WTI framed international law as a standard of humanity against which the actions of individuals and states could be, and were, judged. It was a language of solidarity too. The thousands of participants in the national hearings and in Istanbul, with their different backgrounds and priorities, were brought together by a shared sense that the Iraq War was not only wrong but *illegal*. The WTI participants rejected the deference to professional expertise displayed by the Iraq Inquiry, insisting that international law was more than a language of experts. They used international law to speak to the perpetrator states and to the experts themselves, challenging them to uphold the law to which they had professed commitment. The participants in the WTI process did not share the formalist view of international law that was expressed by the Report; they expressed an egalitarian view of what international law is and who is authorised to speak it.

1.1.3 What the Stories Tell Us

In their treatments of international law, the Report and the WTI reproduce a distinction that historians Ann Curthoys and John Docker have located in the legacies of the ancient historians Herodotus and Thucydides: the question of who is authorised to speak.[42] Both Herodotus and Thucydides wrote about war, but the legacy of their different approaches privileged state-based, masculinist histories. Thucydides regarded war – and its associated public and male politics – as the only subject worthy of recording for posterity.[43] In his claim to be writing an account of the 'truth' of the Peloponnesian Wars, Thucydides

---

[41] Falk (n 2) 179.
[42] Ann Curthoys and John Docker, *Is History Fiction?* (UNSW Press, 2010) 12–32.
[43] Thucydides, *History of the Peloponnesian War*, tr Rex Warner (Penguin Classics, 1974). Thucydides described his approach as 'better evidence than that of ... the prose chroniclers, who are less interested in telling truth than in catching the attention of their public,

recorded the views and actions of a narrow band of people – the leaders of the warring parties. Thucydides' exclusions governed the contours of military and political history for centuries; everything outside of this canon was 'not only irrelevant but *unserious*'.[44] Herodotus, on the other hand, investigated war for what it revealed about the culture, habits and motivations of the warring people; his accounts tell of the personal motivations of the protagonists and the details of everyday lives.[45] Herodotus' multi-vocal style and his fondness for authorial intervention meant that his *Histories* of the Greco-Persian wars included multiple versions of the same event. Herodotus' work is an example of the kinds of stories that are told through histories that take multiple voices as their subject.[46]

The Report and the WTI can be seen as instantiations of Thucydidean and Herodotean approaches towards international law. In the monologic view of the Iraq Inquiry, only a properly constituted international court was authorised to pronounce on legality. This construction of international law denied even that the Iraq Inquiry members, experts who had been tasked by the State with assessing the UK government's decision-making process, were empowered to make a determination on legality. In contrast, the polyphonic WTI process took seriously the views on international legality of writers, civil society activists, journalists and others without formal legal training. Their approach cast international law as a language of both power and resistance, and one that could be democratised for the purposes of holding governments and international institutions to account.

---

whose authorities cannot be checked, and whose subject-matter, owing to the passage of time, is mostly lost in the unreliable streams of mythology': at 46–47.

[44] Peter Green, 'The Great Marathon Man' (online, 15 May 2008) 55 *The New York Review of Books* 33 (emphasis in original).

[45] Herodotus told, for example, of the advantage given to the Persians by 'the braying of the asses and the appearance of the mules . . . [which] . . . frightened the Scythian cavalry', of the dreams of the Athenian Hippias who was guiding the Persians to Athens, and of the strange blinding of the Athenian Epizelus during battle 'untouched either by sword or arrow': Herodotus, *The Histories*, tr George Rawlinson (*The Internet Classics Archive*) http://classics.mit.edu/Herodotus/history.html bk 4. See also Jennifer T Roberts, *Herodotus: A Very Short Introduction* (Oxford University Press, 2011) 99–112; Rosalind Thomas, 'Introduction' in Robert B Strassler (ed.), *The Landmark Herodotus: The Histories* (First Anchor Books, 2009); ix.

[46] Curthoys and Docker (n 42) 37, drawing on the work of Mikhail Bakhtin. See, for example, Mikhail Bakhtin, *Problems of Dostoevsky's Poetics* (Caryl Emerson trans, University of Minnesota Press, 1984). The twentieth-century moves to social, cultural and postmodern histories have opened up the imaginary possibilities of Herodotus' 'dazzlingly dissociative style': Robert D Kaplan, 'A Historian for Our Time' (Jan/Feb 2007) *The Atlantic Monthly* 78, 84.

Yet, while they differed on who had authority to speak international legal language, the Iraq Inquiry members and the WTI Jury shared a view that it was possible to arrive at a definitive determination on legality. The reluctance of both groups to acknowledge openly the indeterminacy of law seems to have arisen from a desire for a final determination of legality to have a measurable effect on the world, whether that was to justify or restrain government action or to avoid impunity of government and institutions. The unity on this point between the Iraq Inquiry and the WTI process points to commonalities in the ways that all participants in public debates think about the purposes of international law, even when they disagree on who can speak it. I explore these commonalities and differences briefly in the next section, and in detail in Chapters 3, 4 and 5.

1.2 Overview of the Book

1.2.1 Choosing Australia and Choosing Wars

In this book, I examine international law in the public debates about war in Australia and thus the generalisations about international law that I make are cautious ones. Any examination of public debate must take place in a context though – and my aim to trace the trajectory of international law in public debates across time has necessitated a deep look at one place. I chose to focus on Australia because it is my home, and the state with which I am most familiar. Choosing Australia as an object of international legal analysis also prises open some of the assumptions about eurocentrism in international law. Scholarship about eurocentrism in international legal histories nearly always uses the terms 'European' and 'Western' interchangeably, often without defining either.[47] This work assumes a shared understanding, at least

---

[47] See, for example, Antony Anghie, 'Western Discourses of Sovereignty' in Julie Evans, et al. (eds.), *Sovereignty – Frontiers of Possibility* (University of Hawai'i Press, 2013) 19; Arnulf Becker Lorca, 'Eurocentrism in the History of International Law' in Bardo Fassbender and Anne Peters (eds.), *The Oxford Handbook of the History of International Law* (Oxford University Press, 2012) 1034; Martti Koskenniemi, 'Histories of International Law: Dealing with Eurocentrism' (2011) 19 *Rechtsgeschichte*; Emmanuelle T Jouannet and Anne Peters, 'The *Journal of the History of International Law*: A Forum for New Research' (2014) 16 *Journal of the History of International Law* 1; Jean D'Aspremont, 'Critical Histories of International Law and the Repression of Disciplinary Imagination' (2019) 7 *London Review of International Law* 89. See also Arnulf Becker Lorca, *Mestizo International Law: A Global Intellectual History 1842–1933* (Cambridge University Press, 2014) for what Becker Lorca describes as a 'different, non-Eurocentric account' of the history of international law.

between the writers and their audiences, of who or what is meant by 'Europe' and the 'West'. To this extent, the terms represent what Dipesh Chakrabarty has described as 'hyperreal terms in that they refer to certain figures of imagination whose geographical referents remain somewhat indeterminate'.[48]

The figure of 'Australia' sits uncertainly within these shared understandings of 'Europe' and the 'West'. Not 'Europe' either geographically or historically, Australian society nevertheless shares many characteristics with 'Europe' and the 'West'. Australia's multiple past and present laws include those of a multicultural western liberal democracy, white settler-colony, British Dominion, constitutional monarchy and, pre-contact, home to an estimated 750,000 people who spoke up to 400 distinct languages.[49] Australians have played key roles in many international institutions, including in advocating for the racial exclusions and preservations of domestic sovereignty under the Charters of both the League of Nations and the United Nations.[50] In their separate work, Antony Anghie and Cait Storr have explored the many ways in which Australian governments in the first half of the twentieth century sought to assert Australian nationhood through sub-imperial authority over Papua New Guinea and Nauru.[51] These pluralities make it difficult to situate Australia within either the 'Europe' or the 'non-Europe' of

---

[48] Dipesh Chakrabarty, *Provincializing Europe: Postcolonial Thought and Historical Difference* (Princeton University Press, 2000) 27.

[49] These figures are from the Australian Museum, available at australianmuseum.net.au/indigenous-australia-introduction.

[50] See, for example, LF Fitzhardinge, *The Little Digger 1914–1952: William Morris Hughes, A Political Biography*, Vol II (Angus & Robertson, 1979) 370–418; Alison Pert and Hitoshi Nasu, 'Australia and International Organisations' in Donald R Rothwell and Emily Crawford (eds.), *International Law in Australia 3rd ed.* (Thomson Reuters 2016), Chapter 5; Madelaine Chiam, 'International Law in Australia (3rd ed.): Book Review' (2018) 35 *Australian Yearbook of International Law* 228. See also Madelaine Chiam, '*Tasmanian Dams* and Australia's Relationship with International Law' (2015) 24 *Griffith Law Review* 89; Madelaine Chiam, 'International Human Rights Treaties and Institutions in the Protection of Human Rights in Australia' in Matthew Groves, Janina Boughey and Dan Meagher, *The Legal Protection of Rights in Australia* (Hart 2019) 229; Hilary Charlesworth et al., 'Deep Anxieties: Australia and the International Legal Order' (2003) 25 *Sydney Law Review* 423; Donald R Rothwell and Emily Crawford (eds.), *International Law in Australia* (Thomson Reuters 2017).

[51] Antony Anghie, 'Race, Self-Determination and Australian Empire' (2018) 19 *Melbourne Journal of International Law* 1; Cait Storr, '"*Imperium in Imperio*": Sub-Imperialism and the Formation of Australia as a Subject of International Law' (2018) 19 *Melbourne Journal of International Law* 335; Cait Storr, *International Status in the Shadow of Empire: Nauru and the Histories of International Law* (Cambridge University Press, 2020).

traditional international legal histories.[52] They highlight the ambivalent position of Australia – and the other settler colonies – within the concept of eurocentrism in international law. This book offers stories from an unusual location for international law as a way of opening up the 'figures of imagination' for the field. Complicating the eurocentrism of international law is a necessary part of coming to terms with it.[53]

My examination of the role of international law in public debate in this book also focuses on debates about whether a state should participate in a war. As my analysis compares the uses of international legal language across three different time periods, I have focused on three events called 'war' that have raised questions over the nature and extent of Australia's participation in that war. The 2003 Iraq War, the Vietnam War and the First World War were all traditional inter-state wars between two or more states, but what matters for my analysis is that the debates of 2003, 1965–66 and 1916 occurred in a context that was called 'war' in public debate, not whether they were considered 'wars' by an international legal standard or any other measure. I have excluded consideration of the Second World War because that war did not generate in Australia a mass movement in the way that each of the three case studies in this book did.[54] While a small peace movement remained active in Australia between 1939 and 1945, the overwhelming sense that Australian society was engaged 'in a war of survival' meant that the Second World War peace movement did not gain the level of support that peace movements garnered in other conflicts.[55] The book has focused on the three inter-state wars in which Australia has participated over the last 100 years that have generated mass public debate.

---

[52] The figure of the United States occupies a similar position: western but not 'European'. Nevertheless, there are significant works on the role of international law in the US and on American influences on the development of international law. See, for example, Mark Janis, *America and the Law of Nations 1776–1939* (Oxford University Press, 2010); John Fabian Witt, *Lincoln's Code: The Laws of War in American History* (Free Press, 2012); Benjamin Allen Coates, *Legalist Empire: International Law and American Foreign Relations in the Early Twentieth Century* (Oxford University Press, 2016).

[53] A longer version of this argument is contained in Madelaine Chiam, 'Tom Barker's "To Arms!" Poster: Internationalism and Resistance in First World War Australia' (2017) 5 *London Review of International Law* 125.

[54] Malcolm Saunders and Ralph Summy, 'One Hundred Years of an Australian Peace Movement, 1885–1984: Part I: From the Sudan Campaign to the Outbreak of the Second World War' (1984) 10 *Peace & Change* 39 ('Peace Movement, Part I'); Malcolm Saunders and Ralph Summy, 'One Hundred Years of an Australian Peace Movement, 1885–1984: Part II: From the Second World War to Vietnam and Beyond' (1984) 10 *Peace & Change* 57.

[55] Saunders and Summy, 'Peace Movement, Part I' (n 54) 51.

1.2.2 The Argument

My analysis in this book draws on the Herodotean tradition of polyphony to explore the ways that a range of speakers have used, understood and characterised international law in public debates. My argument that international law has a long provenance in public debate and that it has generated a form of popular international law is structured as follows. Chapter 2 explains the scholarly traditions of 'popular' law on which I have drawn, describes the analytical approach to law as language that I have used, and situates the smaller histories contained in this book within the wider scholarship on international legal history. Chapters 3, 4 and 5 give an account of the role of international law in public debates about war in Australia in 2003, 1965–66 and 1916. In these three chapters, I also explore how the uses of international legal language have changed across the three case studies and how those changes have generated a popular international law. Chapter 5 concludes the book. This book draws one picture, and not the whole picture, of the role that international law has played in public debate within Australia across the twentieth and early twenty-first centuries.

Each of Chapters 3, 4 and 5 examines the views on international law of the speakers of each period, the ways in which they employed the language and how they responded to the other positions on international law in the public debates. These stories about international law are situated in the relevant social and political contexts of Australia at the time of each public debate. These contexts included the international legal structures, the Australian legal and political structures, the events surrounding the decision to engage in war, and the tenor and content of the public and political responses to that decision. Chapters 3, 4 and 5 present my argument about international law in reverse chronological order; that is, my analysis begins with 2003, and then works backwards to consider 1965–66 and then 1916. This order is intended to signal to readers that, while each chapter gives a contextualised historical account of particular periods in Australia, the book as a whole is not intended as a traditional history. Rather, the reverse chronology is designed to make transparent that I began this book with a puzzle about the present, and used questions arising from that puzzle to inform my examinations of the past. The order of the chapters emphasises that I have studied three moments in the history of Australia and in the history of international law in order to untangle questions about the present. In this sense, this book is more aligned with 'histories of the present' than with the intellectual and conceptual histories that have generally been the mode of international legal histories.[56] The reverse chronology reflects my authorial interest not only in 'what happened' in each period, but also in how 'what happened' contributes to how we might understand ongoing popular uses of international law in public debate.

I argue in this book that the vocabulary and grammar used by speakers in public debates largely cohered with that of the expert language of international law, and that there were distinct competences required to be persuasive. The key competence that emerges in Chapters 3, 4 and 5 is the ability of a speaker to understand and deploy a distinction between international law as an element of collective justifications for or against war and international law as an autonomous justification for or against war. When international law was used as a collective justification, it consisted of a vocabulary that carried a group of undifferentiated standards, such as those of law, morality, strategy, economics and ethics. Use of this language to justify or challenge government decisions relied on the collection of implications that the concepts carry. For example, depending on the context of a particular intervention, an argument about 'self-defence' conveyed meanings that were legal, philosophical, historical, ethical or any combination. Examples of the collective language of international law in this book include self-defence, humanitarianism, aggression and the just war. Two collective justifications appeared most frequently – international law as a standard of morality and international law as evidence of support for an alliance relationship.

When international law was used as an autonomous justification, the requirement of legality was a criterion separated from other considerations. Autonomous justifications feature in two ways in the public debates in this book. First, speakers used the requirement of legality independently of other considerations such as morality or alliance. The assessment of 'legality' on its own was a primary measure of the legitimacy of government action and it was important for speakers to identify a justification as 'legal' or 'illegal'. Autonomous justifications of legality

---

[56] Michel Foucault, *Discipline and Punish: The Birth of the Prison* (Pantheon, 1977). For discussion, see, for example, David Garland, 'What is a "history of the present"? On Foucault's Genealogies and their Critical Preconditions' (2014) 16 *Punishment & Society* 365; Kate Purcell, 'On the Uses and Advantages of Genealogy for International Law' (2019) *Leiden Journal of International Law* 1.

appeared in the public debates of each period, but the naming of 'legality' or 'illegality' took on a power in 2003 that was absent in both 1965–66 and 1916. Second, calls to 'legality' consisted of careful readings of existing legal rules and assessments of the situation against those rules. As such, legality as an autonomous justification in public debates consisted of arguments that were used by all speakers and that were coherent with the vocabulary and grammar of professional speakers of international law.[57]

In Chapter 3, I argue that international law appeared in the 2003 debates primarily as an autonomous reason for or against war. Speakers invoked the legality or illegality of the invasion of Iraq as reason enough, on its own, to justify or condemn Australia's actions. Participants who used international legal language did not just debate the international legal standards relevant to the government's decisions, they deliberately named these standards as international law. Speakers constructed international law as a measure of the justifiability of government action separate from any other measure such as morality or participation in an alliance, calling on a power that they believed international legal status would create. The 2003 debates included some examples of international law as a collective justification, but these were generally subordinate to the autonomous form of international legal language.

In Chapter 4, I examine the debates of 1965–66 over Australia's participation in the Vietnam War. In 1965–66, the UN Charter regulated the use of force by states and the international legal language of those debates resembled in many ways that of 2003. Even so, the success of international legal arguments in the 1965–66 public debates did not depend on the ability of the speaker to characterise an argument as a 'legal' one. Indeed, Prime Minister Robert Menzies dismissed such talk as a 'parlour game'.[58] Successful use of international legal language in the 1965–66 debates turned instead on the ability of the speaker to cast international law as something more than merely law – as either a standard of morality or a manifestation of an alliance. Speakers were negotiating an Australian nationalism in flux, one moving from its traditional reliance on the United Kingdom to its developing relationship with the United States, and international legal language may have supported arguments about other concepts but it did not stand apart from them. The legality or illegality of

---

[57] On coherence, see Vaughan Lowe, 'The Iraq Crisis: What Now?' (2003) 52 *International and Comparative Law Quarterly* 85.

[58] Commonwealth, *Parliamentary Debates*, House of Representatives, 19 August 1965, 282 (Robert Menzies).

Australia's actions was not enough, on its own, to provide a persuasive justification for war in 1965–66.

For Australians, the language of international law in the First World War was both the law of nations as it existed at the time, and the dominion and constitutional law that governed Australia's relationships beyond its territorial borders. In Chapter 5, I describe how participants in the 1916 debates used these different international legal languages to deliberate the justifications for war and for conscription. The languages of these debates included, for example, arguments about the preservation of White Australia, about the need to protect Australians' civil liberties, and about the unequal claims made on the different classes of Australian society as a result of the First World War. The persuasiveness of uses of international legal language in 1916 depended on speakers' abilities to navigate the complications of Australia's colonial nationalism. Speakers made sophisticated arguments about the duties of the Dominion of Australia to the British Empire on the one hand, and to its own emerging nationhood on the other. The accounts in Chapters 3, 4 and 5 suggest a long and complex practice of speaking international legal language in Australian public debates.

2

A 'Popular' International Law

The accounts of the Iraq Inquiry and the WTI in Chapter 1 are examples of attempts to regulate the voices that matter in public discussions involving international law. They illustrate the appearance in different contexts of questions such as whose views in relation to international legal matters are considered 'serious', whether opinions on questions of legality are the domain only of experts, what kinds of international law are invoked by speakers, and what role there is for perspectives of a diverse range of people on international legal questions. I explore these questions using a method of textual analysis that focuses on the contributions from three groups of people who participated in the Iraq War, Vietnam War and First World War debates in Australia: politicians, trade union groups and leaders, and religious groups and leaders. I analyse a series of texts produced by those individuals and groups as interventions in those debates – speeches, media releases, pamphlets, interviews and letters to newspapers. These individuals, groups and their texts are not a traditional focus of analysis for international law, and paying attention to them brings to light the ways in which their contributions to public debate have generated a popular form of international law. To make this argument, I draw on scholarship that has attempted to understand ideas about domestic and international laws that have been held by people beyond traditional legal contexts.[1] To help understand the forms and characteristics of international law in public debate, I draw on approaches that treat international law as a language and a practice, one

---

[1] See, for example, John M Conley and William M O'Barr, *Rules versus Relationships: The Ethnography of Legal Discourse* (University of Chicago Press, 1990); Elizabeth Mertz, 'Language, Law and Social Meanings: Linguistic/Anthropological Contributions to the Study of Law' (1992) 26 *Law & Society Review* 413; Sally Engle Merry, *Getting Justice and Getting Even: Legal Consciousness among Working-Class Americans* (University of Chicago Press, 1990); Steven Wilf, *Law's Imagined Republic: Popular Politics and Criminal Justice in Revolutionary America* (Cambridge University Press, 2010); Christopher W Schmidt, 'Conceptions of Law in the Civil Rights Movement' (2011) 1 *UC Irvine Law Review* 641.

with its own vocabulary, grammar and competence.² This chapter describes the method and theories that underpin my argument.

2.1 Producing Legality through 'Popular' Law

Scholarship in a range of fields argues for the inclusion of a broad range of people and groups as creators of law. There is an extensive body of scholarship in anthropology and sociology contending that the everyday speech of people in domestic and international legal contexts both constitutes and is constituted by formal laws. In their study of the stories that people tell about 'trouble' in their lives, Patricia Ewick and Susan Silbey describe lawmaking as a process through which 'by telling stories of our lives, we not only report, account for, and relive portions of those lives, we participate in the production of legality'.[3] By taking seriously the everyday rather than the official discourse of law, Silbey, Ewick and others show how analysing law, language and society as integrated rather than separate can create opportunities for creativity in legal discourse, generate different forms of legal consciousness or reveal the justice in silence.[4] Work in global and imperial history similarly exposes the multiple ways in which international and imperial law was made outside of interstate conferences and state palaces. Lauren Benton and Lisa Ford, for example, find intellectual origins of international law in 'the correspondence of middling officials ... notes on colonial scandals, [and] communications across political communities by merchants and sojourners'.[5]

---

[2] Martti Koskenniemi, *From Apology to Utopia: The Structure of International Legal Argument* (Cambridge University Press, reissue, 2005) ('*From Apology to Utopia*').
[3] Patricia Ewick and Susan S Silbey, *The Common Place of Law: Stories from Everyday Lives* (University of Chicago Press, 1998) 30.
[4] See, for example, Conley and O'Barr, *Rules versus Relationships* (n 1); Mertz (n 1); Merry, *Getting Justice and Getting Even* (n 1); Sally Engle Merry, *Human Rights and Gender Violence: Translating International Law into Local Justice* (University of Chicago Press, 2006); Marianne Constable, *Just Silences: The Limits and Possibilities of Modern Law* (Princeton University Press, 2005); Luis Eslava, *Local Space, Global Life: The Everyday Operation of International Law and Development* (Cambridge University Press, 2015); Genevieve Renard Painter, 'A Letter from the Haudenosaunee Confederacy to King George V: Writing and Reading Jurisdictions in International Legal History' (2017) 5 *London Review of International Law* 7.
[5] Lauren Benton and Lisa Ford, *Rage for Order: The British Empire and the Origins of International Law 1800–1850* (Harvard University Press, 2016) 21; see also, Lisa Ford, *Settler Sovereignty: Jurisdiction and Indigenous People in America and Australia, 1788–1836* (Harvard University Press, 2009); Luis Eslava, Michael Fakhri and Vasuki Nesiah (eds.), *Bandung, Global History, and International Law: Critical Pasts and Pending Futures* (Cambridge University Press, 2017).

Scholarship on popular constitutionalism in state contexts offers a parallel for the analysis in this book. For Larry Kramer, it is a fundamental aspect of the US legal system that authority to interpret and enforce the Constitution rests not with the Supreme Court but with the people of the United States. Indeed, according to Kramer, 'ordinary citizens are [the] most authoritative interpreters of the Constitution'.[6] Kramer's is both a historical and a normative account. He argues that US society has its roots in a popular constitutionalism that was diminished as deference to judicial review became supreme, and he urges a transformation of the US constitutional system in order to check the power of the Supreme Court and restore that power to the people.[7] In his work on the Indian Constitution, Rohit De also argues for a constitutionalism that recognises manifold ways of reading and interpreting the text.[8] De's argument is based on extensive analysis of historical material, and he presents multiple examples of political action by ordinary Indians that brought the Constitution to life in public imagination and influenced its interpretation by the courts.

In an international legal context, as the WTI example in Chapter 1 illustrates, paying attention to the uses and constructions of international law by non-state actors recalls peoples' tribunals more generally. The modern tradition of 'peoples' tribunals is generally traced to the Russell Tribunals of the late 1960s, and there have been multiple instantiations since then, including later Russell Tribunals such as the Russell Tribunal on Palestine, the Permanent Peoples' Tribunal and the Tokyo Women's Tribunal.[9] While constituted differently and concerned with a range of

---

[6] Larry D Kramer, 'Undercover Anti-Populism' (2005) 73 *Fordham Law Review* 1343, 1344. See also Larry D Kramer, 'The Supreme Court, 2000 Term – Foreword: We the Court' (2001) 115 *Harvard Law Review* 4 ('Foreword'). Kramer's arguments have attracted considerable criticism: for an overview, see Tom Donnelly, 'Making Popular Constitutionalism Work' (2012) 1 *Wisconsin Law Review* 159.

[7] Kramer, 'Foreword' (n 6).

[8] Rohit De, *A People's Constitution: The Everyday Life of Law in the Indian Republic* (Princeton University Press, 2018).

[9] For a general history of peoples' tribunals, see Andrew Byrnes and Gabrielle Simm, 'International Peoples' Tribunals: Their Nature, Practice and Significance' in Andrew Byrnes and Gabrielle Simm (eds.), *Peoples' Tribunals and International Law* (Cambridge University Press, 2017) 11. See also Peter Limqueco and Peter Weiss (eds.), *Prevent the Crime of Silence: Reports from the Sessions of the International War Crimes Tribunal Founded by Bertrand Russell* (Allen Lane, 1971); Tor Krever, 'Remembering the Russell Tribunal' (2017) 5 *London Review of International Law* 483; Tina Dolgopol, 'The Judgment of the Tokyo Women's Tribunal' (2003) 28 *Alternative Law Journal* 242; Karen Knop, 'The Tokyo Women's Tribunal and the Turn to Fiction' in Fleur Johns, Richard Joyce and Sundhya Pahuja (eds.), *Events: The Force of International Law* (Routledge, 2010) 145.

issues, these tribunals have shared a desire to hold states, individuals and institutions publicly to account for egregious violations of international law where such accountability has not been found any other way. The tribunals have decentred the state by claiming the authority of individuals to judge states and their leaders against the standards of international law. In doing so, the tribunals have also aimed to galvanise popular opinion in support of their findings. In their overview of peoples' tribunals, Andrew Byrnes and Gabrielle Simm argue that a common feature of peoples' tribunals is a claim that ordinary people can assert 'for themselves the benefit of international law . . . and to interpret and develop international law'.[10] Sara Dehm explicitly situates peoples' tribunals as exhibiting a form of popular international law that 'claims the authority to speak in the name of the "people"', and Christine Chinkin, who acted as one of the judges in the Tokyo Women's Tribunal, has described a founding principle of peoples' tribunals to be that international law does not belong exclusively to states. '[W]here the state fails to assert the law', Chinkin argues, 'civil society can and should step in to reaffirm [law's] authority'.[11]

Kramer's work on popular constitutionalism has been criticised for minimising the role of the judiciary and leaving American constitutionalism open to the tyranny of majoritarianism.[12] The legitimacy of peoples' tribunals has been challenged too, with accusations that they are 'kangaroo courts', lacking in both legal and political legitimacy.[13] At the core of these critiques is a struggle for the authority to speak legal language. In constitutional contexts, the work of both Kramer and De suggests that the people of the United States and India have claimed this authority for themselves in the past. And in the international legal

---

[10] Byrnes and Simm (n 9) 15.
[11] Sara Dehm, 'Accusing "Europe": Articulations of Migrant Justice and a Popular International Law' in Andrew Byrnes and Gabrielle Simm (eds.), *Peoples' Tribunals and International Law* (Cambridge University Press, 2017) 157, 179; Christine Chinkin, 'Peoples' Tribunals: Legitimate or Rough Justice' (2006) 24 *Windsor Year Book of Access to Justice* 201, 216–17.
[12] See, for example, Erwin Chemerinsky, 'In Defense of Judicial Review: The Perils of Popular Constitutionalism' [2004] *University of Illinois Law Review* 673; Cass R Sunstein, 'If People Would be Outraged by Their Rulings, Should Judges Care?' (2007) 60 *Stanford Law Review* 155.
[13] See, for example, Arundhati Roy, 'Opening Statement on Behalf of the Jury of Conscience of the World Tribunal of Iraq' (Speech, World Tribunal on Iraq, Istanbul, 24 June 2005). See also Andrew Byrnes and Gabrielle Simm, 'Reflections on the Past and Future of International Peoples' Tribunals' in Andrew Byrnes and Gabrielle Simm (eds), *Peoples' Tribunals and International Law* (Cambridge University Press, 2017) 259.

context, the continued formation of peoples' tribunals suggests that previous tribunals have held a power for those who engaged them, however ineffable that power may be. The arguments about the role of a diversity of people in relation to constitutions and tribunals highlight different ways in which individuals have seized for themselves the authority to speak law and have generated different forms of legality as a consequence.

My argument that international law in public debate has created a form of international legality that I call 'popular international law' shares with the broader scholarship on 'popular law' an interest in the manifold ways that a range of people and groups have constructed their engagements with law. In this book, my specific focus is international law and the locus in which I have studied international law is public debate. I explain in section 2.2 the reasons for focusing on public debate and the characteristics of that debate that underpin my argument that international law in public debate is a form of popular international law.

2.2 Public Debate and Law as Language

2.2.1 Public Debate and Its Texts

For each of the three public debates examined in this book, I have analysed a series of texts: speeches, media releases, pamphlets, interviews and letters to newspapers. I chose these particular types of texts because they were 'public'; that is, they were contributions to debate in the public sphere, designed to be read or heard by the wider Australian population, in the hope of persuading that population to agree with the message of the text.[14] In my analysis, the spaces that constituted that public sphere include Parliament, media outlets (such as newspapers and television), public meetings of institutions and groups, and independently produced pamphlets for public distribution. There are limitations and exclusions to

---

[14] I understand 'public sphere' as an 'institutional arena of discursive interaction' in which denizens of a liberal democracy 'deliberate about their common affairs' and can, in principle, be 'critical of the state': Nancy Fraser, 'Rethinking the Public Sphere: A Contribution to the Critique of Actually Existing Democracy' (1990) 25/26 *Social Text* 56, 57. Fraser is critiquing what she calls the 'indispensable resource' of Jurgen Habermas' work on the 'public sphere': see Jurgen Habermas, *The Structural Transformation of the Public Sphere: An Inquiry into a Category of Bourgeois Society*, tr Thomas Burger and Frederick Lawrence (MIT Press, 1991); Jurgen Habermas, *Between Facts and Norms: Contributions to a Discourse Theory of Law and Democracy* (MIT Press, 1998).

2.2 PUBLIC DEBATE AND LAW AS LANGUAGE

this understanding of a 'public sphere', in particular that it occludes some of the class, gender and race divisions within liberal democracies and ignores the structural obstacles that compromise the power of public debates.[15] My argument proceeds, however, on the premise that there exist in liberal democracies one or more discursive spaces in which residents can deliberate issues that affect them, however limited those spaces may be.[16]

As one of the few spaces in which individuals and groups can openly confront, engage and interact with international legal arguments in their own domestic public spheres, public debate is an important context through which to understand popular uses of international law.[17] Two particular characteristics of public debate give rise to my argument that it generates popular international law. The first is that public debate is a process of argument and persuasion. It is a dialogue intended to persuade one or more audiences to a point of view, and to give those audiences an opportunity to respond.[18] Legal argument too is a dialogic process. Through debate in a range of institutional settings – a courtroom, a lawyer's office, a government department – lawyers attempt to convince a judge, a client or a minister that their position on a legal issue is the preferable one. In Chapters 3, 4 and 5, I give multiple examples of similar exercises of negotiation and persuasion through public debates. Participants in the debates used international legal language to express support or opposition for the proposed actions of the Australian Government, and provided justifications for their views to multiple audiences. Each of the chapters also contains examples of speakers adjusting the expression of their positions in response to arguments made

---

[15] Nancy Fraser, 'Transnationalizing the Public Sphere: On the Legitimacy and Efficacy of Public Opinion in a Post-Westphalian World' European Institute for Progressive Cultural Policies (Article, March 2007) https://eipcp.net/transversal/0605/fraser/en.html.

[16] See, for example, Gerard A Hauser, *Vernacular Voices: The Rhetoric of Publics and Public Spheres* (University of South Carolina Press, 1999); Christian J Emden and David Midgley, 'Beyond Habermas? From the Bourgeois Public Sphere to Global Publics' in Christian J Emden and David Midgley (eds), *Beyond Habermas: Democracy, Knowledge and the Public Sphere* (Berghahn Books, 2012) 1.

[17] Cf Eslava (n 4).

[18] See, for example, This should be 'Hauser (n 16)'. This idea is also present in the law as rhetoric theory developed by Peter Goodrich: see, for example, Peter Goodrich: *Reading the Law: A Critical Introduction to Legal Method and Techniques* (Blackwell, 1986) ('*Reading the Law*'). Goodrich has also pointed out that, in order for persuasion (public debate) to be effective, the society's political conditions need persuasion to be the means of decision-making, rather than force or coercion: Goodrich, *Reading the Law*, 171–73.

by others. These interventions in international legal language only occasionally claimed to rely on the expert views of professional international lawyers. Most of the time, contributions by politicians, trade unions, religious and other speakers used international law in their own voices and generated a different form of international law in the process.

The second characteristic of public debate is the role of the state. While I share with peoples' tribunals a desire to decentre the state, this is rarely possible in public debates about international action, where the state is almost always both an actor and an intended audience. This element of public debate – of having the state as both actor and audience – echoes the structures of international law. The debates in each of Chapters 3, 4 and 5 provide context for the various Australian governments' articulations of their international legal justifications. The arc and content of the debates influenced some government statements on international law, and some of the language of politicians can be read as responding to public concerns about international law. In this very direct way, the public debates examined in this book have shaped the Australian state's positions on international law.

This book has concentrated on interventions authored by politicians, trade union leaders, religious leaders and some anti-war activists and journalists. These groups and individuals participated in each of the public debates and provided a consistent focus for the book's analysis.[19] The texts highlighted in Chapters 3, 4 and 5 do not represent every argument that was made during the public debates, but taken together they provide a representative picture of the uses of international law in each of these public debates. I have engaged with the texts in this book using a method of close textual reading and detailed examination of the forms and characterisations of international law in each period. This method is consistent with that employed by others who have mapped the characteristics of international legal language in various contexts.[20] I use textual analysis to examine the questions that drive my analysis: who spoke, and who was considered authorised to speak, international legal language; what forms of international legal language did they use? I have

---

[19] There is one exception in relation to the role of the trade unions in the Vietnam War debates, which I explain in Chapter 4.
[20] See, for example, Nathaniel Berman, '"But the Alternative Is Despair": European Nationalism and the Modernist Renewal of International Law' (1992–93) 106 *Harvard Law Review* 1792; Nathaniel Berman, 'A Perilous Ambivalence: Nationalist Desire, Legal Autonomy, and the Limits of the Interwar Framework' (1992) 33 *Harvard International Law Journal* 353; Guy Fiti Sinclair, *To Reform the World: International Organizations and the Making of Modern States* (Oxford University Press, 2017).

parsed the different elements – vocabulary, grammar and competence – of international legal language in public debate, which has then generated my argument about the forms of international legal language in that debate. In underpinning the arguments about vocabulary, grammar and competence, the textual analysis method opens the possibility for the existence of a popular international law.

2.2.2 International Law as Language

Engaging in close readings of texts of public debate as examples of international law means that I take in this book a primarily linguistic view of international law.[21] There is a long tradition of scholarship that explores law as a language. Peter Goodrich has described law as a 'system of communication and non-communication' that takes place between a 'community of speakers' using a range of different techniques.[22] The language of law includes 'sounds, units of meaning, and grammatical structures, as well as the contexts in which they occur'.[23] It is language in particular contexts that makes contracts, statutes and judgments; it is language in which the exchanges of the courtroom, of lawyers' offices, of university learning take place. Law is not thus 'just words',[24] and law and language scholars have demonstrated the myriad ways in which the power of law is manifested through the language of legal texts, institutions and interactions.[25] In doing so, they have also demonstrated the

---

[21] For overviews of work in law and language, see, for example, John M Conley and William M O'Barr, *Just Words: Law, Language and Power* (University of Chicago Press, 2nd ed., 2005); the contributions of Penelope Pether, Jay Mootz, Ravit Reichman and Harriet Murav in Austin Sarat, Matthew Anderson and Cathrine O Frank (eds.), *Law and the Humanities: An Introduction* (Cambridge University Press, 2014); Michael Freeman and Fiona Smith (eds.), *Law and Language* (Oxford University Press, 2013). Some key texts on the field include Peter Goodrich, *Languages of Law: From Logics of Memory to Nomadic Masks* (Weidenfeld & Nicholson, 1990); Peter Tiersma, *Legal Language* (University of Chicago Press, 1999); Harold J Berman, *Law and Language: Effective Symbols of Community* (Cambridge University Press, 2013) ('*Law and Language*'); James Boyd White, *The Legal Imagination: Studies in the Nature of Legal Thought and Expression* (University of Chicago Press, abridged ed., 1973) ('*Legal Imagination*'); Constable (n 4); Robert Cover, 'Violence and the Word' (1985–86) 95 *Yale Law Journal* 1601.

[22] Peter Goodrich, 'Law and Language: An Historical and Critical Introduction' (1984) 11 *Journal of Law and Society* 173, 174. See also John L Austin, *How to Do Things with Words* (Harvard University Press, 1962); Goodrich, *Reading the Law* (n 18).

[23] Conley and O'Barr (n 21) 6.

[24] Ibid.

[25] See, for example, Jothie Rajah, *Authoritarian Rule of Law: Legislation, Discourse and Legitimacy in Singapore* (Cambridge University Press, 2012); Martha Minow, Michael Ryan

limits of legal language. There are occasions, James Boyd White has argued, where the 'narrowing of concern' of legal language is appropriate: a 'technical language suited to technical ends'.[26] There are many others, White argues, where law 'maintains a false pretence that it can be used as a language of description or naming, when in fact it calls for a process of complex judgment'.[27]

Scholarship on international law as a language has developed largely along a separate trajectory from the wider law and language movement. While international law scholars have recognised the importance of language for some time,[28] the work of David Kennedy and Martti Koskenniemi in bringing the insights of structuralism to international law has had particular impact.[29] Treating international law as a distinctively legal language with its own vocabulary and grammar,

---

and Austin Sarat (eds.), *Narrative, Violence and the Law: The Essays of Robert Cover* (University of Michigan Press, 1983); Richard Jackson, *Writing the War on Terrorism: Language, Politics and Counter-Terrorism* (University of Manchester Press, 2005); Mahmood Mamdani, *Good Muslim, Bad Muslim: America, the Cold War and the Roots of Terror* (Doubleday, 2005).

[26] White, *Legal Imagination* (n 21) 111.

[27] Ibid., 111–12.

[28] Deborah Z Cass, 'Navigating the Newstream: Recent Critical Scholarship in International Law' (1996) 65 *Nordic Journal of International Law* 341, especially 359–62.

[29] See Koskenniemi, *From Apology to Utopia* (n 2) especially 562–73; Martti Koskenniemi, *The Politics of International Law* (Hart, 2011) ('Politics'); David Kennedy, 'Theses about International Law Discourse' (1980) 23 *German Yearbook of International Law* 353; David Kennedy, *International Legal Structures* (Nomos, 1987); David Kennedy, 'When Renewal Repeats: Thinking against the Box' (1999–2000) 32 *New York Journal of International Law and Politics* 335 ('When Renewal Repeats'). Kennedy reflects on the questions that both he and Koskenniemi wanted to pursue early in their careers in David Kennedy, 'The Last Treatise: Project and Person (Reflections on Martti Koskenniemi's *From Apology to Utopia*)' (2006) 7 *German Law Journal* 982 ('The Last Treatise'). For a useful contextualisation of structuralism in international law, see Justin Desautels-Stein, *The Jurisprudence of Style: A Structuralist History of American Pragmatism and Liberal Legal Thought* (Cambridge University Press, 2018); Justin Desautels-Stein 'International Legal Structuralism: A Primer' (2016) 8 *International Theory* 201 ('A Primer'). For an analysis of the early critical work on international law as language, see Cass (n 28) especially 359–62. See also James Boyle, 'Ideals and Things: International Legal Scholarship and the Prison-House of Language' (1985) 26 *Harvard Journal of International Law* 327; Dino Kritsiotis, 'The Power of International Law as Language' (1997–98) 34 *California Western Law Review* 397; Outi Korhonen, 'New International Law: Silences, Defence or Deliverance?' (1996) 7 *European Journal of International Law* 1. For a critical view of Kennedy and Koskenniemi, see, for example, Anthony Carty, 'Language Games of International Law: Koskenniemi as the Discipline's Wittgenstein' (2012) 13 *Melbourne Journal of International Law* 859.

2.2 PUBLIC DEBATE AND LAW AS LANGUAGE

Kennedy and Koskenniemi have argued that international law, while deeply political, is also separated from politics by the distinctiveness in what Justin Desautels-Stein describes as the 'operation of [its] grammar, and the modes in which the grammar governed forms of lexical argument'.[30] Many scholars have since built on the insight that international law is a language that constitutes 'a powerful social practice with very real effects'.[31] Some have traced how particular terminology has been used within international law scholarship and institutions.[32] Others have examined how particular groups have framed their claims within the institutions of international law,[33] or the ways in which international law has constructed language rights.[34] Along with their focus on how the language of international law has been used in different settings, this scholarship shares with general law and language scholarship a desire to unravel the relationships between power and legal language.

---

[30] Desautels-Stein, 'A Primer' (n 29) 205.
[31] Cass (n 28) 360.
[32] There are now, for example, genealogies of terms, including 'progress': Thomas Skouteris, *The Notion of Progress in International Law Discourse* (TMC Asser Press, 2010); Tilmann Altwicker and Oliver Diggelmann, 'How Is Progress Constructed in International Legal Scholarship?' (2014) 25 *European Journal of International Law* 425; 'great powers': Gerry Simpson, *Great Powers and Outlaw States: Unequal Sovereigns in the International Legal Order* (Cambridge University Press, 2004); Stephane Beaulac, *The Power of Language in the Making of International Law: The Word Sovereignty in Bodin and Vattel and the Myth of Westphalia* (Brill, 2004); 'proportionality': Grigory Vaypan, 'Choosing among the Shades of Nuance: The Discourse of Proportionality in International Law' (2015) 15 *Global Jurist* 237; 'culture': Pok Yin S Chow, 'Culture as Collective Memories: An Emerging Concept in International Law and Discourse on Cultural Rights' (2014) 14 *Human Rights Law Review* 611; 'self-determination': Christopher J Borgen, 'Language of Law and the Practice of Politics: Great Powers and the Rhetoric of Self-Determination in the Cases of Kosovo and South Ossetia' (2009) 10 *The Chicago Journal of International Law* 1; 'sustainable development': Tim Stephens, 'International Courts and Sustainable Development: Using Old Tools to Shape a New Discourse' in Kim Rubenstein and Brad Jessup (eds.), *Environmental Discourses in Public and International Law* (Cambridge University Press, 2012) 195; 'rule of law': Christopher May, *The Rule of Law as the Common Sense of Global Politics* (Edward Elgar, 2014). On conceptual genealogy in international law generally, see Ulf Linderfalk, 'The Functionality of Conceptual Terms in International Law and International Legal Discourse' (2013/14) 6 *European Journal of Legal Studies* 27.
[33] Michelle L Burgis, *Boundaries of Discourse in the International Court of Justice: Mapping Arguments in Arab Territorial Disputes* (Brill, 2009); Michelle Leanne Burgis-Kasthala, 'Over-stating Palestine's UN Membership Bid? An Ethnographic Study on the Narratives of Statehood' (2014) 25 *European Journal of International Law* 677.
[34] Jacqueline Mowbray, *Linguistic Justice: International Law and Language Policy* (Oxford University Press, 2012).

A different strand of international law as language scholarship concentrates on the internal rules of the grammar of international law and attempts to identify recurring patterns and styles within that argument itself.[35] Some of this work also theorises the role of international legal language in the formation of the discipline and profession of international lawyers.[36] In a similar vein are bodies of scholarship dedicated to the techniques of interpretation in international law,[37] and to the semiotics of international law more generally.[38] This form of scholarship overwhelmingly takes as its subject the internal uses of international legal language – that is, the uses of international law by professional international lawyers or within formal international legal settings, such as international courts and tribunals, academic writing, international institutions, government departments and non-government organisations.[39]

[35] Koskenniemi's *From Apology to Utopia* (n 2) is the major contribution here, but there are others who build on this work, including, for example, Jean D'Aspremont, 'Wording in International Law' (2012) 25 *Leiden Journal of International Law* 575 ('Wording in International Law'); Geoff Gordon, 'Legal Equality and Innate Cosmopolitanism in Contemporary Discourses of International Law' (2012) 43 *Netherlands Yearbook of International Law* 183; Fiona Smith, 'Power, Rules and the WTO' (2013) 53 *Boston College Law Review* 1063.

[36] Jean D'Aspremont, *Epistemic Forces in International Law: Foundational Doctrines and Techniques of International Legal Argumentation* (Elgar, 2015) ('*Epistemic Forces in International Law*'); Gleider I Hernandez, 'The Responsibility of the International Legal Academic' in Jean D'Aspremont et al. (eds.), *International Law as a Profession* (Cambridge University Press, 2017) 160; Outi Korhonen, *International Law Situated: An Analysis of the Lawyer's Stance towards Culture, History and Community* (Kluwer Law International, 2000) ('*International Law Situated*'); Ulf Linderfalk, 'The Post-9/11 Discourse Revisited: The Self-Image of the International Legal Scientific Discipline' (2010) 2 *Gottingen Journal of International Law* 893; Lianne JM Boer and Sofia Stolk (eds), *Backstage Practices of Transnational Law* (Routledge, 2019).

[37] See, for example, Ingo Venzke, *How Interpretation Makes International Law: On Semantic Change and Normative Twists* (Oxford University Press, 2012); Andrea Bianchi, Daniel Peat, Matthew Windsor (eds.), *Interpretation in International Law* (Oxford University Press, 2015).

[38] See, for example, Susan Tiefenbrun, *Decoding International Law* (Oxford University Press, 2010); Evandro Menezes de Carvalho, *Semiotics of International Law: Trade and Translation*, tr Luciana Carvalho Fonseca (Springer, 2011); Clara Chapdelaine-Feliciati, 'The Sense, Meaning and Significance of the Twin International Covenants on Political and Economic Rights' (2013) 196 *Semiotica* 325; Wouter G Werner, 'The Curious Career of Lawfare' (2010) 43 *Case Western Reserve Journal of International Law* 61; Ronen Shamir and Dana Weiss, 'Semiotics of Indicators: The Case of Corporate Human Rights Responsibility' in Kevin Davis et al. (eds.), *Governance by Indicators: Global Power through Quantification and Rankings* (Oxford University Press, 2012).

[39] Susan Tiefenbrun's semiotic exploration of international law in art, literature and film is a notable exception here; see Tiefenbrun (n 38).

2.2 PUBLIC DEBATE AND LAW AS LANGUAGE

There is a smaller body of scholarship that examines what it means to do or speak international law from outside the traditional settings of international law. Charlotte Peevers and Philip Liste, for example, explore the processes and outcomes that have produced public, and in particular legal, justifications by governments for the use of force.[40] They analyse public debate in order to examine how that external discourse has influenced the internal determinations of governments. In adapting international relations theories, Peevers and Liste also connect with projects in international relations scholarship that trace the structures of political discourses.[41] In general, these international relations projects have paid little attention to international law, and even when they have, the object of analysis has been the language of professional international lawyers.[42] The work of Anna Dolidze also expands linguistic understandings of international law by focusing not on the context in which international law is used, but on the states participating in the international system.[43] If international law is a language, Dolidze argues, then like any language it must have native and non-native speakers. With a focus on Russia, Dolidze uses the metaphor of the non-native speaker as a tool to understand 'the often confusing and contradictory positions of states that have not perceived themselves to be part of the foundations of international law'.[44] She argues in particular that some of the postures Russia has adopted in its international relations can be explained by its status as a non-native speaker of international law.[45]

---

[40] Charlotte Peevers, *The Politics of Justifying Force: The Suez Crisis, the Iraq War and International Law* (Oxford University Press, 2013); Philip Liste, '"Public" International Law? Democracy and Discourses of Legal Reality' (2011) 42 *Netherlands Yearbook of International Law* 177.

[41] See, for example, Jack Holland, *Selling the War on Terror: Foreign Policy Discourses after 9/11* (Taylor and Francis, 2012); Kathleen Gleeson, *Australia's 'War on Terror' Discourse* (Routledge, 2014).

[42] See, for example, Shirley V Scott and Olivia Ambler, 'Does Legality Really Matter? Accounting for the Decline in US Foreign Policy Legitimacy Following the 2003 Invasion of Iraq' (2007) 13 *European Journal of International Relations* 67; Shirley V Scott, 'The Political Life of Public International Lawyers: Granting the Imprimatur' (2007) 21 *International Relations* 411. See also River Cordes-Holland, 'The national interest or good international citizenship? Australia and its approach to international and public climate law' in Kim Rubenstein and Brad Jessup (eds), *Environmental Discourses in Public and International Law* (Cambridge University Press, 2012) 286.

[43] Anna Dolidze, 'The Non-Native Speakers of International Law: The case of Russia' (2015) 15 *Baltic Yearbook of International Law* 77.

[44] Ibid., 79. Dolidze identifies Iran, Japan, China and Turkey as other 'non-native' speakers of international law.

[45] Ibid. These postures are the 'disaffected foreigner' and the 'empowered multilingual subject'.

International law, then, is understood by a cohort of international legal scholars to be a language spoken by professional international lawyers in formal international law contexts. Most of this work traces the internal language of international law from within the discipline itself. The work of Peevers, Dolidze and Liste points to some of the different ways in which studying groups or individuals who are considered to fall outside the traditional boundaries of international law can contribute to understanding how and why speakers of international law use that language. This book builds on the scholarship of international law as language by examining the ways that a diverse range of speakers has used international law in the context of public debate – subject matter to which international lawyers have paid relatively little attention.

2.2.3 Speakers and Analytical Tools

2.2.3.1 Who Spoke? Professional, Political and Public Speakers

In trying to understand how politicians, trade union leaders, religious leaders, anti-war activists, journalists and lawyers conceived of international law, I have distinguished between their professional identities and the modes in which they spoke international legal language. Specifically, I have divided the participants in public debates into three analytical categories – professional, political and public. I use these categories in relation both to the identity of the speakers and to the mode in which they used international legal language. These analytical categories have allowed for an in-depth examination of the questions of 'who spoke', who was considered authorised to speak, and how those individuals characterised international law.

These three categories are, of course, problematic. Membership of each type is historically contingent, the boundaries between them are blurred, and individuals can cross categories or shift between them in the course of the debates. Notwithstanding these imperfections, the categories are a useful heuristic in tracing uses of international law in public debate. They highlight differences between which speakers used international law in the public debates, how they used it and the extent to which they considered themselves, and were considered by others, to be able to speak it with authority. These distinctions have applied both within each period and between periods. For example, in 2003, professional international lawyers had a significant presence in public debate, while they were relatively absent in 1965–66 and 1916. The presence or absence of professional speakers of international law seems to have influenced the degree to which political and public speakers were considered able to speak international legal language with authority.

So what does it mean to be 'professional, political, and public' speakers of international law? There is a sense for those who work in the field that 'professional international lawyers' are intuitively identifiable.[46] The scholarship outlined in section 2.2.2, for example, focuses on contexts and participants considered to have formal roles in the creation and deployment of international law. In this sense, international legal literature recalls Lawrence Friedman's famous distinction between internal and external legal cultures. Freidman considered external legal culture to be 'the legal culture of the general population', while the internal culture was 'the legal culture of insiders – lawyers, jurists, judges, law professors'.[47] Friedman's concept of legal culture has been criticised for being of such 'magnitude' as to be conceptually almost impossible to pin down,[48] and for being simultaneously measurable and evident and yet diffuse and abstract.[49] Friedman himself never offered a fully theorised account of the interactions between external and internal legal cultures, preferring instead to think of them as an heuristic; a way of 'lining up a range of phenomena into one very general category'.[50]

Despite these limitations, Friedman's work helps to clarify why and how professional speakers and contexts of international law have come to

---

[46] For scholarship on how international lawyers are constituted, see, for example, D'Aspremont, *Epistemic Forces in International Law* (n 36) especially 1–27; Korhonen, *International Law Situated* (n 36).

[47] Quoted in footnote 1 of Lawrence M Friedman, 'The Concept of the Self in Legal Culture' (1990) 38 *Cleveland State Law Review* 517. Friedman's key work here is Lawrence Friedman, *The Legal System: A Social Science Perspective* (Russell Sage Foundation, 1975). See also Lawrence M Friedman, *Total Justice: What Americans Want from the Legal System and Why* (Russell Sage Foundation, 1985); Lawrence M Friedman, *The Republic of Choice: Law, Authority and Culture* (Harvard University Press, 1990). For an overview of the impact of Friedman's work, see, for example, Robert W Gordon and Morton J Horowitz (eds.), *Law, Society and History: Themes in the Legal Sociology and Legal History of Lawrence W Friedman* (Cambridge University Press, 2011).

[48] De Carvalho (n 38) 9. See also Roger Cotterell, 'The Concept of Legal Culture' in David Nelken (ed.), *Comparing Legal Cultures* (Routledge, 1997).

[49] Susan S Silbey, 'Legal Culture and Cultures of Legality' in John R Hall, Laura Grindstaff and Ming-Cheng Lo (eds.), *Handbook of Cultural Sociology* (Routledge, 2010) 473. See also Roger Cotterell, *Law, Culture and Society: Legal Ideas in the Mirror of Social Theory* (Routledge, 2006).

[50] Lawrence W Friedman, 'The Concept of Legal Culture: A Reply' in David Nelken (ed.), *Comparing Legal Cultures* (Routledge, 1997) 33.

be constructed and understood. International lawyers are, in Friedman's sense, a self-constituted internal legal culture.[51] Policing the field is a key part of maintaining a professional identity. In David Kennedy's words, '[a]rguments about who is and is not within the discipline, whose arguments are and are not plausible, or what expert work has what consequences in the world are all part of expert practice'.[52] The 'professional' speakers thus consist of self-constituted international lawyers with specific educational and professional qualifications, who work in international courts, tribunals or institutions, for government, in academia or for non-government organisations.[53] They share a commitment to 'the general, the global – and not the particular, the local, the cultural'.[54] This cosmopolitan sensibility manifests in a desire to understand, develop or critique a universally applicable rule-bound system within which international relations are conducted.[55]

Political and public speakers of international law sit outside this internally constituted culture of international law. They do not necessarily share the world-view of international lawyers, nor do they have a common sensibility between or amongst themselves. The distinction between political and public speakers arises primarily through their societal roles in each period. Political speakers in this book were members of governments or Parliaments at the time that they participated in the public debate. They include leaders and ministers, as well as ordinary members of the federal or state parliaments in Australia. Public speakers consist effectively of everyone who was not a professional or political speaker. That is, public speakers in this book were participants in public debates who did not hold formal roles as either elected politicians or as professional international lawyers (to the extent that this latter category

---

[51] See, for example, James Crawford, 'International Law as a Discipline and a Profession' (2012) 106 *American Society of International Law Proceedings* 471.

[52] David Kennedy, *A World of Struggle: How Power, Law, and Expertise Shape Global Political Economy* (Princeton University Press, 2016) 122.

[53] See, for example, Martti Koskenniemi, *The Gentle Civilizer of Nations: The Rise and Fall of International Law 1870–1960* (Cambridge University Press, 2001) ('*Gentle Civilizer of Nations*'); D'Aspremont, 'Wording in International Law' (n 35); D'Aspremont, *Epistemic Forces in International Law* (n 36) especially 1–27.

[54] David Kennedy, 'The Twentieth-Century Discipline of International Law in the United States' in Austin Sarat, Bryant Garth and Robert A Kagan (eds.), *Looking Back and Law's Century* (Cornell University Press, 2002) 386, 392.

[55] This understanding of 'professional' international lawyers is historically contingent: see, for example, Koskenniemi, *The Gentle Civilizer of Nations* (n 53). It applies less clearly in 1916 Australia, for example, than it does in both 1965–66 and 2003. But its heuristic value remains.

was identifiable). This book traces the contributions of specific public speakers, namely trade unions and religious groups, and it also examines contributions from journalists and civil society activists. Some of these individuals had qualifications as lawyers, some had other forms of expertise in law, but they acted in the public debates as neither professional nor political speakers of international legal language.

It is, in one sense, inconsistent with international legal doctrine to describe certain political figures as outside the internal culture of international law. Under traditional sources doctrine, public statements by Prime Ministers, Foreign Ministers and a limited number of other government representatives can be considered to be evidence of the existence of customary international law.[56] Their statements can have a formal role in determining the content of international law. It is possible that some of the statements of Prime Ministers and Foreign Ministers examined in this book could be considered evidence of custom. Nevertheless, I distinguish political speakers from professional speakers in public debate. The role of political speakers in public debates was to prosecute a specific agenda connected to a position of their political party. This contrasted with the professional speakers whose role was, and was perceived to be, to provide independent or unbiased opinions on the law. Sometimes, professional opinions bolstered the positions of the political speakers, but the place of professional speakers in public debates was linked to the perception that they remained 'above' party politics.[57]

2.2.3.2 Vocabulary, Grammar and Competence

To understand the ways that international law has been used in public debate, my analysis draws on Martti Koskenniemi's construction of international law as language with its own vocabulary, grammar and required competence for successful communication.[58] 'Vocabulary'

---

[56] See, for example, James R Crawford, *Brownlie's Principles of Public International Law* (Oxford University Press, 8th ed., 2012) 24.

[57] See the complications of these roles in the reflections of 'professional international lawyers' who participated in the Iraq War debates in, for example, Hilary Charlesworth, 'Saddam Hussein: My Part in His Downfall' (2005) 23 *Wisconsin International Law Journal* 127; Matthew Craven et al., 'We Are Teachers of International Law' (2004) 17 *Leiden Journal of International Law* 363.

[58] Koskenniemi, *From Apology to Utopia* (n 2). Koskenniemi's categories are an inheritance of structural linguistics, see, for example, Ferdinand de Saussure, *Course in General Linguistics* (Bloomsbury, 2013); Noam Chomsky, *Current Issues In Linguistic Theory* (Mouton, 6th ed., 1975). For a discussion of Koskenniemi's linguistic approach see, for example, Anne Orford, 'A Journal of the Voyage from Apology to Utopia' (2006) 7

refers to the words that speakers use; and 'grammar' is the ways in which speakers structure those words in order to communicate. The ability to use both the vocabulary and the grammar of international law in order to create a persuasive argument is determined to some degree by a speaker's understandings of the unspoken (and sometimes unconscious) conventions of international legal language. This is the speaker's 'competence' in that language. The distinction between vocabulary, grammar and competence applies not just to international law as a language but to international law as a practice of argument. Thus, in addition to being able to speak international law through knowledge of its vocabulary and grammar, a fluent speaker of international law uses those elements to create competent international legal argument which, for Koskenniemi, is international legal practice.

The limitation in using this reading of Koskenniemi's scheme to analyse international legal language in public debate arises from a view that this linguistic scheme is a closed project of professional international lawyers. Koskenniemi has argued that international law is what international lawyers do. 'There is no access to legal rules or the legal meaning of international behaviour that is independent from the way competent lawyers see those things', he wrote.[59] As described in section 2.2.2, there is a body of work premised on the understanding that international law is what international lawyers say and do. Public debate is not part of the internal dialogue of the international courts, tribunals, institutions, government departments and universities that are the usual venues for professional international lawyers. Most of the contributors to public debates have also not been professional international lawyers. An argument that public debate generates international law does not sit easily within a scheme that regards international law as primarily what international lawyers say and do. And yet, interventions in the vocabulary of international law by political and public speakers have occurred and

---

German Law Journal 993. There are other critiques of Koskenniemi's overall argument in *From Apology to Utopia*, though perhaps not as many as one might expect. David Kennedy has suggested that this is because 'the book's symbolic meaning has somehow overtaken its analysis': Kennedy, 'The Last Treatise' (n 29) 991. See also, 'Special Issue - From Apology to Utopia: A Symposium' (2006) 7 *German Law Journal* 977–1108; B.S. Chimni, *International Law and World Order: A Critique of Contemporary Approaches* (Cambridge University Press, 2017) 246–357.; Carty (n 29); Iain Scobbie, 'Towards the Elimination of International Law: Some Radical Scepticism about Sceptical Radicalism' (1990) 61 *British Yearbook of International Law* 339. See also Koskenniemi's responses to some of the critiques in Koskenniemi, *From Apology to Utopia* (n 2) 589–615.

[59] Koskenniemi, *From Apology to Utopia* (n 2) 568.

continue to occur, and there seem to be no consistent articulations about why and how these interventions should be excluded as international law. Koskenniemi has expressed uncertainties over his closed linguistic scheme. 'It may be too much to say that international law is only what international lawyers think and do', he wrote in 2001, 'but it is at least that'.[60] Other international law scholars have articulated similar arguments. Balakrishnan Rajagopal reflected in 2006, 'I am not sure that there is a clear consensus that all practitioners need to be international lawyers, especially in the post-modern world of the early twenty-first century when international law-talk is occurring at the popular level'.[61]

I take a broader view of international legal language than that produced by an insular reading of Koskenniemi's linguistic scheme. The examples in Chapters 3, 4 and 5 suggest that there is much 'international law' that is recognisable regardless of who is speaking it.[62] The vocabulary of international law is identifiable for example where it is employed to address a problem of world order, including war and peace, or the movement across borders of people or goods. International legal vocabulary includes that of the sources of international law (custom and treaties); of foundational precepts of international law (including sovereignty, equality, territory, jurisdiction); of the institutions of international law (including the UN and the League of Nations); and of writings or claims by professional speakers of international law.[63] The key grammars of

---

[60] Koskenniemi, *The Gentle Civilizer of Nations* (n 53) 7.
[61] Balakrishnan Rajagopal, 'Martti Koskenniemi's *From Apology to Utopia*: A Reflection' (2006) 7 *German Law Journal* 1089, 1091–92. See also David Kennedy, *Of War and Law* (Princeton University Press, 2006).
[62] The vocabulary and grammar of international law have developed their own internal characteristics and these characteristics have, in turn, made the language identifiable even when spoken by outsiders. See Koskenniemi, *From Apology to Utopia* (n 2) esp 562–73; Koskenniemi, *Politics* (n 29); Kennedy, 'Theses' (n 29); Kennedy, *International Legal Structures* (n 29); Kennedy, 'When Renewal Repeats' (n 29).
[63] Some of the vocabulary of international law is the vocabulary of law in general. In Australia, for example, the vocabulary of 'sovereignty', 'treaty' and 'jurisdiction' are relevant to the internal distribution of legal authority, and to the relationships between Australian and Indigenous laws. See, for example, Christine Black, Shaun McVeigh and Richard Johnstone, 'Of The South' (2007) 16 *Griffith Law Review* 299; Mark McMillan, '*Koowarta* and the rival Indigenous international: Our place as Indigenous peoples in the international' (2014) 23 *Griffith Law Review* 110; Larissa Behrendt, 'Aboriginal Sovereignty: A Practical Roadmap' in Julie Evans et al. (eds.), *Sovereignty: Frontiers of Possibility* (University of Hawai'i Press, 2012). International legal language maintains its distinctiveness, however, through the cosmopolitan sensibility of its speaker or the global nature of the question to which the language is directed.

international law are recognisable too, consisting primarily of argumentative oscillations between law and politics, justice and consent.

For each of the debates examined in this book, I have asked three questions: Who spoke – and who was considered to have authority to speak – international legal language? What forms of international legal language did speakers use? How did speakers characterise their uses of international law? Combining the tools of vocabulary, grammar and competence with theorisations of 'popular' law generated a range of supplementary questions. These include: did speakers treat international law as separate from politics, society or morality? Did they describe international law as bringing virtue and justice, or as politics in another guise? What effect did they appear to imagine that speaking international law would have on their audiences? Were they calling on international law in order to make a larger claim of solidarity with a group, to critique a course of action, to rally public support?

Exploring these questions has given rise to my argument that the debates in this book, directed at the question of whether Australia should participate in a war, were conducted in the vocabulary and grammar of international law. The vocabulary, grammar and competences of professional, public and political speakers of international law were not the same, however. The public debates in Chapters 3, 4 and 5 suggest close correlations between the vocabulary and grammar of professional, political and public speakers of international law but differences in what it meant to make a competent argument in that language. In particular, public and political speakers employed different competences from professional international lawyers in order to be persuasive in public debate. These distinctions emerge from the readings presented in Chapters 3, 4 and 5.

2.3 Some Final Notes on Historical Method

With its accounts of Australian public debate about war during each of 2003, 1965–66 and 1916, this book contributes to the histories of international law by presenting a small history of international law within a particular place. Each chapter includes an account of the contexts that help to make sense of public debate, and, as explained in Chapter 1, I have presented these moments in Australian life in reverse chronological order. While the book as a whole is non-linear, the story of the public debates in each of Chapters 3, 4 and 5 includes a chronological description of the relevant contexts for each period. In situating these accounts

2.3 SOME FINAL NOTES ON HISTORICAL METHOD

within particular contexts, I have engaged with scholarship on one of the ongoing issues in international legal historiography: the debate over the appropriate context for international legal histories.[64] This debate has its roots in critiques of some international legal histories for failing to respect the need to avoid the 'great taboo' of anachronism by allowing the concerns of the present to interfere with the analysis of the past.[65] Ian Hunter, for example, critiqued Antony Anghie's classic *Imperialism, Sovereignty and the Making of International Law* on this basis.[66] Randall Lesaffer ranged a similar argument against international legal histories, arguing that they engage in a 'deplorable' exercise of anachronism by trying to 'understand the past for what it brought about and not for what it meant to the people living in it'.[67]

---

[64] International legal history is a species of legal and historical scholarship with its own trajectory of methodological debates. While they draw on historiographical traditions from other kinds of legal histories, the methodological debates in histories of international law have unfolded (and continue to unfold) differently. See, for example, Matthew Craven, 'Introduction: International Law and its Histories' in Matthew Craven et al. (eds.), *Time, History and International Law* (Brill, 2007) 1; Randall Lesaffer, 'International Law and its History: The Story of an Unrequited Love' in Matthew Craven et al. (eds.), *Time, History and International Law* (Brill, 2007) 27. See also Martti Koskenniemi, 'A History of International Law Histories' in Bardo Fassbender and Anne Peter (eds.), *The Oxford Handbook of the History of International Law* (Oxford University Press, 2012, online version); Martti Koskenniemi, 'Histories of International Law: Significance and Problems for a Critical View' (2013) 27 *Temple International and Comparative Law Journal* 215 ('Significance and Problems'); Jean D'Aspremont, 'Critical Histories of International Law and the Repression of Disciplinary Imagination' (2019) 7 *London Review of International Law* 89; Matilda Arvidsson and Miriam Bak McKenna, 'The Turn to History in International Law and the Sources Doctrine: Critical Approaches and Methodological Imaginaries' (2020) 33(1) *Leiden Journal of International Law* 37.

[65] See, for example, Quentin Skinner, 'Meaning and Understanding in the History of Ideas' (1969) 8 *History and Theory* 3. See also Richard Tuck, 'History of Political Thought' in Peter Burke (ed.), *New Perspectives on Historical Writing* (Pennsylvania State University Press, 2001) 218; Constantin Fasolt, *The Limits of History* (Chicago University Press, 2004) 6.

[66] Antony Anghie, *Imperialism, Sovereignty and the Making of International Law* (Cambridge University Press, 2007). Anghie, Hunter argued, misread the European *jus gentium* discourses that formed the subject matter of his book because he failed to situate them in 'the immanent conflicts among the rival intellectual cultures on which they were based, and the clashing religious and political programs in which these discourses were anchored': Ian Hunter, 'Global Justice and Regional Metaphysics: On the Critical History of the Law of Nature and Nations' in Shaunnagh Dorsett and Ian Hunter (eds.), *Law and Politics in British Postcolonial Thought: Transpositions of Empire* (Palgrave MacMillan, 2010) 11, 12.

[67] Lessafer (n 64) 34. See also Annabel Brett, *Changes of State: Nature and the Limits of the City in Early Modern Natural Law* (Princeton University Press, 2011) 14–15.

Some international legal scholars have resisted the critiques of anachronism by maintaining that the characteristic of being *legal* makes international legal history different from intellectual histories. This characteristic means that an international legal history relies on contexts that are distinctive from those of an intellectual history, and that an international legal historian employs different notions of time and space because studying the law necessarily requires an application of past ideas to the present. Anne Orford and Martti Koskenniemi both have written sustained defences of a method in international legal histories that studies texts, events and people in context (and thus agree at least in part with the contextualist argument), but that also allows for meanings to move across time.[68] Koskenniemi rejects 'pure' contextualism on two grounds. First, even on its own terms, Koskenniemi argues, complete contextualism is not possible because historians make choices in the present about what contexts of the past to study – intellectual, social, economic and more. These choices mean that the past is never studied on its own terms or in all of its contexts.[69] Koskenniemi's second argument is a normative one. He suggests that the past should not be studied merely for its own sake but precisely for what it can teach us about the alleviation of injustice in the present.[70]

Orford extends this argument by drawing on the 'histories of the present' of Michel Foucault, and arguing for the necessity of contextualisation and anachronism in international legal histories.[71] Citing the training of common law lawyers, who are taught in their first year of law school how to make a plausible argument for treating a past case as a binding precedent or not,[72] Orford proposes thinking about international law by holding two notions of time simultaneously. The first is contextualised human time, in which laws are seen and studied as the creations of particular times and

---

[68] See also the discussion in Craven (n 64) 8–15. Others have also argued for historical methods that explicitly confront the present: see, for example, Christopher Tomlins and John Comaroff, '"Law As . . . ": Theory and Practice in Legal History' (2011) 1 *UC Irvine Law Review* 1039.

[69] Koskenniemi, 'Significance and Problems' (n 64) 230–32.

[70] Ibid., 230.

[71] Anne Orford, 'On International Legal Method' (2013) 1 *London Review of International Law* 166 ('On Method'). Orford drew in particular on Michel Foucault, *The Birth of Biopolitics: Lectures at the College de France 1978–1979* tr G Burchell (Palgrave Macmillan, 2008). See also Michel Foucault, 'Nietzsche, Genealogy, History' in Paul Rabinow (ed.), *The Foucault Reader* (Pantheon Books, 1984) 76. For a useful commentary, see David Garland, 'What is a "history of the present"? On Foucault's Genealogies and their Critical Preconditions' (2014) 16 *Punishment & Society* 365.

[72] Orford, 'On Method' (n 71) 172.

2.3 SOME FINAL NOTES ON HISTORICAL METHOD

places. The second is a time beyond human time, in which laws are also understood to have a life and meaning that travel, in some cases across centuries.[73] Holding these ideas together, Orford argues for an international legal historical method that 'accepts the legitimate role of anachronism in international legal method'.[74] 'The past [of international law]', according to Orford, 'is constantly being retrieved as a source or rationalisation of present obligation'.[75]

Justin Desautels-Stein has built on the arguments of Koskenniemi and Orford to present a particular defence of structuralist international legal histories.[76] These linguistic histories, Desautels-Stein argues, relied on a context that was different from that of the intellectual historian. Desautels-Stein draws in particular on the 'conceptual histories' developed by Reinhart Koselleck to argue that the context for structural linguistic histories of international law was the grammar of that law – 'the structures of legal argument animating the legal concept ... in a particular mode of legal thought'.[77] The work of thinkers of the past is read for the structures of arguments in their *legal* register, rather than for their religious, political or cultural context.[78] Desautels-Stein concludes that structural historians and intellectual historians were searching for different but complementary objects of analysis. Structuralists, he says, sought the structure of legal thought in the context of a legal concept, whereas intellectual historians sought the politico-social-cultural-theological contexts of the thought of particular individuals.[79]

I draw from this debate about context that there is no obvious criteria for choosing between the appropriate contexts for international legal histories and that therefore the choice of context(s) both drives and is driven by the type of history that the author seeks to write.[80] In trying to

---

[73] Ibid., 176.
[74] Ibid., 175.
[75] Ibid. See also Anne Orford, 'The Past as Law or as History? The Relevance of Imperialism for Modern International Law', *International Law and Justice Working Papers* 2012/2, New York University School of Law. For a genealogical critique of Orford's argument, see Kate Purcell, 'On the Uses and Advantages of Genealogy for International Law' (2019) *Leiden Journal of International Law* 1.
[76] Desautels-Stein, 'International Legal Structuralism' (n 29) 216–27. Desautels-Stein is concerned here with defending the uses of history in particular in Koskenniemi, *From Apology to Utopia* (n 2) and Kennedy, *International Legal Structures* (n 29).
[77] Desautels-Stein, 'International Legal Structuralism' (n 29) 223–27.
[78] Ibid., 226.
[79] Ibid.
[80] For a thoughtful meditation on this question of context in international legal histories, see Painter (n 4).

identify the forms in which international legal language has appeared in a particular context in different periods, this book shares with structuralist histories an interest in the ways the vocabulary and grammar of international law have been used. By incorporating public debate, however, which is situated within its own social, political and cultural frameworks, the contexts included in this book are broader than the legal context as understood by Desautels-Stein. This book's investigation into international legal language in public debate is a linguistic history situated in the social and political contexts of Australia that mattered for the uses of international law within those public debates. For each period I examine, these contexts included how 'international law' was constituted, the international legal structures, the Australian legal and political structures, the events surrounding the decision to engage in war, and the tenor and content of the public and political response to that decision.

3

Public Debate in 2003: The Iraq War

3.1 Introduction

In this chapter, I focus on the public debates of the 2003 Iraq War. Within the different justifications that were given for the Iraq invasion, international legal language was used both as an autonomous justification and in combination with other factors to form collective justifications for war. The most surprising aspect of the 2003 debates was the frequency with which legality was used as an autonomous justification and how often it was employed by public and political, as well as professional, speakers of international law. Indeed, in 2003, international law was used as an autonomous justification for war by nearly all the participants in the public debate. It is this prominence of the language of legality in particular that most distinguishes the Iraq War public debates from the public debates of 1916 and 1965–66.

The 2003 Iraq War debates took place within the international legal system established by the *Charter of the United Nations* ('UN *Charter*'). The prohibition on the use of force under Article 2(4) of the UN *Charter* and the recognition of a state's 'inherent' right to self-defence under Article 51 are cornerstones of that regime, though their meaning and their application have always been contested.[1] Before 2003, two key sites of dispute were the 1999 North Atlantic Treaty Organization ('NATO') bombing of Kosovo and responses to the terrorist attacks on the United States ('US') on 11 September 2001 ('9/11'). Both events generated long-term implications for the international legal system. Within the framework of this book, the Kosovo bombing, ultimately framed as a question of

---

[1] See, for example, Marc Weller (ed.), *The Oxford Handbook of the Use of Force in International Law* (Oxford University Press, 2015) ('*Oxford Handbook of the Use of Force*').

legality versus legitimacy,[2] illustrates the fluidity of international legal argument. And one of the consequences of the 9/11 attacks was that, for at least a decade afterwards, the war on terror became the prism through which threats to international peace and security were addressed.[3] Since 2003, flashpoints for the law on the use of force have included the Security Council's operationalisation of the 'responsibility to protect' doctrine in Libya in 2011 and the debate over whether states are justified in using force against non-state actors located in states that are 'unwilling or unable' to take action themselves.[4] The expanding authority to use force that these examples embody exemplifies David Kennedy's argument that the UN *Charter* provides in practice a range of ways for states to justify their uses of force. The UN *Charter* is, in other words, an 'institutional framework for transforming sovereign power and violence into right'.[5]

In this chapter, I first outline the sources I have relied on. I then set out the context of Australia in 2002–3 and the major elements of the public debate about the Iraq War. Last, I analyse a series of texts from the debates as illustrations of the way international legal language was used.

3.2 Timing and Sources

Operation Iraqi Freedom, the 'invasion phase' of the US-led coalition attack on Iraq, began on 19 March 2003. The war, in the form of 'major combat operations', was declared 'over' five weeks later on 1 May 2003.[6] The

---

[2] For a description and analysis of this debate, see, for example, Hilary Charlesworth, 'International Law: A Discipline of Crisis' (2002) 65 *Modern Law Review* 377 ('Discipline of Crisis').

[3] For a description of Security Council actions on terrorism up to 2008, see Jane Boulden, 'The Security Council and Terrorism' in Vaughan Lowe, Adam Roberts and Jennifer Welsh (eds.), *United Nations Security Council and War: The Evolution of Thought and Practice Since 1945* (Oxford University Press, 2008) 608. For a description of more recent activities, see Helen Duffy, *The 'War on Terror' and the Framework of International Law* (Cambridge University Press, 2015). See also William J Aceves, Everard Meade and Gershon Shafir (eds.), *Lessons and Legacies of the War on Terror: From Moral Panic to Permanent War* (Routledge, 2013).

[4] SC Res 1973, UN SCOR 65th sess, 6498th mtg, UN Doc S/RES/1973 (17 March 1990); Spencer Zifcak, 'The Responsibility to Protect after Libya and Syria' (2012) 13 *Melbourne Journal of International Law* 59 ('Responsibility to Protect'); Monica Hakimi, 'Defensive Force against Non-State Actors: The State of Play' (2015) 91 *International Law Studies* 1.

[5] David Kennedy, *A World of Struggle: How Power, Law and Expertise Shape Global Political Economy* (Princeton University Press, 2016) 257 ('*World of Struggle*').

[6] George W Bush, 'Speech Declaring End of Major Combat Operations' (delivered on USS *Abraham Lincoln*, 1 May 2003), quoted in Jarrett Murphy, 'Text of Bush Speech' (1 May 2003) CBS News www.cbsnews.com/stories/2003/05/01/iraq/main551946.shtml.

international effort to rehabilitate Iraq then began. Australian troops participated in Operation Iraqi Freedom and in the reconstruction until they were withdrawn from operational roles on 31 July 2009.[7] The last American combat troops withdrew from Iraq on 18 December 2011,[8] eight and a half years after the initial invasion. During the invasion and occupation of Iraq, interim and then elected Iraqi governments were installed; the former Iraqi dictator Saddam Hussein was tried and executed; approximately 100,000 civilians were killed;[9] and 4.3 million Iraqis became refugees, with approximately half of those internally displaced.[10] The coalition forces also found no weapons of mass destruction ('WMD'), proving the lie that had formed the basis of one of the justifications for the Iraq invasion.

In this chapter, I examine material that was part of the public debate about the Iraq War in Australia from mid-2002 to 1 May 2003. It was during this period that the Australian Government moved to support a policy to invade Iraq. The end date of 1 May 2003 was when George W Bush declared the end of major combat operations in Iraq, which marked a shift to the 'post-invasion' phase of the Iraq conflict.[11] For political speakers, I focus in this chapter on Prime Minister John Howard and the Minister for Foreign Affairs, Alexander Downer, both of whom led the public case against the Saddam Hussein regime. I also examine the contributions of some members of the Opposition Labor Party. For public speakers, I examine statements by representative bodies of the unions and religious orders, including the Australian Education Union and the Catholic Bishops of Australia. I also describe in this chapter the contributions of professional international lawyers to the public debate.

My analysis of the public debate in this chapter is built around a selection of documents and statements made by these public and political speakers that provides a picture of the content and trajectory of the Iraq War debate in Australia. A number of themes emerge from these documents: the prominence of an autonomous language of legality spoken by all participants in the debates; the shifting framings of expertise; the reliance on

---

[7] See 'Iraq: The Second Gulf War, 1990–91', Australian War Memorial (Web Page) www.awm.gov.au/atwar/gulf/#secondgulfwar.
[8] See, for example, Tim Arango and Michael S Schmidt, 'Last Convoy of American Troops Leaves Iraq', *The New York Times* (New York, 18 December 2011).
[9] *Iraq Body Count* (Web Page) www.iraqbodycount.org/.
[10] United Nations High Commissioner for Refugees, *Global Report 2008: Facing New Challenges* (Geneva, 2008) 148.
[11] Bush's claim was false. For reflections on the legacy of the 2003 invasion, see, for example, Benjamin Isakhan (ed.), *The Legacy of Iraq: From the 2003 War to the 'Islamic State'* (Cambridge University Press, 2015).

international law through the languages of pre-emption, humanitarianism and the 'just war'; and the competing visions of international solidarity through law. These themes are described in detail in section 3.4. Next, I give an account of the different contexts in which the Iraq War debates in Australia took place.

3.3 The Context

3.3.1 The Howard Government's Australia

Australia's Prime Minister John Howard was the driving force behind the country's participation in the Iraq War. The conservative Coalition government of the Liberal and National parties that Howard led was in government from 1996 until 2007, making Howard the second-longest-serving Prime Minister in Australia's history.[12] Howard's time as Prime Minister included being re-elected in October 2004 in the aftermath of the Iraq War and remaining Prime Minister until the Labor Party, led by Kevin Rudd, won the election of 2007.[13]

Two elements of the Howard government's foreign policy agenda underpinned its positions in the Iraq War debates. These were the centrality of the Australian alliance with the US and the need to preserve Australia's physical and metaphorical borders from outside threats. This approach relied on a construction of Australian identity as Western and aligned with the great powers of the US and the United Kingdom ('UK'), rather than with Australia's regional Asian neighbours, which had been the focus of the predecessor Labor governments.[14] The approach also emphasised the physical and existential dangers to Australia from the foreign 'outside'. It was these threats whose existence Howard was keen to establish in order to demonstrate his government's ability to protect against them. Australian political scientist Jack Holland has described this phenomenon thus:

[12] See, for example, 'Australia's Prime Ministers: John Howard', *National Archives of Australia* (Web Page) http://primeministers.naa.gov.au/primeministers/howard/. See also John Howard, *Lazarus Rising: A Personal and Political Autobiography* (HarperCollins, 2013); Wayne Errington and Peter Van Onselen, *John Winston Howard: The Definitive Biography* (Melbourne University Press, 2008). Note that the 'National' Party was called the Australian Country Party from 1920 until 1975, when the Party formally changed its name to the 'National Party of Australia', https://nationals.org.au/about/our-history/key-dates-and-events/ accessed 13 December 2019.

[13] For an account of the 2007 campaign, see Christine Jackman, *Inside Kevin07: The Plan, the People, the Prize* (Melbourne University Press, 2008).

[14] See, for example, Adam Henry, 'Keating: The Man who Discovered Asia?' (2006) 5 *ISAA Review* 21.

> Howard's foreign policy discourse ... told Australians who 'we' were (Westerners, part of the Anglosphere) and who 'they' were (... definitely not Western).... [D]ifference was equated with potential danger.... [The discourse] tapped into the cultural terrain of 'mainstream Australia' ... reinforcing long-held geographical imaginations that viewed the Australian border as a 'dread frontier' to be defended.[15]

Howard's construction of Australia as an 'inside' that needed protection from the 'outside' was evident, too, in his government's attitude towards the international legal system.[16] In 2000, for example, after a critical review of Australia by the Committee on the Elimination of Racial Discrimination, the Howard government chose to withdraw from interactions with the human rights treaty committees, in favour of a 'strategic engagement' with the human rights system that would ensure a 'better deal from the UN treaty committees for Australia'.[17] Howard's scepticism towards international law emerged also in his government's reluctant 2002 ratification of the Rome Statute of the International Criminal Court, an outcome achieved only on the basis that Australia's 'sovereignty' would be maintained. Australia's ratification of the statute was accompanied by a declaration that stated, 'no person can be surrendered to the Court unless the Australian Attorney-General issues a certificate allowing surrender'.[18]

Two events of 2001 confirmed Howard's conviction in his foreign policy approach and contributed to his openness to an Iraq invasion. The first was the 9/11 terrorist attacks on the US. Howard had been on an official visit to Washington DC on the day of the attacks. His personal experience of that day gave him 'an enormous sense of empathy towards

---

[15] Jack Holland, 'Howard's War on Terror: A Conceivable, Communicable and Coercive Foreign Policy Discourse' (2010) 45 *Australian Journal of Political Science* 643, 648.

[16] See, for example, Hilary Charlesworth et al., 'Deep Anxieties: Australia and the International Legal Order' (2003) 25 *Sydney Law Review* 423.

[17] Australian Minister for Foreign Affairs, Alexander Downer; Attorney-General, The Hon Daryl Williams AM QC MP; Minister for Immigration and Multicultural Affairs, The Hon Philip Ruddock MP, 'Improving the Effectiveness of United Nations Committees' (Joint Media Release, 29 August 2000). See also Hilary Charlesworth and Gillian Triggs, 'Australia and the International Protection of Human Rights' in Donald R Rothwell and Emily Crawford (eds.), *International Law in Australia* (Thomson Reuters, 3rd ed., 2017); Madelaine Chiam, '*Tasmanian Dams* and Australia's Relationship with International Law' (2015) 24 *Griffith Law Review* 89.

[18] Australian Declaration accompanying ratification of the *Rome Statute of the International Criminal Court*, 1 July 2002. For an account of the events leading up to this ratification, see Hilary Charlesworth et al., *No Country Is an Island: Australia and International Law* (UNSW Press, 2006) 71–82.

the American people',[19] and furthered his resolve that Australia would participate in any military response.[20] Australia's domestic reactions to 9/11 included joining the war in Afghanistan and passing a raft of new counterterrorism legislation, some of which was highly restrictive.[21] While the shock of 9/11 made Australians more open to such changes, the severity of the responses was made more palatable to the Australian people by the second key event of 2001: the *Tampa* affair.

In the two weeks preceding 9/11, the Howard government had been locked in a standoff with the captain of a Norwegian ship – the *MV Tampa* – over the government's refusal to allow the ship to enter Australian territorial waters. The *Tampa* was carrying more than 400 asylum seekers (most of them Hazaras from Afghanistan) whom it had rescued from an Indonesian fishing boat that had been stranded in international waters.[22] The Howard government was determined not to let the asylum seekers arrive in Australian territory and rapidly arranged for their claims to be processed in Nauru. Howard and his ministers linked the events of 9/11 with the *Tampa* by arguing that a restrictive security approach to asylum seekers arriving by boat was necessary in order to protect Australians from the risk that asylum seekers may be terrorists.[23]

The Howard government's foreign policy narratives about the dangers to Australia from the physical and imagined 'outside' were magnified by the threats posed by the 'new' (post-9/11) terrorism and the arrival of boats characterised as possibly carrying terrorists. Howard further amplified these fears during the federal election campaign of October–November 2001, maintaining that only the Liberal–National Coalition could properly protect Australia's borders. Howard made

---

[19] Commonwealth, Parliamentary Debates, 17 September 2001, 30739 (John Howard).

[20] James Grubel, 'Australia's Howard a Surprise 9-11 Witness', *Reuters* (online, 5 September 2011) www.reuters.com/article/us-sept11-howard-idUSTRE78406N20110905.

[21] For an overview of Australia's counterterrorism legislation under Howard, see, for example, Greg Carne, 'Neither Principled nor Pragmatic? International Law, International Terrorism and the Howard Government' (2008) 27 *Australian Year Book of International Law* 11; George Williams, 'A Decade of Australian Anti-Terror Laws' (2011) 35 *Melbourne University Law Review* 1136.

[22] See, for example, Jane McAdam and Kate Purcell, 'Refugee Protection in the Howard Years: Obstructing the Right to Seek Asylum' (2008) 27 *Australian Year Book of International Law* 87; David Marr and Marian Wilkinson, *Dark Victory: How a Government Lied Its Way to Political Triumph* (Allen & Unwin, 2004).

[23] See Pene Mathew, 'Resolution 1371: A Call to Pre-Empt Asylum Seekers' (or 'Osama, the Asylum Seeker') in Jane McAdam (ed.), *Forced Migration, Human Rights and Security* (Hart Publishing, 2008) 21.

a statement during that campaign that became emblematic of his government's approach to the 'outside': 'We will decide who comes to this country and the circumstances in which they come'.[24] Howard's assertion that his government alone was able to control external threats to Australia was crucial to his government's electoral victory in November 2001.[25]

3.3.2 Alignment with the Bush Administration

The Howard government's perception of new threats from terrorists, its scepticism about the international legal system, and its foreign policy realignment with the US combined to make Australia a receptive partner for US President George W Bush's administration and its aggressive stance on the policy of 'regime change' in Iraq.[26] The Howard government indicated its support for Bush's Iraq policy during the first half of 2002. In March 2002, Australian Defence Minister Robert Hill told Parliament there was clear evidence of Saddam Hussein's continuing development of WMD and that the consequences would be 'devastating' if terrorists were to have access to them.[27] Howard told the Joint Meeting of the US Congress in June of that year that 'America has no better friend anywhere in the world than Australia'.[28] Around the same time, Foreign Minister Alexander Downer was taking a forceful public stance against

---

[24] John Howard, 'Address at the Federal Liberal Party Campaign Launch, Sydney', *Parliament of Australia* (Transcript, 28 October 2001) https://parlinfo.aph.gov.au/parlInfo/search/display/display.w3p;query=Id:%22library/partypol/1178395%22.

[25] Marr and Wilkinson (n 22).

[26] This policy had been in place since the Clinton administration passed the *Iraq Liberation Act of 1998*, PL 105–338, 112 STAT 3178 (1998). The Act authorised, among other things, supporting Iraqi democratic opposition organisations while also explicitly prohibiting in section 8 'the use of the United States armed forces ... in carrying out this Act'. In January 2001, at the first meeting of the new National Security Council, Bush positioned the 'destabilizing' influence of Saddam Hussein at the top of the Council's agenda: Ron Suskind, *The Price of Loyalty: George W Bush, the White House, and the Education of Paul O'Neill* (Simon & Schuster, 2004) 72.

[27] Commonwealth, *Parliamentary Debates*, Senate, 21 March 2002, 1266 (Robert Hill). This statement was made shortly after Bush delivered the 2002 State of the Union address identifying 'regimes that sponsor terror' as a threat to American security: George W Bush, 'State of the Union Address' (Speech, Joint Session of Congress, Washington DC, 29 January 2002). For other examples of these kinds of statements, see, for example, Dick Cheney, 'Remarks to the Council on Foreign Relations' (Speech, Council on Foreign Relations, Washington DC, 15 February 2002).

[28] John Howard, 'Address to Joint Meeting of US Congress' (Speech, US Congress, Washington DC, 12 June 2002).

the Iraqi regime, accusing those who opposed strong action against Hussein of supporting 'a policy of appeasement'.[29]

Iraq's development, possession and use of WMD had long been of concern to the international community. These concerns became particularly acute after Iraq ceased complying with UN weapons inspectors in 1998.[30] The combination of the Bush administration's disquiet about WMD and its desire for regime change in Iraq meant that the WMD issue emerged as the key justification for the action taken against Iraq by the US, the UK and Australia.[31] In August 2002, Alexander Downer stated that 'the critical issue is Iraq's possession of weapons of mass destruction. . . . For me, there is no doubt about it. I think this whole question of weapons of mass destruction is a profoundly serious and a profoundly important issue'.[32]

One of the main challenges for the US government, and consequently for the Australian Government, was to present convincing evidence of Iraq's apparently flourishing WMD programmes. Although it was established shortly after the end of formal hostilities that those WMD programmes did not exist, many people did believe until that time that Saddam Hussein possessed some level of WMD. The questions in 2002 were over the nature, quality and quantity of those weapons and the evidence available to demonstrate this, rather than whether the WMD existed in the first place.[33] To overcome these evidentiary difficulties, the Australian and US governments adopted two approaches. The first was to emphasise Iraq's known WMD history and the intelligence demonstrating Hussein's desire to acquire more. This argument relied not only on the presence of WMD evidence but also on the absence of evidence of their destruction.[34] Downer's speech to

---

[29] 'Downer rattles sabre over Iraq', *The Age* (online, 12 July 2002) www.theage.com.au/articles/2002/07/12/1026185101517.html.

[30] The then new President Bush identified weapons of mass destruction as a key security concern in his January 2001 inaugural address, and in February 2001, he explicitly warned Saddam Hussein against the further development of such weapons. See George W Bush, 'First Inaugural Address' (Speech, West Front of the US Capitol Building, Washington DC, 20 January 2001); George W Bush, 'The President's News Conference with President Vicente Fox of Mexico' (Speech, press corps, San Cristobal, Mexico, 16 February 2001).

[31] Paul Wolfowitz, quoted in John Shovelan, 'Wolfowitz Reveals Iraq PR Plan', *The World Today* (ABC Broadcasting Corporation, 29 May 2003) www.abc.net.au/worldtoday/content/2003/s867453.htm.

[32] Commonwealth, *Parliamentary Debates*, House of Representatives, 19 August 2002, 4792 (Alexander Downer).

[33] See, for example, Hans Blix, 'An Update on Inspections' (Speech, Security Council, New York, 27 January 2003 and 14 February 2003).

[34] See, for example, Interview with Dick Cheney, US Vice-President (Tim Russert, *Meet the Press*, NBC, 8 September 2002); George W Bush, 'Address by Mr George W Bush, President of the United States of America', UN Doc A/57/PV.2 (Speech, United Nations General

Parliament on 17 September 2002 was an example of this approach, with the details of Iraq's known WMD programme interspersed with references to the inability of UN weapons inspectors to establish whether warheads and quantities of chemical and biological weapons had been destroyed.[35]

The second approach was to maintain that Saddam Hussein's resistance to renewed weapons inspections was itself evidence of the possession of those weapons. Downer argued, for example, that the onus was not on the international community to prove that Hussein had WMD but rather on Hussein to prove that he did not. Thus, Downer concluded his 17 September speech as follows:

> It is Iraq which, after four years without inspections, has to disprove that it possesses weapons of mass destruction. . . . We must not reverse the onus of proof by taking it away from Iraq, the transgressor, and placing it on the international community.[36]

The US, UK and Australia also argued that states had a responsibility to prevent WMD from falling into the hands of terrorists, a position ultimately formalised by the Bush administration as the doctrine of pre-emption.[37] The US argued that the existing law on self-defence, which allowed military action in order to prevent an imminent attack, should encompass a broader understanding of 'imminent attack' – one that included the potential danger of a state such as Iraq providing WMD to terrorists who might use them against the US.[38]

Assembly', 12 September 2002) 8 ('Address to UN'); George W Bush, 'Remarks on Iraq' (Speech, Cincinnati Museum Centre, Cincinnati, 7 October 2002); George W Bush, 'State of the Union Address' (Speech, Joint Session of Congress, Washington DC, 28 January 2003) ('State of the Union Address 2003').

[35] Commonwealth, *Parliamentary Debates*, House of Representatives, 17 September 2002, 6379–80 (Alexander Downer).

[36] Ibid., 6383. See also Commonwealth, *Parliamentary Debates*, House of Representatives, 16 September 2002, 6245–46 (John Howard).

[37] In his 1 June 2002 speech, Bush said, inter alia, 'If we wait for threats to fully materialize, we will have waited too long . . . . We must take the battle to the enemy, disrupt his plans, and confront the worst threats before they emerge'. George W Bush, 'Graduation Speech' (Speech, West Point Military Academy, West Point, 1 June 2002); National Security Council, *The National Security Strategy of the United States of America* (President of the United States of America, 2002) ('*National Security Strategy of the United States*').

[38] It said, in part, 'For centuries, international law recognized that nations need not suffer an attack before they can lawfully take action to defend themselves against forces that present an imminent danger of attack . . . . We must adapt the concept of imminent threat to the capabilities and objectives of today's adversaries': *National Security Strategy of the United States*, ibid., 15. See generally Andrew Garwood-Gowers, 'Pre-Emptive Self-Defence: A Necessary Development or the Road to International Anarchy' (2004) 23 *Australian Year Book of International Law* 51; W Michael Reisman and Andrew Armstrong, 'The

The Howard government chose to support the US in principle on pre-emption, although it did not frame the argument as forcefully as did its counterpart. When Defence Minister Robert Hill explained the Australian position to Parliament in September 2002, he argued that the principles of international law needed to change as time, circumstance and weapons also changed. Thus, he said, the definition of self-defence needed to evolve with changing circumstances, 'in particular, the circumstances of terrorism and the development of weapons of mass destruction'.[39] Howard himself was more enthusiastic than his colleagues about pre-emption.[40] Asked in a television interview in December 2002, for example, if he would launch a pre-emptive strike against terrorists in another country if he had evidence they were about to attack Australia, Howard answered:

> Oh, yes. I think any Australian Prime Minister would. It stands to reason that if you believed that somebody was going to launch an attack against your country, either of a conventional kind or of a terrorist kind, and you had a capacity to stop it and there was no alternative other than to use that capacity, then of course you would have to use it.[41]

While the Howard government's attitude of committed support for the US policy on Iraq was a marker of Howard's foreign policy commitment to the US, it was also consistent with the support that previous Australian governments had given to the US policies towards Iraq. With bipartisan support from the Australian Parliament, the Labor government of Bob Hawke, for example, had joined the US-led, and UN-authorised, coalition to expel Iraq from Kuwait in 1991.[42]

Past and Future of the Claim of Preemptive Self-Defense' [2006] *Yale Law School Faculty Scholarship Series* 957; Belinda Helmke, *Under Attack: Challenges to the Rules Governing the International Use of Force* (Ashgate, 2013).

[39] Commonwealth, *Parliamentary Debates*, Senate, 17 September 2002, 4232 (Robert Hill).

[40] See, for example, Nicole Abadee and Don Rothwell, 'The Howard Doctrine: Australia and Anticipatory Self-Defence against Terrorist Attacks' (2007) 26 *Australian Yearbook of International Law* 19.

[41] Interview with John Howard, Prime Minister of Australia (Laurie Oakes, *Sunday*, 1 December 2002). See also 'Leaders Push UN to Legitimise Strike', *The 7.30 Report* (Australian Broadcasting Corporation, 9 September 2002, Fran Kelly).

[42] See generally Commonwealth, *Parliamentary Debates*, House of Representatives and Senate, 21 and 22 January 1991. Not all Australians had been convinced that a military response was justified in 1991. The Democrats, for example, had argued that the UN sanctions should be given more time to work. Public protests were also vigorous, with thousands of Australians joining protestors around the world to object to the military action. Large demonstrations occurred across the country, while some took their protests directly to Parliament: see Commonwealth, *Parliamentary Debates*, Senate, 21 January 1991, 13–19 (Janet Powell). See also 'Hawke: Sometimes Peace Can Be at

3.3.3 *Australia, the Security Council and the Final Push to War*

September and October 2002 were key months in the lead-up to the Iraq War. With a focus on Security Council action, the pressure was on the members of the Security Council to agree to a new resolution on Iraq. In Australia, the parliamentary debate on Iraq that occurred in mid-September received extensive media coverage. A looming war in Iraq was part of the public conversation, and the public was generally sceptical about the war. A Newspoll conducted in September 2002 reported that 47 per cent of people surveyed were against the US attacking Iraq, 33 per cent were in favour and 20 per cent were undecided.[43] The terrorist attacks in Bali in October 2002 gave greater impetus to the Howard government's case. Bali has long been one of Australia's most popular holiday destinations, and the death of eighty-eight Australians that day made the attacks feel personal for many.[44] For Howard, the attacks intensified a determination to confront terrorism with 'unrelenting vigour and with an unconditional commitment'.[45]

At the Security Council, concentrated diplomatic efforts by the US and UK resulted in the passage of Resolution 1441 on 8 November 2002. This resolution gave Iraq a 'final opportunity to comply with its disarmament obligations [arising from earlier Security Council resolutions]' and warned Iraq of 'serious consequences' if it continued to violate its previous obligations or the new inspection regime set out in Resolution 1441.[46] As a consequence of the pressure applied by Resolution 1441,

---

Too Great a Price', *The Canberra Times* (Canberra, 18 January 1991) 5; 'Recalled Parliament "A Chance for Protest"', *The Canberra Times* (Canberra, 18 January 1991) 5; 'Anti-War Protests Escalate', *The Canberra Times* (Canberra, 28 January 1991) 4; 'Thousands Rally for Peace', *The Canberra Times* (Canberra, 17 January 1991) 2. Operation Desert Storm was authorised by Security Council Resolution 678. For commentary on the 1991 Iraq War, see, for example, James Cockayne and David M Malone, 'The Security Council and the 1991 and 2003 Wars in Iraq' in Vaughan Lowe, Adam Roberts and Jennifer Welsh (eds.), *United Nations Security Council and War: The Evolution of Thought and Practice Since 1945* (Oxford University Press, 2008) 384.

[43] Newspoll, 'Iraq Poll' (Public Opinion Poll, 15 September 2002) http://polling.newspoll.com.au/image_uploads/cgi-lib.16527.1.0912iraq_poll.pdf.

[44] See, for example, Shandon Harris-Hogan, 'Remembering the Bali Bombings Ten Years On', *The Conversation* (online, 12 October 2012) https://theconversation.com/remembering-the-bali-bombings-ten-years-on-10040.

[45] John Howard, quoted in David Fickling, '"Lucky Country" in shock after its worst peacetime disaster', *The Guardian Online*, 14 March 2002 www.theguardian.com/world/2002/oct/14/indonesia.alqaida.

[46] SC Res 1441, UN SCOR, 57th sess, 4644th mtg, UN Doc S/RES/1441 (8 November 2002) [1, 13].

Iraq agreed to a new round of weapons inspections, and the team of inspectors, led by the head of the International Atomic Energy Agency, Hans Blix, was due to report to the Security Council on 27 January 2003. On 23 January, Australian troops left for the Middle East, although the Howard government maintained that no decision to commit Australian forces to an invasion of Iraq had been made.[47] The justification for the troop movement was instead that the 'government believes, however, that the forward deployment adds to diplomatic pressure on Saddam Hussein'.[48]

In Australia, media coverage in January 2003 concentrated on the question of whether the war would occur and, if so, whether Australia would participate.[49] Popular opinion was generally opposed to war without UN sanction. A Newspoll from January 2003 cited 61 per cent of those surveyed as against Australian forces being part of a US-led military action against Iraq, 30 per cent in favour and 9 per cent uncommitted. In that same poll, 61 per cent of people said they would be in favour of Australian forces being part of military action if it were authorised by the UN, 32 per cent said they would oppose it, and 7 per cent were uncommitted.[50] At least according to this poll, the authority of the UN was a key issue for the Australian people.

Neither Hans Blix's report to the Security Council on 27 January 2003 nor US Secretary of State Colin Powell's speech in February 2003 produced convincing evidence of an immediate threat of force from Iraq or of a 'material breach' of Iraq's Security Council obligations.[51] The Howard government then developed an argument that relied on Resolution 1441 in combination with two earlier Security Council

---

[47] See, for example, Interview with John Howard, Prime Minister of Australia (Kerry O'Brien, *The 7.30 Report*, Australian Broadcasting Corporation, 23 January 2003) http://pmtranscripts.pmc.gov.au/release/transcript-20633 ('Interview with John Howard, 23 January 2003').

[48] 'Troops to leave for Middle East tomorrow', *The Age* (online, 22 January 2003) www.theage.com.au/articles/2003/01/22/1042911424779.html.

[49] See, for example, Interview with John Howard, Prime Minister of Australia (Heather Ewart, *The 7.30 Report*, Australian Broadcasting Corporation, 10 January 2003) https://pmtranscripts.pmc.gov.au/release/transcript-20618; Interview with John Howard, 23 January 2003 (n 47).

[50] Newspoll, 'Iraq Poll', 21 January 2003, http://polling.newspoll.com.au.tmp.anchor.net.au/image_uploads/cgi-lib.22318.1.0102iraqi_military.pdf.au.

[51] See, for example, Dan Plesch, 'US Claim Dismissed by Blix', *The Guardian* (online, 5 February 2003) www.theguardian.com/world/2003/feb/05/iraq.unitednations; Michael White and Brian Whittaker, 'UK War Dossier a Sham, Say Experts', *The Guardian* (online, 7 February 2003) www.theguardian.com/politics/2003/feb/07/uk.internationaleducationnews; 'Ritter Dismisses Powell Report', *Kyodo News* (online, 6 February 2003) www.globalpolicy.org/component/content/article/167/35189.html.

resolutions, 678 and 687, to justify the use of force. Resolution 678 had provided the Security Council authorisation for the collective use of force to repel Iraq's forces from Kuwait in 1990.[52] Resolution 687 established the terms of the permanent ceasefire agreement following Iraq's withdrawal from Kuwait, including the destruction of all of Iraq's chemical, biological and nuclear weapons capability.[53]

The argument over the meaning and effect of these resolutions eventually became the central focus of the debate over the legality of the Iraq War. Broadly put, those who opposed war argued that it was for the Security Council to determine whether the terms of Resolution 1441 had been breached and that a further resolution was necessary to authorise military action. The states that adopted this approach generally wanted to give the ongoing weapons inspections more time to work, and without a deadline. Those who supported war – the coalition of the willing – argued that a state (in this case the US) could unilaterally determine whether Resolution 1441 had been violated and that the 'serious consequences' it threatened amounted, through resolutions 687 and 678, to an authorisation to use force in the event a violation was established.[54]

This technical issue of the interpretation of Security Council resolutions eventually became a key part of the public debate in Australia. The question in particular of whether a second Security Council resolution – a follow-up to Resolution 1441 – was necessary and achievable was prominent in Australia's public debate in February and March 2003. Towards the end of this debate, the Howard government took the unusual step of releasing its legal advice regarding the war, to which the Labor Party responded with two separate pieces of legal advice of its own.[55] International lawyers became regular participants in the public debate – appearing in the media to give their views on plausible interpretations of

---

[52] SC Res 678, UN SCOR 45th sess, 2963rd mtg, UN Doc S/RES/678 (29 November 1990).
[53] SC Res 687, UN SCOR 46th sess, 2981st mtg, UN Doc S/RES/687 (3 April 1991).
[54] For an outline of the legal debate, see, for example, Alex J Bellamy, 'International Law and the War with Iraq' (2003) 4 *Melbourne Journal of International Law* 497; Ronli Sifris, 'Operation Iraqi Freedom: United States v Iraq' (2003) 4 *Melbourne Journal of International Law* 521; Gerry Simpson, 'The War in Iraq and International Law' (2005) 6 *Melbourne Journal of International Law* 167; Dino Kritsiotis, 'Arguments of Mass Confusion' (2004) *European Journal of International Law* 233.
[55] The competing legal opinions of the Australian Government and the Opposition were reproduced as a 'Special Feature' called 'Advice on the Use of Force Against Iraq' (2003) 4 *Melbourne Journal of International Law* 177.

Security Council resolutions.[56] An open letter, signed by a group of forty-three international law academics condemning the legality of war and published in both *The Age* and *The Sydney Morning Herald* generated its own short bubble of media commentary.[57]

The broader protests against the war reached a peak in March 2003. On 11 March, Andrew Wilkie, then a senior analyst at the Office of National Assessment and responsible for assessing the state of WMD intelligence on Iraq, had resigned in protest at the Howard government's policy.[58] There were multiple mass public demonstrations against the war in all Australian cities, with estimates of nearly 40,000 participants across Australia on 20 March alone.[59] Newspoll results from 18 March reported 68 per cent of respondents were against Australian troops being involved in military action in Iraq without UN authority, and 33 per cent were against military action with UN authority.[60]

A final consensus that there would be no further resolutions on Iraq was confirmed in Australia on 18 March 2003, the same day that Howard formally committed Australian troops to the coalition of the willing. During the days leading up to 18 March, politicians from all sides were

---

[56] See, for example, 'Legal Implications of Iraq War', *Lateline* (Australian Broadcasting Corporation, 6 February 2003); Hilary Charlesworth and Andrew Byrnes, 'No, This War is Illegal', *The Age* (online, 19 March 2003) www.theage.com.au/articles/2003/03/18/1047749770379.html; 'Law Experts on Legality of Use of Force against Iraq', *PM* (Australian Broadcasting Corporation, 14 March 2003).

[57] 'Coalition of the Willing? Make that War Criminals', *The Sydney Morning Herald* (online, 26 February 2003) www.smh.com.au/articles/2003/02/25/1046064028608.html. I was one of those 43 signatories. Responses to the letter included Don Greig, 'War, Legality and Iraq', *The Canberra Times* (Canberra, 17 March 2003); 'The Case for a Legal Attack', *The Australian* (Sydney, 18 March 2003) 11. For reflections on the interventions by international lawyers in the Iraq debate in Australia, see, for example, Andrew Byrnes, '"The Law Was Warful": The Iraq War and the Role of International Lawyers in the Domestic Reception of International Law' in Hilary Charlesworth et al. (eds.), *The Fluid State: International Law and National Legal Systems* (Federation Press, 2005) 229; Hilary Charlesworth, 'Saddam Hussein: My Part in His Downfall' (2005) 23(1) *Wisconsin International Law Journal* 127.

[58] See Andrew Wilkie's personal account of this time in Andrew Wilkie, *Axis of Deceit: The Extraordinary Story of an Australian Whistleblower* (Black Inc. Agenda, 2nd ed., 2010).

[59] For reports on the mass anti-war protests, see, for example, Jacqueline Maley, 'Thousands Protest across Australia', *The Sydney Morning Herald* (online, 20 March 2003) www.smh.com.au/articles/2003/03/20/1047749876856.html; 'Anti-War Rally Makes Its Mark', *BBC World News* (online, 19 February 2003) http://news.bbc.co.uk/2/hi/uk_news/2767761.stm; 'Anti-War Demonstrators Rally around the World', *CNN* (online, 18 January 2003) http://articles.cnn.com/2003-01-18/us/sproject.irq.us.protests_1_rally-inspection-team-iraq?_s=PM:US.

[60] Newspoll, 'Iraq Poll', 18 March 2003 http://polling.newspoll.com.au.tmp.anchor.net.au/image_uploads/cgi-lib.26256.1.0303war.pdf.

regularly in the media, defending their various positions on the war. Howard, in particular, seemed to be everywhere, taking his government's justifications to the Australian people to ask for their support. Following the hectic events of 18 March, including the confirmed commitment of Australian troops to an Iraq invasion, on 19 March the aerial bombardment of Iraq began. Public protests against the war continued during the first few days of the campaign – perhaps most famously, two anti-war activists painted 'No War' across the sails of the Sydney Opera House.[61] Howard delivered an 'Address to the Nation' via television on the evening of 20 March 2003. It was the final pre-war statement of the Howard government's justifications for war in Iraq. After this address, most of the public debate turned to logistical and strategic issues around the conduct of hostilities, the treatment of civilians during the military campaign and, finally, the reconstruction of Iraq.

Australians have not had the opportunity to scrutinise the Howard government's decision-making in the same way as their British and American counterparts have.[62] The political and public pressure that forced revelations about government conduct in the US and the UK did not arise in the same way in Australia, and the Howard government was able to resist the pressure that did exist. Wide-ranging inquiries into official conduct in Australia have never occurred; the two inquiries that did occur were confined to issues around the intelligence that led to the

---

[61] See, for example, 'Opera House defaced in war protest', *The Age* (online, 18 March 2003) www.theage.com.au/articles/2003/03/18/1047749763708.html.

[62] United States inquiries include the following: https://fas.org/irp/offdocs/wmd_report.pdf; Inspector General, United States Department of Defense, https://fas.org/irp/agency/dod/ig020907-decl.pdf; United States Senate Select Committee on Intelligence, https://fas.org/irp/congress/2004_rpt/ssci_iraq.pdf; United States Senate Select Committee on Intelligence, www.intelligence.senate.gov/sites/default/files/publications/109331.pdf. The UK Iraq Inquiry released its final report in July 2016; see *The Report of the Iraq Inquiry: Report of a Committee of Privy Counsellors* (6 July 2016) www.iraqinquiry.org.uk/ ('*The Report of the Iraq Inquiry*'): see text accompanying footnotes 9–25 in Chapter 1. Memoirs from people involved include Tony Blair, *A Journey: My Political Life* (Alfred A Knopf, 2010); George W Bush, *Decision Points* (Broadway Paperbacks, 2010); Richard A Clarke, Against all Enemies: Inside America's War on Terror (Free Press, 2004); Dick Cheney, *In My Time: A Personal and Political Memoir* (Threshold Editions, 2011); Condoleezza Rice, *No Higher Honor: A Memoir of My Years in Washington* (Crown Publishers, 2011); Donald Rumsfeld, *Known and Unknown: A Memoir* (Sentinel, 2011). Two of the investigative books include Ron Suskind, *The Price of Loyalty: George W. Bush, the White House, and the Education of Paul O'Neill* (Simon & Schuster, 2004); Bob Woodward, *Plan of Attack: The Definitive Account of the Decision to Invade Iraq* (Simon & Schuster, 2004).

war.[63] Of the main players in the Iraq enterprise in Australia, only Howard chose to present his version of events – in his published memoirs.[64] Few other decision-makers have written about Australia's role in the war, although the former intelligence officer who became a federal Member of Parliament Andrew Wilkie recorded his story and continued to call for an independent inquiry into the Australian Government's conduct over Iraq.[65] Australian academics and commentators have reflected on and investigated Australia's participation in the Iraq War, and the ten-year anniversary of the invasion in 2013 produced a further push for an Australian inquiry.[66] Neither major political party in Australia has expressed interest in convening one. The Howard government participated in the coalition of the willing despite a forceful anti-war push both from the Opposition parties and from the public more generally.

3.4 The Public Debate

At the core of the justifications presented by the coalition of the willing was the threat posed by Iraq's possession of WMD. The WMD justification formed the basis of three of the key arguments used by the Howard government, each of which was an argument framed in a collective form of international legal language. These were, first, military action against Iraq was necessary to prevent the proliferation of WMD (which included chemical and biological weapons as well as the potential of nuclear weapons) in general but in particular to prevent its use by a rogue state like Iraq; second, military action against Iraq was necessary to prevent it from providing WMD to terrorists who might then use those WMD anywhere in the world; and third, military action against Iraq was necessary to enforce a series of Security Council resolutions authorising the destruction of Iraq's WMD programme. Two other justifications featured in the Australian public debate: the

---

[63] See Parliamentary Joint Committee into ASIO, ASIS and DSD, *Intelligence on Iraq's Weapons of Mass Destruction* (Commonwealth of Australia, 2004); Philip Flood, *Report of the Inquiry into Australian Intelligence Agencies* (Commonwealth of Australia, 2004).

[64] Howard (n 12) chapter 34.

[65] Wilkie (n 58); Jeremy Thompson, 'Wilkie Wants Howard to Front Iraq Inquiry', *ABC News* (online, 11 August 2011) www.abc.net.au/news/2011-08-11/wilkie-wants-iraq-inquiry/2834732.

[66] Information about this campaign, which has since become a campaign to reform Australia's war-making powers, is available at the website of Australians for War Powers Reform www.warpowersreform.org.au/.

3.4 THE PUBLIC DEBATE

humanitarian outcome of war, which, according to the Howard government, was to rescue the Iraqi people from the brutality of the Saddam Hussein regime; and the importance of maintaining a strong Australia–US alliance. 'Regime change' was a major theme of the US debates,[67] but Australia's leaders were reluctant to press this cause. Indeed, the Howard government framed regime change not as a basis for intervention but as the happy consequence of a war that was justifiable on other grounds.[68]

The WMD, humanitarian and alliance justifications were 'collective justifications' for war: justifications that incorporated international legal reasoning within larger claims to rightness, ethics or strategy. These justifications were most prominent in the early stages of the Iraq debates. In the later stages of the public debate, particularly as the meaning and role of Security Council resolutions captured the public's interest, international law became prominent as an autonomous justification. In the following sections, I examine texts from the 2003 debates that illustrate each of these uses of international legal language: as an autonomous claim to legality, as a basis for WMD enforcement, as a measure of humanitarianism and as a representation of alliance.

3.4.1 International Legal Language and Legality

3.4.1.1 The Vocabulary of Law and the Challenge of Legality: Speech to Parliament by Foreign Minister Alexander Downer, September 2002

An early contribution that evidenced the developing significance of international legality as a measure in Australian public debate was Foreign Minister Alexander Downer's September 2002 speech to the House of Representatives (and the almost identical version delivered by Defence Minister Robert Hill to the Senate). Downer's speech was the first major speech by a member of the Howard government on Australia's position against Iraq. It set out in comprehensive terms the state of the case against Iraq in September 2002. This timing is significant because it was in September 2002 – after a summit at Camp David between George W Bush and Tony Blair – that its proponents shifted how they framed

---

[67] See, for example, Michael MacDonald, *Overreach: Delusions of Regime Change in Iraq* (Harvard University Press, 2014).
[68] See, for example, Commonwealth, *Parliamentary Debates*, House of Representatives, 18 September 2002, 6594 (Alexander Downer).

their reasons for invading Iraq.[69] During the second half of 2002, the three justifications that had been favoured by the Americans – WMD, links to terrorism and Iraq's brutal human rights record – had coalesced to form the basis for a public justification for the invasion of Iraq that was centred on Iraq's failure to comply with Security Council resolutions. The speeches of Bush, Downer and UK Foreign Secretary Jack Straw to the General Assembly in September 2002 all evidenced this change.[70] All three men argued that Iraq posed a grave threat to the international community by its failure to comply with the Security Council resolutions aimed at ending its WMD programme. Each of the speeches contended (in differing language) that 'the authority of the United Nations itself is at stake'.[71] Alexander Downer's version of the challenge posed to the UN was framed thus:

> Let us also be very clear: Iraq's flagrant and persistent defiance is a direct challenge to the United Nations, to the authority of the Security Council, to international law, and to the will of the international community.[72]

Until this point, the Australian Government's justifications for war in Iraq had centred on the WMD argument – that is, rogue regimes like Saddam Hussein's must be prevented from obtaining and using WMD. The argument that a failure to discipline Iraq constituted a challenge to the authority of the UN was a new combined front for the coalition of the willing, and signalled a turn to justifications based on the defiance of law upon which the US and Australia in particular relied. It also indicated that Australia was prepared in September 2002 to join its coalition partners in doing what they considered necessary in order to bend the Security Council to their will.

Downer built on the themes of his speech to the General Assembly in his September 2002 speech to Parliament. He argued that the case against Iraq consisted of two major elements: first, Iraq's failure to comply with

---

[69] Reports of the Camp David summit between Bush and Blair on 9 September 2002 reveal that Cheney was still resistant to taking the issue to the UN for resolution, but Blair was insistent that his government would be destroyed if they did not use the UN route. See, for example, David Rose, 'Bush and Blair Made Secret Pact for Iraq War', *The Observer*, 4 April 2004; *The Report of the Iraq Inquiry* (n 62) 159–68.

[70] See, for example, the extracts of speeches delivered to the General Assembly in September 2002: *The Report of the Iraq Inquiry* (n 62) 182–92.

[71] Jack Straw, UN Doc A/57/PV.6 (Speech, United Nations General Assembly, 14 September 2002) 11. See also Bush, 'Address to UN' (n 34) 6–9; Alexander Downer, UN Doc A/57/PV.4 (Speech, United Nations General Assembly, 13 September 2002) 23–26 ('Speech to UN').

[72] Downer, 'Speech to UN' (n 71) 24.

3.4 THE PUBLIC DEBATE

a series of Security Council resolutions and, second, Iraq's existing and planned WMD programme to which the Iraqi regime's 'involvement with international terrorism' was also relevant.[73] Downer used this speech to set out in some detail the international community's knowledge about Iraq's WMD programme. After setting out the case, Downer then outlined likely developments in the Security Council to advance action against Iraq and explained Australia's national interest in the resolution of the Iraq issue. Downer said explicitly that the international community was still in a 'diplomatic phase' and that the government was 'not at the stage of making decisions about possible military commitments'.[74]

With a focus on the Security Council, Downer's presentation was replete with the language of international law. Indeed, in the context of the public debate, where the autonomous form of international legal language became significant in the later stages, this speech was distinctive for its explicit focus on legality. This language was evident in Downer's discussion of Iraq's failure to comply with Security Council resolutions and its WMD programme. Downer described how, for 'over a decade, Iraq has persistently defied legally binding obligations to disclose and eradicate its weapons of mass destruction program and capabilities'.[75] He characterised Iraq's actions as constituting 'clear and material breaches of Security Council resolutions'[76] and called the Saddam regime 'a serial transgressor'.[77] Later, Downer recounted how his discussions about Iraq at the UN focused on how 'the authority of the UN was at stake' and that the Security Council needed 'to meet its responsibilities in addressing the threat to international peace and security'.[78] He said that he 'judged that Australia should leave no stone unturned in our efforts to get Iraq to comply with international law and disarm and destroy its weapons of mass destruction'.[79]

In their attempts to resist the Howard government's moves against Iraq, the Labor Opposition and the Australian Democrats, a minor party, also relied on international legal argument. The day before Downer's speech, for example, the leader of the Labor Party, Simon Crean, had posed this question to John Howard:

---

[73] Commonwealth, *Parliamentary Debates*, House of Representatives, 17 September 2002, 6381 (Alexander Downer).
[74] Ibid., 6379.
[75] Ibid.
[76] Ibid.
[77] Ibid.
[78] Ibid., 6381.
[79] Ibid., 6382.

> Does the Prime Minister support Labor's policy that the United Nations Security Council should adopt a fresh resolution stipulating a timetable for Iraq's readmission of weapons inspector from UNMOVIC? Does the government also support Labor's policy position that, if Iraq fails to readmit weapons inspectors within the stipulated time frame, the Security Council should adopt a further resolution outlining the necessary action to be taken against Iraq under chapter VII of the United Nations charter?[80]

Here, Crean focused on the specific legal issues of Security Council process and authorisation in a targeted attempt to combat the Howard government on Iraq. Crean's question identified one of the legal questions that came to be crucial in the legal justifications for the Iraq War: how many Security Council resolutions did the Howard government believe were required in order to authorise the use of force? In response to Crean, John Howard gave an answer that mirrored Downer's approach and the attitude of both the US and the UK. Howard's answer placed responsibility for resolving the Iraq problem with the UN while reserving the ability to be part of a future coalition force in Iraq, with or without UN authorisation. He said, 'I can inform [the Leader of the Opposition] that the government do support very strongly the United Nations taking action. We believe the appropriate vehicle *at this stage* is the Security Council of the United Nations'.[81]

Compliance with international law was, thus, a key element of Downer's speech. But it was a dual sense of legality – one that relied in part on forcing obedience to the law and in part on gaining legitimacy through the defiance of law.[82] In Downer's conception, while it was unacceptable for Iraq to continue to flout its own international legal obligations, it was justifiable for Australia, and its partners in the coalition of the willing, to defy that same international law in order to force Iraq into compliance. A failure by the UN to enforce its own resolutions would amount, in Downer's argument, to a failure not only of the institution but also of the entire international legal system. Such a dual failure was not simply a challenge to the enforceability of international law; it was a challenge to the authority of the institution that created those

---

[80] Commonwealth, *Parliamentary Debates*, House of Representatives, 16 September 2002, 6240 (Simon Crean).
[81] Commonwealth, *Parliamentary Debates*, House of Representatives, 16 September 2002, 6240 (John Howard); emphasis added.
[82] Nathaniel Berman, 'Legitimacy through Defiance: From Goa to Iraq' (2005) 23 *Wisconsin International Law Journal* 93.

obligations in the first place. In the opening paragraphs of his speech, for example, Downer described the Iraqi regime thus:

> Combined with his record of aggression, both within and across Iraq's borders, [Saddam Hussein] threatens international security and directly challenges the authority of the United Nations and international law.[83]

In constructing the argument about the UN in this way, Downer repeated the stance he had taken in his speech to the General Assembly a few days earlier. In both speeches, Downer portrayed international law as a standard he respected, but his words simultaneously undermined the authority of that law. The power of international law for Downer in this example seemed to come from the comfort that it could offer the coalition of the willing if the international legal system chose to legitimise the coalition's actions, rather than from any normative pull that international law had on his government. In the event that the international legal system rejected the coalition's proposed military action, Downer's response would not be that Australia would remain within the system and persist in an argument within the law – this was not a construction of international law as indeterminate – but to reject the international legal system altogether.[84] Downer was seeking to justify his government's actions through defiance of an international law that he constructed as obstructing the proper aims of three democratic governments. This view of international law became a central plank of the coalition of the willing's justifications for war. The US, the UK and Australia continued to challenge the UN to 'serve the purpose of its founding'[85] and 'demonstrate a clear, collective determination to uphold the authority of the Security Council'.[86]

Downer expressed no sense of contradiction between his insistence that the UN be willing to punish Iraq's repeated non-compliance with its international obligations – by force if necessary – and his own position that Australia was justified in defying obligations created by that same international legal system in order to secure Iraq's conformity. Downer's careful outlining of the international legal positions on Iraq during his September 2002 speech, and his professed willingness to defy the

---

[83] Commonwealth, *Parliamentary Debates*, House of Representatives, 17 September 2002, 6379 (Alexander Downer) 6378.
[84] This was also the US position. The UK position was more ambivalent than either the Australian or the US positions. See *The Report of the Iraq Inquiry* (n 62) 94–181.
[85] Bush, 'Address to the UN General Assembly' (n 34) 8.
[86] Downer, 'Speech to the UN General Assembly' (n 71) 24.

international system in order to bring Iraq to heel, are consistent with Nathaniel Berman's argument that governments that have sought legitimacy through defiance of international law 'listen very attentively to the voice of law'.[87] It is only in situations where an understanding of international law is relatively commonplace that legitimacy through defiance of law can succeed, that such attempts at justification 'gain their "edge"'.[88] Downer's September 2002 speech to Parliament was, in many ways, a conventional attempt to set out the government's justifications for its position on Iraq. That the speech relied so much on international law to do so underlined the power of international legal language in the 2003 public debate. The boldness of Downer's speech, however, came not from his reliance on law but from his stated willingness to defy that law in order to enforce it.

3.4.1.2 The Competence of Public Speakers: Speech by Rob Durbridge to the Conference of the Australian Education Union, January 2003

One of the distinctive features of international legal language in the 2003 public debate was its use by public speakers. In this section, I examine the speech of an individual trade unionist who could not be described as a professional speaker of international law. Rob Durbridge was a high school teacher and anti-Vietnam War activist who served as federal secretary of the Australian Education Union ('AEU') for 12 years.[89] Acting in his capacity as federal secretary, Durbridge delivered a speech to the Annual Federal Conference of the AEU, held 15–17 January 2003, in support of a 'No War in Iraq' resolution adopted during the conference. It was a passionate speech, hitting notes of anger and disaffection that hinted at Durbridge's past as an anti-Vietnam War activist.

Durbridge's speech focused on the key themes of the public debate on Iraq, including the role of the UN, the doctrine of pre-emption and the humanitarian consequences of war. His construction of those arguments was distinctive, however, for his faith in a redemptive power of international law. Durbridge began by claiming that war in Iraq was inevitable and that it was most likely that the US would create a pretext to invade and to cause 'appalling trauma, death and destruction, including possibly tens or hundreds of thousands of children and other

---

[87] Berman, 'Legitimacy through Defiance' (n 82) 94.
[88] Ibid., 95.
[89] 'A Giant of a Man, Gone but Never Forgotten' (2015) 40(1) *AEU SA Branch Journal* 10.

innocent civilians'.⁹⁰ He then emphasised the lack of public support for the war and cited some of the many civil society groups that were opposed to an Iraq war, including the Australian Medical Association, the Returned Soldiers' League and the main Christian churches.

Durbridge rejected the arguments that a war in Iraq would be justified as an action in pre-emptive self-defence. He was careful to state that, while there were limited circumstances in which war was sometimes justified, this was not one of them: '[T]he Howard government has not provided any adequate justifications, no reason which stands up, and we should say so clearly, now'. In identifying the circumstances in which force may be justified, Durbridge relied on what he considered the standards provided by the international law of self-defence. He said,

> It is a patent lie, spread by that Tory twerp Tony Blair, that there is a clear and present danger to Britain, Australia or the US from Iraq. That is the standard international law requires and it has not been met.⁹¹

Durbridge's argument here presented a determinative view of international law. Durbridge considered that the international law standard for self-defence was clear and that it did not encompass situations of pre-emption. Nor did Durbridge accept that the international standard for self-defence might need to develop alongside changed circumstances, as the Howard government argued. For Durbridge, the standard was definite and static, and it was a straightforward matter to determine whether a sufficient threat of use of force existed to justify military action in self-defence. In this case, in his view, it did not. This reasoning, based on a belief in the precision and certainty of the international law on self-defence, was evident, too, in the terms of the AEU's 'No War' resolution itself, which included the following paragraph:

> International Law and UN Conventions provide a means whereby military action can be taken by states where a real and present danger exists to their security or where their borders have been violated. No such danger has been demonstrated by any nation in relation to Iraq.⁹²

The AEU's vision of international law relied on a belief in its certainty and predictability, painting a picture of that law as a rational framework under which 'bad' political decisions and the excesses of governmental power could

---

⁹⁰ Rob Durbridge (Speech delivered to the Australian Education Union Annual Federal Conference, 15–17 January 2003).
⁹¹ Ibid.
⁹² Australian Education Union, 'No War' Resolution, adopted 15–17 January 2003.

be constrained. This was a conception of international law not merely as separated from politics but international law as a curative for politics. For Durbridge and the AEU, the 'standard' required by international law was clear and objectively determinable – it was something about which Durbridge and the AEU could reasonably form a view, not something that demanded the opinion of a professional international lawyer.

Durbridge's speech gave vitality to the rhetorical force of legality as an autonomous justification. The manner in which he used the argument assumed that his audience would be moved, even outraged, by the argument that the Iraq War might be illegal. Durbridge was not simply choosing to use law to resist the government's arguments; he was using the idea of illegality as a galvanising force to protest the government's actions. The success of this tactic depended on Durbridge's successful translation of the international legal standards of self-defence into language that would resonate with his union audience.

Questions about the relationship between international law and politics are as perennial to the field of international law as they are contested. They are central to Martti Koskenniemi's constructions of the grammar of international law,[93] and Michelle Burgis has described the law/politics distinction as 'the main grammar' of international legal language.[94] Durbridge's ideas of international law depicted a kinder positivism, one that regarded the standards of international law as distinct from politics and able to temper the latter's excesses. The speech by Rob Durbridge suggests that this grammar of international law has been internalised by public speakers when using international legal language.

3.4.1.3 Public and Political Speakers' Debate: Interview of John Howard by Kerry O'Brien, *The 7.30 Report*, ABC Television, 18 March 2003

On 18 March 2003, Kerry O'Brien, journalist and host of the Australian Broadcasting Corporation's current affairs television programme, *The 7.30 Report*, interviewed John Howard about Australia's participation in the invasion of Iraq.[95] O'Brien focused most of his questions on international

---

[93] Martti Koskenniemi, *From Apology to Utopia* (Cambridge University Press, reissue, 2006) 562–689.
[94] Michelle Leanne Burgis, *Boundaries of Discourse in the International Court of Justice: Mapping Arguments in Arab Territorial Disputes* (Brill, 2009) 266.
[95] Interview with John Howard, Prime Minister of Australia (Kerry O'Brien, *The 7.30 Report*, Australian Broadcasting Corporation, 18 March 2003). For a transcript of this interview, see https://pmtranscripts.pmc.gov.au/release/transcript-20738.

3.4 THE PUBLIC DEBATE

law, thus making this interview a public debate conducted in the vocabulary of international law between a political and a public speaker of that language. These distinctive features of this interview point to two aspects of the role of international legal language in the 2003 public debates. The first was the foregrounding of legal expertise by both the political and the public speakers; the second, a consequence of the first, was the attempt by these speakers to naturalise a single concept of law and of legality.

On the day of the interview, Howard had given a speech to Parliament explaining his decision to commit troops to the Iraq invasion. At the end of that speech, Howard took the unusual step of tabling his government's legal advice on the Iraq War, which had been signed by senior legal officers of the Australian Attorney-General's Department and Department of Foreign Affairs and Trade.[96] This legal advice set out the 'reactivation' argument that Howard had hinted at in earlier speeches when he had argued that a further Security Council resolution to underpin military action in Iraq was unnecessary legally, though desirable politically.[97] The failure of the US and the UK to secure a further Security Council resolution authorising force, however, meant that from 18 March Howard relied solely and explicitly on 'reactivation' as the legal justification for the Iraq War. Kerry O'Brien's decision to focus in this interview almost exclusively on the legal justifications for the Iraq War occurred in the context of the events of that day, including the public release of legal advice to government.

O'Brien's opening gambit was to ask where the 'moral authority' for an Iraq invasion came from. Howard answered by avoiding the language of morality, arguing instead that the invasion was 'in the medium- and long-term interests of Australia' and that, while law was 'important' to underpin the invasion, 'I don't argue that it's just a legal issue'. O'Brien nevertheless zeroed in on the weaknesses in the legal justifications for war. O'Brien framed legality as a factor of importance in itself, 'because if you're going to risk so many young Australian lives, you would want to be on rock solid legal ground, would you not?' O'Brien and Howard then sparred over the core legal justification for the Iraq invasion – the interpretation of the Security Council resolutions. Howard presented

---

[96] Bill Campbell and Chris Moraitis, 'Memorandum of Advice to the Commonwealth Government on the Use of Force against Iraq', reproduced in (2003) 4 *Melbourne Journal of International Law* 178.
[97] Ibid. See also Commonwealth, *Parliamentary Debates*, House of Representatives, 4 February 2003, 10642–52 (John Howard). For an explanation of this argument, see n 54 and accompanying text.

the argument as if it were straightforward, stating that 'the failure of Iraq to fully disarm reactivates the authority to use force contained in the earlier Resolutions of 678 and 687'. As a consequence of this reactivation, no further Security Council resolutions were, nor were ever, required to authorise force. Howard explained in the interview:

> Never did I regard going back to the Security Council as being a necessary legal exercise, I made that clear in my statement to Parliament on 4th February, when I said we didn't need the 18th resolution of the Security Council on this subject in order get more legal cover, rather to increase the level of international pressure on Iraq.

Howard took a consistently firm line on this legal position, portraying it as undeniable. Earlier that day, to Parliament, he had described his legal advice as 'unequivocal' and as the only 'informed analysis' on this point.[98] Howard's argumentative technique was to denigrate those who took an opposing view, on the grounds that they were either wrong about the law or engaged in questionable conduct. In an interview with O'Brien on 13 March, for example, Howard had described countries that would deny the Security Council the ability to authorise military action (a veiled reference to France) as engaged in 'international political posturing'.[99] In Howard's construction, he had sensible motives and legal justifications, and his opponents had only unmeritorious argument. Howard was himself, of course, engaged in political posturing, but his position allowed him to dismiss, rather than debate, differing views on the Iraq War.

O'Brien relied on the views of professional international lawyers to challenge Howard's arguments. In this 18 March interview, the role of legal expertise in public debate became the subject of analysis itself. O'Brien presented Howard with legal opinions that contradicted his government's legal advice and asked him why Howard's legal position was superior. O'Brien did this on two separate occasions, basing his competing opinions on the views of the Secretary-General of the UN ('Why is your knowledge of the *Charter* superior to the Secretary-General of the UN's?') and on individuals whom O'Brien described as 'eminent professors from Oxford and Cambridge' ('Why would your Attorney-General's Departments' advice be superior to these eminent professors of law?').

---

[98] Commonwealth, *Parliamentary Debates*, House of Representatives, 18 March 2003, 12509 (John Howard).

[99] Interview with John Howard, Prime Minister of Australia (Kerry O'Brien, *The 7.30 Report*, Australian Broadcasting Corporation, 13 March 2003).

3.4 THE PUBLIC DEBATE

Howard responded in two ways. First, he relied on the indeterminacy of law ('you know what lawyers are like ... they do tend on occasions to argue') and, second, he relied on the greater expertise of his experts, making it clear, too, that he was not one of these experts ('I'm not asserting it as John Howard the international legal guru'). The superior abilities of Howard's experts arose first because they were practitioners of international law and second because the Australian Government practitioners agreed with the US and UK government practitioners. Howard said,

> any suggestion that we have lightly embarked on this with a flimsy legal underpinning when you've got the legal advice of the three governments you've mentioned all saying the same thing, I don't think it's a very fair criticism.
>
> ...
>
> Now with all due respect to the learned professors from Oxford and Cambridge, and I'm sure they are very learned, I don't think you can discount somebody whose daily job is to advise not on the theory but on the practice of international law, the Australian Government.

In these exchanges, Howard distanced himself from his own legal advice at the same time as he relied on it. He disclaimed any expertise himself but was happy to trust in the knowledge and opinion of his advisers. That other experts may disagree was of little consequence to him because he knew that his experts were better; indeed, they had the only proper view. Howard had expressed a similar sentiment in an earlier speech to Parliament when he had claimed that his legal experts' opinion was the only one supported by 'informed analysis of the Security Council resolutions'.[100] Howard also disparaged the views of the 'eminent professors' by characterising them as theory rather than practice. For Howard, what he considered theoretical views were more removed from political reality and thus less worthy of respect than the views of the Australian Government's legal advisers. This view of diplomatic relations was consistent with the Howard government's realist approach to international relations,[101] and it captured a superciliousness that emerged periodically during the public debates.

---

[100] Commonwealth, *Parliamentary Debates*, House of Representatives, 4 February 2003, 10642 (John Howard).

[101] See, for example, *Advancing the National Interest: Australia's Foreign and Trade Policy White Paper* (Commonwealth of Australia, 2003). For a critical overview of the Howard government's realism, see, for example, David McGraw, 'The Howard Government's Foreign Policy: Really Realist?' (2008) 43 *Australian Journal of Political Science* 465.

As the interview unfolded, however, Howard's portrayal of legal expertise shifted. Despite claiming no particular proficiency in international law, Howard insisted on framing both the scope of his reliance on the legal advice and the terms of the legal opinion carefully. He objected to what he saw as O'Brien's mischaracterisation of his positions. In response to O'Brien's phrasing of a question on Resolution 1441, Howard said,

> [D]on't misquote me, that's all.... We are relying on advice, the essential gist of which is that the failure of Iraq to fully disarm reactivates the authority to use force contained in the earlier resolutions of 678 and 687. ... [Our] argument is that because Iraq has not [fully disarmed] then the authority to take forcible action is re-activated because of that failure because the deal, if I can put it that way, on which the cease fire was arranged has been dishonoured by the Iraqis. ... that is a matter, I think, of commonsense.

Here, Howard gave a precise account of the legal justification for an Iraq invasion. It was a recitation of the advice given by his legal experts – a version, he argued, that was superior to the competing pieces of advice from other sources. Yet, at the end of his description of this expert advice, Howard described it as a matter of 'common sense'. He portrayed an arcane legal argument – one that would previously have been confined to lawyers – as the natural interpretation of words and as something that any sensible person would understand and agree with.

Howard's move in this interview to distance himself from legal advice while suggesting that the legal position was entirely natural is one example of the shifting ground of legal expertise in the Iraq War debates. In the second example above, union leader Rob Durbridge expressed no doubt about his ability to make an assessment both of the relevant international law and its application in this case. For him, the 'standard' required by international law was clear and objectively determinable – it was something about which he could reasonably form a view, not something that demanded the opinion of a legal expert. Before Parliament and for parts of this O'Brien interview, Howard adopted a different view – one that saw international law as requiring the careful interpretation that only professional international lawyers (though not 'theorists') could provide. Having explained the expert advice, however, Howard argued that it was also 'commonsense' – the plain and natural meaning of words that held myriad other interpretations – and something therefore to which only foolish people would object.[102] The

---

[102] For a range of views on the role of 'commonsense' in law, see, for example, Sally Engle Merry, *Getting Justice and Getting Even: Legal Consciousness among Working-Class Americans* (University of Chicago Press, 1990); John M Conley and William

3.4 THE PUBLIC DEBATE

picture that Howard presented was simultaneously determinate and indeterminate: indeterminate because he acknowledged that different interpretations of the Security Council resolutions existed, and determinate because Howard considered it possible for there to be only one right interpretation – the 'informed' and 'commonsense' view given by his government lawyers. Thus, even while he was acknowledging the limits of international law, Howard presented his government's decision as falling within those limits, and, more importantly, as the only reasonable position to take on the law. This technique effectively neutralised the other legal critiques of his government's position.

The foregrounding of legal expertise that occurred during the O'Brien interview is consistent with Kennedy's analysis of the role of expertise in global governance.[103] In this case, O'Brien and Howard paid close attention to the views of expert international lawyers, although the government's professional speakers themselves remained in the background. The government lawyers in Australia remained silent on the legality question, except for the written legal advice that they signed and that was released to the public. They gave no interviews and did not otherwise defend their legal opinion in any way. Placing the professional speakers in the background while foregrounding their advice allowed the political speaker – Howard – to rely on the professional advice and to disclaim personal responsibility for the legal opinion without allowing the authors of that opinion to be challenged directly. The professional speakers who were 'eminent professors', however, played a prominent role in Australia's public debate. Several international law academics made multiple appearances on television, on radio and in the press.[104]

Notwithstanding the ubiquity of the legal issues, professional speakers of international law did not dominate the public debate; international law academics did not take on the government legal experts in public forums. The Australian debate over expertise occurred through public and political speakers of international law. Kennedy has argued that the foregrounding of legal expertise makes political decisions seem like a 'matter of fact rather than points of choice'.[105] This was not the case in Australia's

---

[*] M O'Barr, *Rules versus Relationships: The Ethnography of Legal Discourse* (University of Chicago Press, 1990); Raimondi Gaita, 'Radical Critique, Scepticism and Commonsense' (1991) 29 *Royal Institute of Philosophy Supplement* 157.
[103] Kennedy, *World of Struggle* (n 5); David Kennedy, 'Challenging Expert Rule: The Politics of Global Governance' (2005) 27 *Sydney Law Review* 5 ('Challenging Expert Rule').
[104] See above n 56.
[105] Kennedy, 'Challenging Expert Rule' (n 103) 14.

decision to participate in the invasion of Iraq. It was clear to all participants in the public debate that the Howard government took responsibility for the decision to go to war, that it justified that decision in particular terms and that those terms could be challenged. Nevertheless, the foregrounding of legal expertise allowed Howard to engage in a kind of ventriloquy, where he spoke the words of the international lawyers without taking responsibility for them. Howard's foregrounding of expertise did not shift responsibility for decision-making – Howard was proud of his decision to participate in the invasion. However, it did give Howard the flexibility to both rely on and distance himself from professional opinions as and when it suited his argument.

The use of the language of international law by public and political speakers in 2003 suggests there was a connection between the foregrounding of legal expertise and the prominence of legality as an autonomous justification in those public debates. When legal decisions form part of the background to government decision-making, the opportunities to challenge those views are limited. This may be because the existence and/or the content of those opinions are not in the public domain or because, as background decisions, they are made in the kind of exclusionary expert language that Kennedy has described.[106] Once foregrounded, however, as it was in the Iraq debates, the question of legality becomes another issue for public debate, along with the political, societal and economic questions.

Kennedy has also argued that foregrounding expertise can push certain groups into wanting to '"do something" ... demanding resolutions, regulations and funds'.[107] In the Iraq War debate in Australia, foregrounding the legal question encouraged participants to demand a legal justification for war. And when legal justifications were provided, legal expertise was no longer exclusive to the professional speakers of international law but became something over which other speakers could form reasoned opinions – just as they did with other social, political or economic issues. In this sense, the seizure of international legal language by public speakers such as Durbridge and the AEU was an act that liberated international law from the realms of the professional. Public speakers of international law took that language from the professionals

---

[106] Kennedy, *World of Struggle* (n 5) chapter 1.
[107] Kennedy, 'Challenging Expert Rule' (n 103) 14.

3.4 THE PUBLIC DEBATE 71

and used it to speak back to them, to challenge their expert positions and to gain advantages over their opponents in the public debate.

Generally, however, the consequences of the foregrounding of expertise were not, as Kennedy has suggested, that the decision-making on the relevant question (legality of the war) became freer or more responsible.[108] Rather, as the focus on international law in the O'Brien interview suggests, towards the end of the Australian public debate, the frame of reference for the debate narrowed to a consideration of the interests and ideologies of the professional language of international law.

3.4.2 *International Law as Self-Defence, Humanitarianism and the Just War*

In this section, I examine international law as an element of three collective justifications for the Iraq War – pre-emptive self-defence, humanitarianism and the just war – through analysis of three documents that responded to the government's arguments: a media release from the Australian Council of Trade Unions ('ACTU') and two separate letters from religious leaders.

3.4.2.1 Pre-Emption and Humanitarianism: ACTU Statements on Iraq, 11 October and 1 December 2002

The ACTU is the peak body for unions in Australia. It intervened relatively early in the Iraq War debate in Australia with the release of two statements on Iraq: on 11 October and 1 December 2002.[109] The timing and content of the short release on 11 October suggest that it was a response to the government's arguments, in particular those presented by Alexander Downer in his speech to Parliament in September 2002 (see section 3.4.1.1 of this chapter). The content of the 11 October Statement placed it in dialogue with the government's Iraq War arguments about WMD, pre-emption and humanitarianism. The 1 December statement echoed the key messages of the 11 October statement, while also providing further details to support the ACTU position.

The ACTU statement on 11 October 2002 emphasised that its opposition to Australian involvement in a war in Iraq was based on their view

---

[108] Ibid., 27.
[109] Australian Council of Trade Unions, 'Unions Oppose Iraq War' (Media Release, 11 October 2002) www.actu.org.au/actu-media/archives/2002/war-is-not-the-alternative. Australian Council of Trade Unions, 'War Is Not the Alternative' (Media Release, 1 December 2002) <https://www.actu.org.au/actu-media/archives/2002/war-is-not-the-alternative>.

that '[t]he threat of a pre-emptive strike by the USA, supported by Australia, contravenes international law, is a threat to world peace and must be resisted by the UN Security Council'. The ACTU stressed its commitment to peace and its continued support for the 'strong presence and authority of the United Nations'. The ACTU statement of 1 December 2002 enumerated a range of other reasons for its objections to a war in Iraq, including that 'it is working men and women and their children who bear the brutal brunt of war' and that war will 'further exacerbate an already desperate humanitarian crisis'. The statement evidenced the ACTU's anti-war position in principle, with statements that 'War is not the answer' and 'War is not the solution'. The statement identified what the ACTU considered the 'real issue' to be – disarmament – and argued for a continuation of weapons inspections over military action:

> UN mandated international inspections of any country currently stockpiling weapons of mass destruction – chemical, biological or nuclear – whether Iraq, USA or Russia would significantly contribute to global peace and security.

The 1 December statement concluded with a critique of the 'unrelenting talk of war', arguing that this rhetoric had drowned out 'solutions for peace'.

The ACTU statements identified two issues that combined international law as an element of collective justifications for opposing war: the pre-emptive self-defence argument that had evolved from the justifications based on Iraq's possession of WMD, and arguments about the humanitarian consequences of war. The statements shared with Downer's September 2002 speech to Parliament a concern with Iraq's WMD programme, and the texts of both Downer and the ACTU expressed a preference for a peaceful and diplomatic resolution to the WMD issue. Downer's speech had not used the language of pre-emption, but by opening its statement with an objection to the potential of a pre-emptive strike against Iraq, the ACTU suggested this issue was central to its concerns.

Earlier in this chapter, I described how the Howard government supported the principle of pre-emptive self-defence, although members of the government were careful in the way they expressed that support. Howard's decision to rely on the language of self-defence to sustain his proposed principle of pre-emption drew on the long-established moral groundings of self-defence, moderated as they have been by the legal regime of the UN *Charter*. By including in both its statements a rejection of the doctrine of pre-emption on the grounds that it both violated international law and threatened world peace, the ACTU confronted the legal and moral bases within the Howard government's pre-emptive self-defence argument.

A state's 'inherent right' to self-defence is acknowledged in the UN *Charter*, underscoring the principle's longstanding status as a justification for war.[110] Before becoming a legal concept, self-defence had long combined moral, ethical and strategic considerations. For example, the ancient Greek historian Herodotus explained the Scythian failure to gain the support of neighbouring kings for their war against the Persian king Darius as a consequence of the Persians having committed no wrong against them that could warrant such an attack.[111] In the thirteenth century, theologian and jurist Thomas Aquinas theorised the Catholic tradition of the just war as requiring the existence of a just cause, which would exist where one party attacked another party who had engaged in an aggressive war against them.[112] By the nineteenth century, war was such an entrenched element of statecraft that the Uruguayan jurist Jiménez de Aréchaga later described claims of self-defence in that period as 'a political excuse for the use of force'.[113] The modern Charter concept of self-defence is a legal one, but it continues to embrace the older conceptions of morality, ethics and strategy.[114] Michael Walzer exemplified this combination in his classic

---

[110] See *Military and Paramilitary Activities in and against Nicaragua (Nicaragua v United States) (Judgment)* [1986] ICJ Rep 1, 94. For a detailed account of the narrowing of the contours of the law on self-defence in the twentieth century, see Ian Brownlie, *International Law and the Use of Force by States* (Oxford University Press, 1963) especially 231–80. See also Yoram Dinstein, *War, Aggression and Self-Defence* (Cambridge University Press, 5th ed., 2011) 191–93; Michael C Alder, *The Inherent Right of Self-Defence in International Law* (Springer, 2013) chapter 1.

[111] Herodotus attributes this quote to the Scythians' neighbouring kings. 'We, on our part, did no wrong to these men in the former war, and will not be the first to commit wrong now. If they invade our land and begin aggressions upon us, we will not suffer them; but, till we see this come to pass, we will remain at home. For we believe that the Persians are not come to attack us, but to punish those who are guilty of first injuring them': Herodotus, *The Histories* tr George Rawlinson, Book 4 (*The Internet Classics Archive*) http://classics.mit.edu/Herodotus/history.html.

[112] Thomas Aquinas, 'Summa Theologica' in Larry May, Eric Rove and Steve Viner (eds.), *The Morality of War: Classical and Contemporary Readings* (Pearson Prentice Hall, 2006) 27–28. See generally Adil Ahmad Haque, *Law and Morality at War* (Oxford University Press, 2017).

[113] quoted in Dinstein: see Dinstein (n 110) 188.

[114] Indeed, the leading authority on self-defence remains the Caroline Incident of 1837–42. See, for example, Tadashi Mori, *Origins of the Right of Self-Defence in International Law: From the Caroline Incident to the United Nations Charter* (Brill/Nijhoff, 2018) 25–40. See also Dinstein (n 110); Weller, *Oxford Handbook of the Use of Force* (n 1).

treatise on the morality of war, where he described all aggressive acts by states as having 'one thing in common: they justify forceful resistance'.[115]

The ACTU statements assessed the arguments about pre-emption against the moral, legal and ethical standards of international law and 'world peace'. They treated international law as part of an undifferentiated collective of justifications that together created a standard of justice against which the actions of the Australian Government could be measured. Pre-emption, the 1 October statement insisted, 'contravene[d] international law' and was 'a threat to world peace'. Other participants in the public debate also rejected pre-emption. The extension of the traditional principles of self-defence to pre-emptive self-defence embraced situations that many professional international lawyers considered were unsupportable – legally and morally.[116] The Australian Catholic Social Justice Council relied on the principles of the just war when it described pre-emption as 'specious, lack[ing] due authority and risk[ing] undermining the fundamental principles of international relations'.[117] The ACTU, then, joined with other governments, professional international lawyers and religious leaders in rejecting the principle of pre-emptive self-defence in its legal, moral and strategic forms.

The second collective justification on which the ACTU statements relied raised the humanitarian consequences of war. The ACTU argued in the 1 December statement that an Iraq invasion would create a humanitarian crisis in multiple ways, including through the suffering of innocent Iraqis ('up to a million families are already displaced'); the displacement and suffering of Iraqis who survived an invasion ('Economies are destroyed, jobs are lost and families dislocated'); the long-term consequences of war for the families of combatants ('any attack will further exacerbate an already desperate humanitarian crisis'); and the violation of a commitment to peace ('Peace has always been a union issue. ... War is not the answer'). The ACTU's ideas of humanitarianism were thus a broad conception that carried a range of moral, philosophical and legal imperatives.[118]

---

[115] Michael Walzer, *Just and Unjust Wars: A Moral Argument with Historical Illustrations* (Basic Books, 5th ed., 2015) 52.

[116] See, for example, Vaughan Lowe, 'The Iraq Crisis: What Now?' (2003) 52 *The International and Comparative Law Quarterly* 859; Bellamy (n 54).

[117] Australian Catholic Social Justice Council, 'Catholic Study Condemns War' (Media Release, 19 March 2003).

[118] For considerations of the uses of the language of humanitarianism in international law, see, for example, B. S. Chimni, 'Globalization, Humanitarianism and the Erosion of Refugee Protection' (2000) 13 *Journal of Refugee Studies* 243; Anne Orford, *Reading*

3.4 THE PUBLIC DEBATE

The clearest legal implications of the ACTU's humanitarianism arose from its advocacy on behalf of the potential victims of war, an advocacy that called on the tradition of humanitarianism that seeks to protect victims of armed conflict. This tradition, embodied by the International Committee of the Red Cross, has been embraced by numerous organisations, including Save the Children, on whose statistics the ACTU Statement relied.[119] Neither ACTU statement identified the particular international humanitarian laws on which its claims relied, but these laws underpin the protection of individuals during war.[120] The law, morality and ethics collected within this conception of 'humanitarianism' were not just standards against which government conduct could be judged but also protections on which all individuals could call in a time of war. In this sense, the humanitarian treatment of victims of war provided a measure of solidarity between civilians around the world. The ACTU called for the protection of the humanity of the people of Iraq and the combatants and their families in the same way that they would want others to call for the protection on humanitarian grounds if members of the ACTU or other civilian Australians were ever threatened by war.

There was another sense in which humanitarianism was employed during the Iraq War debates, and the ACTU statements can be seen at least in part as a response to this different idea of humanitarianism. This alternative version of humanitarianism, which was first used by the Bush administration and subsequently adopted by the Howard government, focused on the consequences of leaving the regime of Saddam Hussein in power. For example, in August 2002, then US Secretary of State Condoleeza Rice had argued that there was a 'powerful moral case for regime change' against the 'evil' Saddam Hussein.[121]

Humanitarian Intervention: Human Rights and the Use of Force in International Law (Cambridge University Press, 2003); David Kennedy, *The Dark Sides of Virtue: Reassessing International Humanitarianism* (Princeton University Press, 2004).

[119] For analyses of this tradition of humanitarianism, see, for example, Michael Barnett and Thomas G Weiss, *Humanitarianism Contested: Where Angels Fear to Tread* (Routledge, 2013); Richard Ashby Wilson and Richard D Brown (eds.), *Humanitarianism and Suffering: The Mobilization of Empathy* (Cambridge University Press, 2009); Michael Barnett and Thomas G Weiss (eds.), *Humanitarianism in Question: Politics, Power, Ethics* (Cornell University Press, 2008).

[120] For a history of the term 'international humanitarian law', see, for example, Amanda Alexander, 'A Short History of International Humanitarian Law' (2015) 26 *European Journal of International Law* 109.

[121] '"Moral Case" for Deposing Saddam', *BBC News World Edition* (online, 15 August 2002) http://news.bbc.co.uk/2/hi/americas/2193426.stm.

In the Australian debate, this version of humanitarianism never amounted to an argument for military intervention to prevent egregious violations of human rights – or humanitarianism as humanitarian intervention – but it came close. Alexander Downer set the scene in his September 2002 speech, where he described Saddam's regime as 'brutal towards his own people' and as having an 'appalling' human rights record.[122] Howard continued to press this argument in the Australian debate, insisting that military intervention would prevent the Iraqi people from continuing to endure life under the brutality of Saddam Hussein. In his speeches of March 2003, as the coalition of the willing was about to invade Iraq, Howard emphasised how 'particularly horrific' the Hussein regime was by identifying practices of torture, rape and abuse of children.[123] In his national televised Address to the Nation on 20 March 2003, Howard provided a particularly graphic example of abuse by citing what he called a 'human shredding machine', which he claimed was used to execute opponents of Saddam Hussein. Howard was careful never to frame this humanitarian argument as a justification for intervention on its own but rather as the fortunate consequence of the removal of Saddam Hussein. Military intervention in Iraq, he said, would 'lift this immense burden of terror from the Iraqi people'.[124]

'Humanitarian intervention' to halt or prevent ongoing serious violations of human rights remains a contested concept in international law. Its successor, the 'responsibility to protect' doctrine, relies on Security Council approval for authority.[125] As brutal as the Iraqi regime was, there were not in 2002–03 the kinds of serious human rights abuses occurring on a widespread and systematic basis that had generally been used to justify earlier military interventions on humanitarian grounds.[126] The

---

[122] Commonwealth, *Parliamentary Debates*, House of Representatives, 17 September 2002, 6378 (Alexander Downer).

[123] John Howard, 'Address to the Nation' (Speech, Australian national television, 20 March 2003) ('Address to the Nation'). See also John Howard, 'National Press Club Address' (Speech, Great Hall, Parliament House, Canberra, 13 March 2003) ('National Press Club Address').

[124] Howard, 'Address to the Nation' (n 123).

[125] For more on both humanitarian intervention and the 'responsibility to protect', see, for example, Simon Chesterman, *Just War or Just Peace: Humanitarian Intervention and International Law* (Oxford University Press, 2002); Anne Orford, *International Authority and the Responsibility to Protect* (Cambridge University Press, 2011); A Hehir and R Murray (eds.), *Libya, the Responsibility to Protect and the Future of Humanitarian Intervention* (Palgrave Macmillan, 2013); Zifcak, 'Responsibility to Protect' (n 4).

[126] As supporters of intervention argued there had been in Kosovo in 1999, justifying the NATO intervention, for example, see Charlesworth, 'Discipline of Crisis' (n 2).

claims to humanitarianism by Howard and his government nevertheless relied on a combination of legal and moral authority held within the doctrines of both 'humanitarian intervention' and the 'responsibility to protect'. By choosing not to justify military intervention on this specific humanitarian ground and instead framing it as a consequence of an intervention that was otherwise justified, Howard minimised the opportunities for debate over this form of humanitarianism. At the same time, he was able to lay claim to some of the legal and moral authority that this humanitarianism gave him and to reject the alternative version advanced by the ACTU.

3.4.2.2 The Just War and Humanitarianism: Interventions by Religious Groups

Nearly all commentary from religious groups on the Iraq War opposed Australia's participation in military action.[127] The only Anglican bishop to have publicly endorsed the Howard government's position on the Iraq War recanted that position in 2004, asking at the same time for 'God's forgiveness for [his] complicity in creating a world in which this sort of action was ever considered by anyone to be necessary'.[128] The near unanimity from Christian groups in opposition to a war proposed by the Australian Government has been described as 'remarkable' by one commentator.[129] In this section, I examine two interventions. The first is a letter to the editor, published in *The Age* on 21 February 2003 and signed by sixteen religious leaders representing the Christian and Muslim faiths. The Christian leaders represented a range of denominations, including the Catholic, Anglican, Baptist, Coptic and Lutheran denominations; the Salvation Army; and the Society of Friends. The second intervention is a media release issued by the Catholic Bishops of Australia on 5 March 2003.[130]

The letter to the editor was relatively short and put the argument against war simply. The letter affirmed that all people, regardless of

---

[127] For a general discussion on the effects that religious groups had on the Iraq War campaign in Australia, see Elisabeth Porter, 'No Just War: Political Reflections on Australian Churches' Condemnation of the Iraq War' (2006) 52 *Australian Journal of Politics and History* 471.

[128] Bishop Tom Frame, 'Forgive me, I was wrong on Iraq', *The Age* (online, 18 June 2004) www.theage.com.au/articles/2004/06/17/1087245036392.html.

[129] Porter (n 127) 473.

[130] 'Letter to the Editor', *The Age* (Melbourne, 21 February 2003); Catholic Bishops of Australia, 'A Statement on Iraq from the Catholic Bishops of Australia' (Media Release, 5 March 2003).

religion, were 'the family of God' and that acts of war 'devalue[d] both humanity and creation'. The letter identified six reasons for concern about war with Iraq, including that war would 'put at risk the lives of many innocent Iraqi citizens', 'lead to unacceptable humanitarian consequences' and 'be an unjust action'. The authors professed to 'reject both terrorism and militarism as a means of achieving justice' and urged the international community to 'seek alternative solutions to the present crisis that will not increase the level of human suffering in Iraq'. Finally, the leaders concluded with a prayer that 'peace will descend from God' and calling for 'compassion for the people of Iraq'.

The Catholic Bishops' Statement was longer. It was explicitly based in the Catholic tradition of the just war, through which the bishops engaged directly with some of the legal arguments about the Iraq War. Thus, the bishops called war 'always a defeat for humanity' and exhorted the international community to 'search exhaustively for peaceful solutions through the United Nations'. They repeated the Pope's comments that the way to avoid war lay in 'observing international law, engaging in honest dialogue and diplomacy and rejecting the culture of death'. They engaged with the just war arguments by asserting that the 'strict conditions' for the use of military force against Iraq had not been met. 'In particular', the bishops continued,

> we question the moral legitimacy of a pre-emptive strike. Indeed, any action against Iraq without broad international support and the mandate of the United Nations Security Council would be questionable.

The bishops considered the impact of a conflict on the Iraqi people. They prayed that the people would be 'spared further conflict and destruction' and that they would one day know 'justice and freedom'. The bishops urged prayers for the Australian Defence Force and for 'cool heads and wisdom' for political leaders everywhere. They concluded with a final exhortation to prayer:

> At this perilous time in world history, we invite all Australians to pray that our world will find ways other than war to secure justice, increase security and promote genuine peace for all of God's people.

The interventions from religious representatives relied on justifications within a frame of humanitarianism. This particular religious conception of 'humanitarianism' was aimed at securing peace through means other than war. The religious leaders urged politicians to avoid acting in a way that would increase the suffering of the people of Iraq, and they all gave an important role to prayer and to the wisdom that they thought prayer would bring.

An emphasis on humanity was common to other religious interventions in the public debate. For many of the religious groups, the importance of the protection of humanity was closely aligned with God's connection to humanity. Another peak religious body, the National Council of Churches in Australia framed its anti-war statement thus: 'God loves all humanity ... The way to peace does not lie through war, but through the transformation of structures of injustice and the politics of exclusion'.[131] Although the humanitarianism of the religious groups was based in the teachings of the Christian and Muslim deities, its foundations were the same as those of the ACTU's humanitarianism – law was connected with the moral and ethical imperatives to prevent the unnecessary suffering of individuals during war. Neither of the religious interventions addressed the Howard government's alternative view of the humanitarian consequences – the humanitarian imperative of ending the brutal regime of Saddam Hussein. As with the ACTU statements, the justification of humanitarianism provided in these religious statements was a standard of solidarity with individuals across the world. All people, the 21 February letter affirmed, 'are the family of God' and deserve protection from war.

The Catholic Bishops' Statement engaged the Catholic tradition of the just war to assess the wisdom of military action in Iraq. Both George W Bush and Tony Blair used the language of the just war in their public cases for war.[132] Commentators both before and after the war assessed the coalition of the willing's military intervention against the criteria of a just war.[133] In Australia, neither Howard nor his ministers used the language of the just war to justify their decisions, preferring instead the

---

[131] National Council of Churches in Australia, 'Statement of the Heads of the National Council of Churches in Australia' (Media Release, 25 August 2002).

[132] See, for example, George W Bush, 'State of the Union Address 2003' (n 34) ('If war is forced upon us, we will fight in a just cause and by just means, sparing, in every way we can, the innocent'); Jimmy Carter, 'Just War: Or a Just War?' *The New York Times* (online, 9 March 2003) www.nytimes.com/2003/03/09/opinion/just-war-or-a-just-war.html; Peter Lee, *Blair's Just War: Iraq and the Illusion of Morality* (Palgrave Macmillan, 2012).

[133] See, for example, Albert L Weeks, *The Choice of War: The Iraq War and the Just War Tradition* (Praeger Security International, 2010); Craig M White, *Iraq: The Moral Reckoning: Applying Just War Theory to the 2003 War Decision* (Lexington Book, 2010); Michael Novak, 'A Just War: Was the War in Iraq Just?' (2004) 9 *Nexus, A Journal of Opinion* 11; Cian O'Driscoll, 'Re-Negotiating the Just War: The Invasion of Iraq and Punitive War' (2006) 19 *Cambridge Review of International Affairs* 405;

languages of legality, pre-emption and WMD and of humanitarianism and alliance as described in this chapter. The justification of the just war still featured in Australian debate, however, through the interventions of particular arms of the Catholic Church, including the Catholic Bishops' Statement.

Long understood as establishing moral and theological, rather than legal, thresholds for war, the modern form of the criteria for a just war nevertheless resemble legal criteria.[134] The threshold requirements to trigger the legal consequences under the 'responsibility to protect' principles, for example, draw heavily on the requirements for a just war.[135] One of these requirements is the approval for the war from a 'legitimate authority', which in the case of the Iraq War was the UN. As described earlier, the presence or absence of UN authority through Security Council resolutions on Iraq was the question on which determination of the legality of the Iraq invasion ultimately rested. In the frame of the just war, the existence of this authority would also help to decide the moral justice of this war. In the view of the Australian Catholic Social Justice Council, the presence of UN authority would not, of itself, have made the Iraq War just or moral, because the war did not fulfil the other criteria of the just war: '[w]ar on Iraq fails to meet the conditions enshrined in the criteria for a just war and hence would be immoral and unjust. . . . [T]here is no just cause'.[136]

The correlations between the criteria of the just war and the criteria for international legality in the use of force make the just war another example of collective justifications in which international law played a role. While the use of the criteria by the Catholic bishops is consistent with the Catholic Church's longstanding theological tradition, the bishops' identification in particular of a lack of 'legitimate authority' in this case paralleled the legal arguments about the lack of Security Council authorisation for the Iraq War. The Catholic Bishops' Statement can be read as an intervention on a theological basis that relies also on parallel standards in international law for persuasive power. Here, the collective

---

Jutta Brunnee and Stephen J Toope, 'Slouching towards New "Just" Wars: The Hegemon after September 11th' (2004) 18 *International Relations* 405.

[134] For a detailed discussion of the just war criteria, see Richard J Regan, *Just War: Principles and Cases* (Catholic University of America Press, 2nd ed., 2013).

[135] See International Commission on Intervention and State Sovereignty, *The Responsibility to Protect* (International Development Research Centre, December 2001) xii–xiii.

[136] Australian Catholic Social Justice Council, 'War on Iraq Unjust and Immoral' (Media Release, 19 March 2003).

justification of the just war called on both the moral underpinnings of Catholicism and the legal underpinnings of the international legal system of collective security for its valence.

The statements from the ACTU, the religious leaders and the Catholic bishops were examples of the manifold ways in which the language of humanitarianism was used as an intervention in the 2003 public debates. The shifting ground of these humanitarian justifications speaks to broader critiques of uses of humanitarian language in international relations. BS Chimni has highlighted the fluidity of the language of the 'humanitarian', arguing that its lack of 'rigid conceptual boundaries ... facilitates ambiguous and manipulative uses and allows ["humanitarian"] practices to escape critique'.[137] Anne Orford has made related critiques in relation to humanitarian intervention, where any radical potential of humanitarian intervention was ultimately confined by 'the way in which international law was narrated ... such that the right of intervention in the name of human rights became profoundly conservative in its meaning and effects'.[138] Anna Hood and I have argued that the consequences of the adoption of a humanitarian focus within nuclear regulation have been limited and, in some instances, acted as impediments to nuclear disarmament.[139] The Howard government's response to the union and religious appeals – that is, maintaining that the interests of humanitarianism would be best served by saving the people of Iraq from the Hussein regime – further supports these critiques of the indeterminacy and conservatism of the language of humanitarianism.

3.4.3 *International Law as Alliance*

3.4.3.1 International Law as Alliance: John Howard, Address to the Nation, 20 March 2003

In the Iraq War public debate, international law was used to represent an alliance with the US via the Howard government's construction of Australia's 'national interest' as almost entirely driven by its relationship with the US. In this section, I use John Howard's televised Address to the Nation on 20 March 2003 to explore the Howard government's reliance on international law as alliance in these debates.

---

[137] Chimni (n 118) 244.
[138] Orford (n 118) 11.
[139] Madelaine Chiam and Anna Hood, 'Nuclear Humanitarianism' (2019) 24 *Journal of Conflict and Security Law* 473.

John Howard's Address to the Nation, broadcast nationally on the evening of 20 March 2003, was the final pre-war statement of the Howard government's justifications for war in Iraq.[140] The address opened with a line that summarised Howard's justifications for war: 'we believe it is right, it is lawful, and it's in Australia's national interest'. Most of Howard's attention in the address was given to the arguments of 'right' and 'national interest'. In explaining why he believed 'passionately' that the war was 'right', Howard merged the pre-emption and WMD arguments that he had presented separately earlier in the Iraq debate. The threat to Australia from Iraq did not arise from an existing or imminent threat of the use of WMD against Australian territory (or that of its allies) but from the possibility of their use by a rogue state such as Iraq or by terrorists who obtained WMD from a rogue state. This argument built on the earlier assertions from Howard and Defence Minister Robert Hill that the international legal principle of self-defence needed to evolve to take into account the changes in circumstances caused by the 'new reality' of terrorism combined with the potential use of WMD.[141] Howard relied on the arguments he had presented earlier as pre-emptive self-defence and made his notion of 'right' a justification that included international legal standards at its core.

The idea of the 'national interest' had appeared often during the Iraq War debate in Australia, although the factors that contributed to the national interest were not always clear. Alexander Downer had identified two 'national interest' issues in his parliamentary speech of September 2002: Australia's 'fundamental interest in global security' and 'stability in the Middle East'.[142] In other places, Howard had asserted that participating in the Iraq War would protect the national interest but not necessarily detailing how. Without elaborating, for example, he told Kerry O'Brien in November 2002 that any intervention in Iraq would be justified 'morally, legally, and in the national interest'.[143]

The one factor that was consistently tied to the national interest was the importance of Australia's alliance with the US. In Howard's Address to the Nation, Australia's 'close security alliance' with the US was

---

[140] Howard, 'Address to the Nation' (n 102).

[141] When asked by a journalist after the Press Club speech about the implications of the pre-emption policy for the future, Howard responded by rejecting that terminology: 'I'm not going to adopt [your] ... language. I choose my own': Howard, 'National Press Club Address' (n 123).

[142] Commonwealth, *Parliamentary Debates*, House of Representatives, 17 September 2002, 6382 (Alexander Downer).

[143] Interview with John Howard, Prime Minister of Australia (Kerry O'Brien, *The 7.30 Report*, Australian Broadcasting Corporation, 11 November 2002).

the second justification he gave for participating in an invasion of Iraq. 'The Americans have helped us in the past', he said, 'and the United States is very important to Australia's long-term security. It is critical that we maintain the involvement of the United States in our own region.'[144] Indications that the US–Australia alliance would be important in relation to Iraq were evident from early in the Iraq War debate. In March 2002, for example, Robert Hill explained to the Senate: 'The issue of that [WMD] program in Iraq is of major concern to Australia in the same way as it is to the United States.'[145] Howard emphasised the quality of the alliance later in 2002, when he asserted that Australia was in as strong a position as any other country to understand US military thinking on Iraq.[146]

The ACTU and many unions disagreed with Howard's characterisation of the US alliance. They described the Howard government variously as 'subservient to the United States';[147] as having 'irresponsibly disregarded Australia's national interest in his subservient commitment to George W Bush's war on Iraq';[148] and as having 'positioned Australia as George Bush's lapdog, committing Australian troops regardless of United Nations approval'.[149] Throughout the public debate, however, Howard remained unapologetic about the alliance being a factor in his decision-making about Iraq. A few days before Downer's speech, on 11 September 2002, Howard had told the National Press Club, 'I will never apologise for the depth and strength of the relationship between Australia and the United States'.[150] And in February 2003, he told Parliament, '[t]he crucial long-term value of the United States alliance should always be a factor in major national security decisions taken by Australia.'[151]

---

[144] Howard, 'Address to the Nation' (n 102).
[145] Commonwealth, *Parliamentary Debates*, Senate, 21 March 2002, 1266 (Robert Hill).
[146] Commonwealth, *Parliamentary Debates*, House of Representatives, 19 August 2002, 4793 (Simon Crean and John Howard).
[147] Australian Council of Trade Unions, 'Parliament Must Debate Iraq War' (Media Release, 23 January 2003).
[148] Australian Council of Trade Unions, 'Iraq War Not in Australia's National Interest' (Media Release, 20 March 2003).
[149] Unions NSW, 'Unions work for Peace' (Pamphlet, 2003).
[150] John Howard, 'Address to the National Press Club' (Speech, National Press Club, Canberra, 11 September 2002).
[151] Commonwealth, *Parliamentary Debates*, House of Representatives, 4 February 2003, 10648 (John Howard). Howard identified the alliance as a reason to support the US on many other occasions, including, for example, John Howard, 'National Press Club Address' (n 123). See also Robert Garran, *True Believer: John Howard, George Bush and the American Alliance* (Allen & Unwin, 2004).

The Howard government had aligned Australia's foreign policy objectives with the US from the beginning of the government's term, including by invoking the terms of the Australia, New Zealand and United States ('ANZUS') collective security treaty for the first time after the terrorist attacks of 11 September 2001.[152] While Howard and his ministers did not refer to the ANZUS treaty obligations during the Iraq War debates, the security treaty formed part of the context of the alliance relationship on which the Howard government placed so much importance. Some commentators have argued that the alliance with the US, in combination with his vision of Australia as a Western society positioned in a threatening region (surrounded by non-Westerners), drove Howard's commitment to the war in Iraq.[153] The Howard government's justifications for the Iraq War certainly mirrored those of the US much more closely than they did those of the UK.[154] Howard's attitude towards pre-emptive self-defence in particular, while more cautious than that of the Bush administration, demonstrated a similar attitude of defiance towards international law and the international system as that of the US.[155] In this sense, not only was international law in the form of the ANZUS treaty part of the context for the Australian public debates, but the US attitudes towards international law also had a role in creating a context in which the Howard government felt empowered to express both scepticism towards and defiance of the international legal system. Parallel approaches towards international law were part of the context of the Howard government's commitment to its 'great friend', the US.

3.5 Conclusion

The vocabulary and grammar of international law were prominent features of the 2003 Iraq War debates. A collective or autonomous form of international legal language was used in nearly all the arguments about the justifiability of the war: WMD, the Howard version of pre-emptive self-defence, the interpretation of Security Council resolutions and the

---

[152] Office of the Prime Minister, 'Application of the ANZUS Treaty to Terrorist Attacks on the United States' (Media Release, 14 September 2001).

[153] Jack Holland and Matt McDonald, 'Australian Identity, Interventionism and the "War on Terror"' in Asaf Siniver (ed.), *International Terrorism Post 9/11: Comparative Dynamics and Responses* (Routledge, 2010).

[154] For a comprehensive account of the Iraq War debates in the UK, see *The Report of the Iraq Inquiry* (n 62).

[155] See, for example, National Security Council, *National Security Strategy of the United States* (n 37).

3.5 CONCLUSION

humanitarian consequences of an invasion. Each of these arguments used both the vocabulary and the grammar of international law, and one of its key grammars – the oscillation between law and politics – was particularly evident. Rob Durbridge relied on a strong construction of international legal language to argue that the 'standard' required of the international law of self-defence had not been met and that Australia was therefore not justified in invading Iraq. He constructed international legal language as a restraint on politics. At the same time, John Howard and Alexander Downer argued, in different ways, that international law had to give way to politics. Thus for Downer, a failure to enforce the Security Council resolutions against Iraq was a failure of the entire international legal system itself, and for Howard, the doctrine of self-defence had to develop in such a way as to take account of political developments and embrace a standard of pre-emption.

The proliferation of international legal language during these debates gave traction to a grammar of defiance in international law. In order for the arguments on pre-emption and on the failure of the international legal system to be persuasive, the Howard government had to assume that its audience understood the significant role of international law in relation to war. It was only in a context of a shared understanding of the importance of international law that a threat to defy that law gained purchase. The Howard government's defiant attitude towards international law throughout the Iraq War debates suggested it was confident its audience would not only understand the place of international law – it would also be sympathetic to the need for defiance in this case.

The Australian Iraq War debates suggest that a key measure of speakers' competence was their ability to construct international law as an autonomous justification for war. The idea that legality, on its own, was enough to justify or condemn an Iraq invasion took hold – in particular, towards the end of Australia's public debates – and was exemplified by Kerry O'Brien's interview with John Howard, dominated as it was by legal argument. The importance of international law as an autonomous justification was also evident in the contributions to the public debate by Alexander Downer in September 2002, John Howard's Address to the Nation on 20 March 2003, the statements by Rob Durbridge and the ACTU, and the unprecedented release of the Howard government's advice on the legality of invading Iraq. Even the statement by the Catholic bishops can be read as emphasising an aspect of the 'just war' reasoning – legitimate authority, which is overlaid with autonomous legal authority.

Collective justifications that included international law as a constitutive element were also a consistent part of the Iraq War debates, particularly through the languages of humanitarianism, pre-emption and the just war. Their persuasive power seemed to wane in the latter stages of the public debates, when the autonomous form of international law captured the public's imagination. The collective justifications offered other opportunities for speakers, however. They allowed the unions and religious groups to express solidarity with others around the world who were opposed to the war and with the potential victims of war. The justification of humanitarianism, in particular, encompassed claims for the protection of civilians in war and the unions and religious leaders who used humanitarian arguments considered these applicable to all who suffer in situations of war. But while the language of humanitarianism allowed the public speakers to call on universal standards of protection, it also allowed the political speakers to construct competing ideas of humanitarianism. Just as arguments in the autonomous form of international law were effectively neutralised by competing constructions of legality, so too these different conceptions of humanitarianism seemed to cancel each other out.

The Howard government took opportunities to express solidarity through international law as the collective justification of alliance. This was a different kind of solidarity – one between governments rather than between members of civil society. The Howard government used international legal language to display scepticism about the international system. Expressing this attitude was part of the Howard government's larger project to maintain a strong alliance relationship with the Bush administration, which had forcefully questioned the role of the international legal system. But scepticism of international law was not a mere posture for the Howard government – it was a defining characteristic of its attitude towards the UN system. Howard's solidarity with Bush on this question was genuine, and joining the coalition of the willing enabled a very public airing of that shared belief.

The Iraq debates illustrate that speakers had different ideas about who could speak international legal language with authority. For public speakers such as Durbridge and the ACTU, no special expertise was required to make a judgment about international law. The foregrounding of international legal language in the public debate opened that language to all speakers and empowered Durbridge and the ACTU to use that language to challenge both political and professional speakers of international law. Within this apparent pluralisation of the speakers of international law,

3.5 CONCLUSION

ideas of who had authority to speak that language changed. John Howard's ventriloquy in the interview with Kerry O'Brien saw the authority to speak international legal language shift within the one conversation from the professional speakers to Howard the political speaker and back to the professional speakers. Even when using international legal language proficiently, Howard the political speaker resisted being portrayed as an authoritative professional speaker, characterising his argument instead as 'commonsense'. In one sense, this expression of technical international legal argument as 'commonsense' liberated all the contributors to the public debates to speak international legal language. If law is, after all, a matter of 'commonsense', then it is easy enough for almost anyone to both understand and speak it without any need to develop the expertise of a professional speaker of international law. Even so, Howard's deflection during the interview, and in other contexts, to the greater authority of his expert international law speakers underpinned his deliberate shifting of authority to use that language.

The contributions to public debate from religious groups point to one other characteristic of the 2003 public debate: the hollowness of the vocabulary of morality. The question of morality was raised periodically during the Iraq debates. A common response from the political speakers was to dismiss or deflect from that question: Howard effectively ignored the question about morality in his interview with Kerry O'Brien, for example. When Howard did consider morality in more depth, he did so in a way that replaced any classical conception of morality with a largely international legal one. In his 20 March Address to the Nation, for example, Howard described the invasion of Iraq as 'right'. Howard's idea of 'right' relied on an international legal construction: he argued that Iraq's failure to disarm combined with the Security Council's failure to enforce its resolutions against Iraq created a threat to Australia and the world. Thus, even in a construction of 'right', which carries with it a sense of moral decision-making, Howard relied on international legal language.

To the extent that considerations of morality were raised in these debates, they occurred most often in the language of humanitarianism. In the absence of a shared sense of morality within a secular Australian society, the public speakers turned instead to the proxy of humanitarianism – with its capacious set of meanings – to serve the purpose that the language of morality might have served in different times. It was with appeals to the needs of humanity that the ACTU and religious leaders framed the human suffering that would result from the war. The absence of a consistent language of morality in 2003 stands in stark contrast with the earlier debates, described in the next two chapters.

The 2003 debates set the scene for the examination of the debates of 1965–66 and 1916. Multiple speakers in the Iraq War debates spoke the language of international law. They used international legal language in both collective and autonomous forms of international law in public debate, although the autonomous form was dominant, especially towards the end of the debates. Speakers also characterised international law variously as a constraint on government decision-making, as a force that needed to yield to political priorities and as a way of establishing solidarity with like-minded people or governments around the world. The uses of international legal language by public speakers were prolific and they influenced the trajectory of the debate as a whole. In the latter stages of the Australian debate, the emphasis on legality forced the political speakers to address technical legal questions about the Iraq invasion and to provide regular assurances that the war was 'legal'. The examinations of the public debates in Chapters 4 and 5 raise similarities and differences between those debates and the Iraq War debates. They provide a greater sense of what it means to do and speak international law in public debates, and of the characteristics of a popular international law that arises out of such debates.

4

Public Debate in 1965–66: The Vietnam War

4.1 Introduction

In this Chapter, I examine the Vietnam War debates of 1965–66. Australia's participation in the Vietnam War has parallels with its participation in the 2003 Iraq War. In both cases, a Liberal–Country (National) Coalition government needed to justify participation in a military intervention led by the United States ('US') into a foreign country that posed no immediate or direct threat to US or Australian security. In both cases, the threat to Australia and the US was said to come from the broader consequences of failing to act – the dominoes of communism in the 1960s and the destructive potential of WMD in 2003. In both cases, there was dispute over the evidence that purported to support the government's case; there was no United Nations ('UN') authority for intervention; and there was no widespread support from a coalition of states for military action. In both cases, the extent of Australia's support for its relationship with its powerful alliance partner – the US – was fundamental to the government's decision to participate.

The international legal regime that regulated uses of force under the *Charter of the United Nations* ('*UN Charter*') in 1965 was also the same as that of 2003. The Vietnam War took place within the modern international system where the use of force is outlawed except in self-defence. The key issues of international law in the 1965–66 Vietnam War debates arose from disagreements over the classification of the conflict between North and South Vietnam and over Australia's treaty obligations.[1] Determining whether the conflict in Vietnam was an international armed conflict or

---

[1] For a comprehensive discussion of the legal issues of the Vietnam War, see Richard Falk (ed.), *The Vietnam War and International Law* (American Society of International Law, republished Princeton University Press, 2015) vol. 1–2. A collection of Falk's essays on the

a civil war turned on arguments about the effect of the Geneva Accords of 1954 ('Accords'), which had brought a negotiated end to the Ho Chi Minh-led battle for Vietnamese independence from France.[2] The Accords created what was intended to be a temporary division of Vietnam into North and South, but the division remained in place in 1965. If, as a result of the ongoing divide, North and South Vietnam had attained the status of independent states, the US and Australia could lawfully provide military assistance to South Vietnam to repel aggression from North Vietnam. If, however, North and South Vietnam were instead separated parts of a single state, then the conflict between them was a civil war, and third states, such as Australia and the US, could not lawfully intervene. The treaty questions arose out of disagreements over whether Australia's actions in Vietnam were justified under its obligations as a member of either the South East Asian Treaty Organization ('SEATO') treaty or the Australia, New Zealand and United States ('ANZUS') security treaty arrangement.[3]

The great power rivalries of the 1960s meant, however, that the UN's work was often stalled, particularly in the Security Council where decisions were routinely vetoed by one or more of the permanent members.[4] Most efforts to bring the Vietnam War to the Security Council failed because of the tensions between the Union of Soviet Socialist Republics ('USSR'), the US and the communist governments of the People's Republic of China and North Vietnam.[5] In 1966, the mere inscription

---

legal issues of the Vietnam War is contained in Stefan Andersson (ed.), *Revisiting the Vietnam War and International Law: Views and Interpretations of Richard Falk* (Cambridge University Press, 2017).

[2] Geneva Agreements 20–21 July 1954, consisting of: *Agreement on the Cessation of Hostilities in Viet-Nam* 20 July 1954; *Agreement on the Cessation of Hostilities in Cambodia* 10 July 1954; *Agreement on the Cessation of Hostilities in Laos* 20 July 1954; *Final Declaration of the Geneva Conference on the Problem of Restoring Peace in Indo-China* 21 July 1954.

[3] There was one question regarding the legality, under Australian domestic law, of sending conscripts to fight overseas without their consent – this resulted in a small exchange between Jim Cairns and Billy Sneddon on 30 and 31 March 1966 in Parliament. Sneddon assured the Parliament that such a process was indeed in conformity with the Australian Constitution. See Commonwealth, *Parliamentary Debates*, House of Representatives, 31 March 1966, 795 (Billy Sneddon).

[4] For a record of the Security Council's voting patterns, see, for example, Peter Wallensteen and Patrick Johansson, 'Security Council Decisions in Perspective' in David Malone (ed.), *The UN Security Council: From the Cold War to the 21st Century* (Lynne Rienne, 2004) 17–34.

[5] Neither the People's Republic of China nor North Vietnam was a member of the UN at this time, but their interests and influence were mediated through the USSR. See, for example, Bernard J Firestone, 'Failed Mediation: U Thant, the Johnson Administration, and the Vietnam War' (2013) 37 *Diplomatic History* 1060.

of the Vietnam War on the Security Council's agenda brought strenuous objections from the USSR.[6] The government of France also objected to US intervention in the former French colony[7] and, even absent the rivalries of the 1960s, it is possible that France would have vetoed any Security Council resolution to approve or assist US action in Vietnam.

The situation in the Security Council meant that the international system that existed at the time of the Vietnam War was different from that of the 2003 Iraq War, but it was a difference of expectation, not of architecture. For the participants in the public debates of 1965, the international legal system purported to regulate matters of international peace and security, but the system's main actor – the Security Council – consistently failed to act as the UN *Charter* had envisaged. The public debates of the Vietnam War are thus an example of the use of international legal language when the public had little faith in the UN's ability to regulate international armed conflict.

Two characteristics emerge from the forms of international legal language used in the 1965–66 public debates. The first is that international law did not function as it did in the 2003 Iraq War debate as an autonomous justification, separated from factors such as morality, strategy and alliances. The persuasiveness of any international legal language depended instead on its relationship with those other justifications. The second characteristic is a corollary of the first. In the 1965–66 Vietnam War debates, international legal language was used, but it was rarely named as such. Characterising an argument as 'legal' or 'illegal' did not in these debates hold the power that it did in 2003. Indeed, for some speakers, a focus on legality demonstrated a misguided interest in process over substance, formalities over merits. International legal language had a role in debating the merits of the Vietnam War, but the idea of legality in itself held limited appeal.

4.2 Timing and Sources

Australia's participation in the Vietnam War began in 1962 and was formally declared at an end by Proclamation of the Governor-General on 11 January 1973. In this chapter, I focus on the period between March 1965 and November 1966, which marks the time from shortly

---

[6] See the account in Charles W Yost, 'The United Nations: Crisis of Confidence and Will' (1966) 45 *Foreign Affairs* 19, 24–25.
[7] Ibid.

before the announcement of the commitment of an Australian battalion in April 1965 to the federal election of November 1966. It was in 1965–66 that Australia's commitment to the war in Vietnam became an issue in public debate. Unusually for Australia, the 1966 election was fought on questions of foreign policy – specifically whether Australia should be fighting in Vietnam and whether conscripts should be part of Australia's military commitments. The years 1965 and 1966 saw the galvanisation of public debate around federal government policies in a way that had not occurred since the conscription debates of the First World War, which are described in Chapter 5.

In concentrating on 1965 and 1966, I exclude from this chapter the debates of the later anti-Vietnam War mass protest movement and, in particular, the debates of the 1970 and 1971 moratoriums, in which hundreds of thousands of people around Australia marched.[8] By late April 1970, both US President Richard Nixon and Australian Prime Minister John Gorton had announced the first withdrawal of their respective troops from Vietnam. The aims of the moratorium movement were the complete withdrawal of Australian troops from Vietnam and the repeal of the *National Service Act 1964* (Cth), under which men were conscripted for Vietnam. The moratorium movement is excluded from this chapter because the aim of the movement was to bring on the end of a conflict rather than to consider the wisdom of entering a conflict (as with the 2003 Iraq War or the 1965–66 Vietnam debates) or the means in which to do so (as with the conscription debates of 1916).[9] Also excluded from this chapter are the public debates that focused on opposing conscription for Vietnam more generally. The question of Australia's participation in the war was of course linked with the conscription question. Many of the conscripts from 1966 who objected to the war were opposed to fighting specifically in the Vietnam War. The objections to the war and to conscription can be analysed separately. I focus in this chapter on the contributions to public debate that discussed entry and participation in the war.

For political speakers, this chapter highlights Prime Minister Robert Menzies and his Minister for External Affairs, Paul Hasluck, as

---

[8] See, for example, Greg Langley, *A Decade of Dissent: Vietnam and the Conflict on the Australian Home Front* (Allen & Unwin, 1992) 135.

[9] For a sample of some of this material, see, for example, Lani Russell, 'Today the Students, Tomorrow the Workers! Radical Student Politics and the Australian Labour Movement 1960–72' (PhD Thesis, University of Technology Sydney, 1999); Kate Murphy, '"In the Backblocks of Capitalism": Australian Student Activism in the Global 1960s' (2015) 46 *Australian Historical Studies* 252.

representatives of the government. Menzies led the decision to commit Australia to military intervention in Vietnam and was actively engaged in the 1965 debates until his retirement in early 1966. Hasluck led the government's public case through 1966, along with new Prime Minister Harold Holt. I also include in this chapter the political figure of Jim Cairns, a Member of Parliament for the Labor Party, a future Deputy Prime Minister and a leading intellectual of Australia's political left.[10] Cairns became one of the leaders of Australia's anti-Vietnam War movement and was instrumental in the moratorium campaigns of the 1970s. He was an important figure in the Australian anti-Vietnam War debates. Public speakers featured in this chapter include religious figures – represented by leaders of the Anglican and Catholic churches – and religious newspapers. Australian trade unions were divided on Australia's decision to send troops to Vietnam, and throughout the Vietnam War their responses to Australia's involvement in the conflict and to conscription reflected these opposing views.[11] This division in the union movement meant that, as a movement, it played only a small role in the Vietnam War debates. In the absence of consistent contributions to the Vietnam debates from the trade unions, I examine instead contributions from individuals and groups that were published in mainstream newspapers.

This chapter proceeds with a description of the social, political and legal contexts in which the Vietnam War debates occurred in 1965–66. In section 4.4, I analyse a series of texts as a means of understanding how international legal language was used in the public debate of 1965–66. Through these texts, a number of themes emerge from the Vietnam War

---

[10] Jim Cairns also wrote extensively on Australian foreign policy, especially in relation to Vietnam: see, for example, JF Cairns, *Vietnam: Is it Truth We Want?* (Victorian Branch of the Australian Labor Party, 1965); JF Cairns, *Eagle and the Lotus: Western Intervention in Vietnam 1847–1968* (Lansdowne Press, 1969). See also Paul Strangio, *Keeper of the Faith: A Biography of Jim Cairns* (Melbourne University Press, 2002).

[11] Nearly all the published and unpublished research on the specific question of the trade unions' response to Australia's Vietnam policies is by Malcolm Saunders. I draw here especially on Malcolm J Saunders, 'The Trade Unions in Australia and Opposition to Vietnam and Conscription: 1965–73' (1982) 43 *Labour History* 64 ('Trade Unions in Australia'); Malcolm Saunders, 'The Vietnam Moratorium Movement in Australia 1969–1973' (PhD Thesis, Flinders University, 1977) ('Vietnam Moratorium Movement'). See also Rick Kuhn, 'The Australian Left, Nationalism and the Vietnam War' (1997) 72 *Labour History* 163; Langley (n 8); John Murphy, *Harvest of Fear: A History of Australia's Vietnam War* (Allen & Unwin, 1993); Barry York, 'The Australian Anti-Vietnam Movement, 1965–73' (1983) 15 *Melbourne Journal of Politics* 24.

public debates. These are the relationships between morality and legality; the nature of Australia's treaty obligations; and differing conceptions of self-determination, aggression and self-defence. Section 4.4 of this chapter illustrates these themes in detail. First, I turn to a description of the contexts in which the 1965–66 debates occurred.

4.3   The Contexts

By 1965, Australia had been governed by the conservative Liberal–Country Coalition led by Robert Menzies for sixteen years. One of the most dominant and divisive figures of Australian politics, Menzies was a lawyer by training, deeply anti-communist and committed to the 'Britishness' of Australia and its continued membership of the Commonwealth.[12] The early 1960s were the twilight of Menzies' Prime Ministership, during which he oversaw Australia's involvement, or potential involvement, in the conflicts that were dominating South East Asia at the time.[13] In 1961, the Menzies Cabinet had agreed in principle to participate in action led either by the US or under the auspices of the

---

[12] The authorised biographies of Menzies are AW Martin, *Robert Menzies: A Life, Volume 1 1894–1943* (Melbourne University Press, 1993); AW Martin, *Robert Menzies: A Life, Volume 2 1944–1978* (Melbourne University Press, 1999). For a more critical view, see Judith Brett, *Robert Menzies' Forgotten People* (Melbourne University Press, 2007). Menzies' colleagues and successors have also written about his life. See, for example, Paul Hasluck, *Sir Robert Menzies* (Melbourne University Press, 1980); Percy Joske, *Sir Robert Menzies 1894–1978: A New, Informal Memoir* (Angus & Robertson, 1978); John Howard, *The Menzies Era: The Years that Shaped Modern Australia* (Harper Collins, 2014). For a brief outline of some of the contrasting views on Menzies, see, for example, Frank Bongiorno, 'The Price of Nostalgia: Menzies, the "Liberal" Tradition and Australian Foreign Policy' (2005) 51 *Australian Journal of Politics and History* 400.

[13] The 'official' histories of Australia's involvement in South East Asia in the 1960s include Peter Edwards, *Crises and Commitments: The Politics and Diplomacy of Australia's Involvement in Southeast Asian Conflicts 1948–1965* (Allen & Unwin and Australian War Memorial, 1992) ('*Crises and Commitments*'); Peter Edwards, *A Nation at War: Australian Politics, Society and Diplomacy during the Vietnam War 1965–75* (Allen & Unwin and Australian War Memorial, 1997) ('*Nation at War*'); Peter Edwards, *Australia and the Vietnam War* (NewSouth Books, 2014) ('*Vietnam War*'); Peter Dennis and Jeffrey Grey, *Emergency and Confrontation: Australian Military Operations in Malaya and Borneo 1950–1966* (Allen & Unwin and Australian War Memorial, 1996). For other views on this period, see, for example, Glen St J Barclay, *A Very Small Insurance Policy: The Politics of Australian Involvement in Vietnam 1954–1967* (University of Queensland Press, 1988); John Murphy (n 11); Gregory Pemberton, *All the Way: Australia's Road to Vietnam* (Allen & Unwin, 1987)('*All the Way*'). Succinct descriptions of Australia's involvement in these conflicts are provided by Peter Dennis et al., *The Oxford Companion to Australian Military History* (Oxford University Press, 2009) and the website of the Australian War Memorial www.awm.gov.au.

regional security pact – SEATO – to suppress the communist insurgency in Laos. A ceasefire agreement between the various Laotian parties, formalised in June and July 1962, meant this commitment was never realised.[14] Threats from communist insurgents in Thailand and a request for assistance from the Thai government had seen the commitment of Australian military aircraft to Thailand in 1962.[15] The Australian Government characterised this action as being in accordance with its SEATO obligations.[16] Between 1963 and 1966, the new federation of Malaysia defended itself against military confrontation from Indonesia, with the aid of Australian and United Kingdom ('UK') forces.[17] The UK remained involved in the defence of its former colony of Malaya for its own strategic reasons, but it was otherwise withdrawing from commitments to South East Asia.[18]

This set of commitments constituted some of the regional security environment in which Australia committed thirty non-combatant military instructors to assist US action in South Vietnam in May 1962. By 1962, conflict between communist-led North Vietnam (the Democratic Republic of Vietnam) and anti-communist South (the Republic of Vietnam) had escalated, as had the US military commitment in South Vietnam.[19] Alert to British withdrawal from the region and committed to a strategic defence requirement to preserve a strong relationship with the US, the Menzies government took the view that, despite its other commitments in the region, Australia had to both support and encourage the US actions in Vietnam. Only in this way, the thinking went, could Australia demonstrate an alliance with the US in strong opposition to the spread of communism across the world and secure Australia's own security in the region.[20]

The alliance with the US was at the foundation of the twin aims of Menzies' foreign policy. These aims were subsequently pursued by Harold Holt, who assumed the Prime Ministership following Menzies'

---

[14] See Edwards, *Crises and Commitments* (n 13) 208–28.
[15] Ibid., 237–44.
[16] Commonwealth, *Parliamentary Debates*, House of Representatives, 17 May 1962, 2451–52 (Garfield Barwick).
[17] See Dennis and Grey (n 11).
[18] Edwards, *Crises and Commitments* (n 13) 206.
[19] Ibid., 234.
[20] Ibid., 244–48. See also Barclay (n 13); John Murphy (n 11); Pemberton, *All the Way* (n 13); Alan Watt, *Vietnam: An Australian Analysis* (FW Cheshire, 1968); David McLean, 'From British Colony to American Satellite? Australia and the USA during the Cold War' (2006) 52 *Australian Journal of Politics and History* 64.

retirement in January 1966. The first aim was to resist the spread of communism in South East Asia (the 'domino theory') and the second to develop even stronger ties with the US (the 'insurance policy'). The theory of the domino effect held that the fall of South Vietnam to the North Vietnamese communists would precipitate a consequential loss of neighbouring countries to communism. And once Cambodia, Thailand, Malaysia and Indonesia had all fallen, the fight against communism would be literally on Australian shores. The spread of communism therefore had to be stopped before the dominoes of South East Asia collapsed. According to the theory of the 'insurance policy', Australia needed to provide unqualified support for the US war in Vietnam in order to ensure that the US would provide military and other assistance to Australia if it were ever necessary (for example, if Indonesia fell to the communists).[21] Menzies and Holt were fiercely anti-communist, as was their Minister for External Affairs, Paul Hasluck.[22] Menzies, Holt and Hasluck in particular viewed the world through Cold War lenses that regarded the government of North Vietnam as a proxy for China and its ambitions in the region.[23] Australia's participation in the Vietnam War thus occurred within a context of conservative Australian governments with a deep-rooted fear of communism, ongoing tensions in South East Asian countries and withdrawal of British interest in the region.

Australia's military commitments in South East Asia and the suspicion that these would increase in the coming years led the Menzies government to introduce conscription for foreign service in November 1964. In his speech on the policy, Menzies argued that conscription was necessary to increase the size of the army for 'a continuing requirement to make

---

[21] The domino theory was originally developed by US President Eisenhower and was adopted by the Australian Government, Edwards, *Vietnam War* (n 13) 42-43. The 'insurance policy' has been at the heart of Australia's foreign policy since the Second World War: see, for example, Malcolm Fraser, *Dangerous Allies* (Melbourne University Press, 2014).

[22] Biographies of Holt and Hasluck include Tom Frame, *The Life and Death of Harold Holt* (Allen & Unwin, 2005); Robert Porter, *Paul Hasluck: A Political Biography* (UWA Press, 1993); Geoffrey Bolton, *Paul Hasluck: A Life* (UWA Publishing, 2015).

[23] See John Murphy (n 11) 99-114; Pemberton, *All the Way* (n 13) 312-22. For speeches by these men expressing these views, see, for example, Commonwealth, *Parliamentary Debates*, House of Representatives, 10 November 1964, 2715-18 (Robert Menzies); Commonwealth, *Parliamentary Debates*, House of Representatives, 5 May 1966, 1561-67 (Harold Holt); Harold Holt, 'Prime Minister's Visit to U.S. and U.K.' (Speech, National Press Club, Washington, 30 June 1966); Commonwealth, *Parliamentary Debates*, House of Representatives, 18 August 1966, 215-26 (Paul Hasluck).

forces available for cold war and anti-insurgency tasks'.[24] These tasks arose from threats that included the ongoing conflicts in Vietnam and on the border between Malaysia and Indonesia, of which the latter, he said, created 'a real risk of war'.[25] While not explicit, this speech indicated that conscripts would most likely be used for overseas service, the issue that had galvanised the debates of 1916.[26]

Public responses to the re-introduction of conscription were muted, although the Labor Party did object in Parliament. Labor Party leader Arthur Calwell was passionately anti-conscription and had been in Australian politics long enough to have participated in the conscription debates of 1916 and 1917.[27] The public, however, appeared relatively unperturbed by the change; polling at the time showed support for both Australian involvement in Vietnam and for conscription.[28] The 1964 polling did not ask specifically about conscription for overseas service but recorded overwhelming support in response to a question asking about the government's programme of military service for two years, including 'overseas if necessary'.[29] Later polling, between 1965 and 1967, specifically asked whether conscripts should be sent overseas or whether they should perform their service in Australia. This was answered by a consistent majority against conscription for overseas service.[30] But at the end of 1964, the Menzies government was comfortable in the knowledge that a majority of the public supported all its policies on both Vietnam and conscription.

Support for Menzies' Vietnam policy remained high, even after Menzies announced that Australia would be sending 800 troops to assist the US and

---

[24] Commonwealth, *Parliamentary Debates*, House of Representatives, 10 November 1964, 2718 (Robert Menzies).

[25] Ibid., 2716.

[26] See *National Service Act 1964* (Cth) and second reading speech in Commonwealth, *Parliamentary Debates*, House of Representatives, 11 November 1964, 2836-39 (William McMahon). See Chapter 5 for a detailed discussion of the 1916 debates.

[27] See, for example, Commonwealth, *Parliamentary Debates*, House of Representatives, 12 November 1964, 2920-28 (Arthur Calwell).

[28] See Murray Goot and Rodney Tiffen, 'Public Opinion and the Politics of the Polls' in Peter King (ed), *Australia's Vietnam: Australia in the Second Indo-China War* (Allen & Unwin, 1983) 129, 134, 142. See also a summary of polling between 1965 and 1968 in Malcolm Saunders, '"Law and Order" and the Anti-Vietnam War Movement: 1965-72' (1982) 28 *Australian Journal of Politics and History* 367, 367.

[29] Goot and Tiffen (n 28) 142.

[30] Ibid., 142-43. See also Michael E Hamel-Green, 'The Resisters: A History of the Anti-Conscription Movement 1964-72' in Peter King (ed.), *Australia's Vietnam: Australia in the Second Indo-China War* (Allen & Unwin, 1983) 100.

South Vietnam in April 1965.[31] Menzies' Cabinet had agreed in 1962 that it would make military commitments in Southeast Asia only after requests from the relevant governments.[32] By early 1965, there were indications from the US that a larger Australian commitment was desired, and Menzies himself was keen to send a battalion, but no specific request was received from the South Vietnamese government.[33] On 17 December 1964, a meeting of five ministers of Menzies' Cabinet agreed, in principle, to commit a military battalion to South Vietnam, but this decision remained secret for some months as negotiations with the US and South Vietnam over the timing and nature of that battalion continued.[34] When the formal decision to send a battalion was made by the Cabinet's Foreign Affairs and Defence Committee on 7 April 1965, its public announcement was delayed, pending receipt of the formal request from the government of South Vietnam. Menzies finally surprised an almost empty House of Representatives on 29 April 1965 with the announcement that Australia would be sending an infantry battalion to Vietnam.[35] Menzies described the Australian commitment as a response to 'a request from the Government of South Vietnam for further military assistance'.[36] This remained the accepted account of these events until the release in 1971 of the Pentagon Papers – the formerly secret US Department of Defence report detailing the US military involvement in Vietnam from 1945 to 1967.[37] The Pentagon Papers revealed that the 'request' from South Vietnam had been procured, if not by force, then at least with considerable prompting from representatives of both the US and Australia.[38] At the time, however, the request was publicly perceived to be genuine.

[31] Goot and Tiffen (n 28) 134.
[32] Pemberton, *All the Way* (n 13) 277.
[33] Accounts of this period are given in, for example, Edwards, *Crises and Commitments* (n 13) 351–75; Pemberton, *All the Way* (n 13) 276–97; John Murphy (n 11) 121–39.
[34] Garry Woodard, *Asian Alternatives: Australia's Vietnam Decision and Lessons on Going to War* (Melbourne University Press, 2004) 191–256. See also Trish Payne, *War and Words: The Australian Press and the Vietnam War* (Melbourne University Press, 2007) 77–128.
[35] The odd circumstances of the announcement were justified on the basis that Menzies needed to pre-empt a journalist planning to publish a story about Australia's military commitment. See Pemberton, *All the Way* (n 13) 292–94; Payne (n 34) 78.
[36] Commonwealth, *Parliamentary Debates*, House of Representatives, 29 April 1965, 1060 (Robert Menzies).
[37] See, for example, Daniel Ellsberg, *Secrets: A Memoir of Vietnam and the Pentagon Papers* (Viking, 2003).
[38] See, for example, 'Menzies Says He Did Not Lie', *The Sydney Morning Herald* (Sydney, 18 June 1971) 1; 'PM on Vietnam Row', *The Sydney Morning Herald* (Sydney, 19 June 1971) 1. For different interpretations of these events by the two historians who have had the most comprehensive access to the Menzies and US government files, see

Reaction to the commitment of Australian troops to fight in Vietnam was generally supportive – polling indicated that a majority of Australians supported Menzies' decision, and newspaper editorials generally expressed support.[39] The Labor Party under Calwell opposed the contribution of a fighting battalion, however, which was a shift from the bipartisanship that had characterised Australia's policies on Vietnam to that point. Parliamentary speeches in May 1965 by Calwell and Cairns made this clear.[40] The ACTU aligned with the Labor Party to oppose sending troops to Vietnam, and it urged support for the anti-war rallies held around the country in May 1965. The ACTU, however, did not support all union anti-war efforts.[41] The ACTU President, for example, ruled that the ACTU would not support either work stoppages or strikes by unions such as the Waterside Workers' Federation to protest the commitment of troops.[42] The ACTU's compromise was designed to appease the anti-communist unions that supported Australia's participation in the Vietnam War. These unions included the Federated Ironworkers Association, which, with the support of at least four other unions, had passed a resolution in May 1965 declaring support for Menzies' decision and for the alliance with the US.[43] The ideological divide that was evident in May 1965 among the unions and within the ACTU continued for the duration of Australia's participation in the Vietnam War.[44]

Menzies' announcement of an Australian troop commitment triggered what became an 'active and angry minority' anti-war movement, which then worked tirelessly to dislodge the Holt government at the November 1966

Pemberton, *All the Way* (n 13) 276–79 and Edwards, *Crises and Commitments* (n 13) 351–75.

[39] Goot and Tiffen (n 28) 134–35. See also Rodney Tiffen, 'The War the Media Lost: Australian News Coverage of Vietnam' in Gregory Pemberton (ed.), *Vietnam Remembered* (Weldon, 1990) 110, 128–29.

[40] For analyses of Labor Party policies towards Vietnam, see, for example, Kim C Beazley, 'Federal Labor and the Vietnam Commitment' in Peter King (ed.), *Australia's Vietnam: Australia in the Second Indo-China War* (Allen & Unwin, 1983) 36; Graham Freudenberg, 'The Australian Labor Party and Vietnam' (1979) 33 *The Australian Outlook* 157; Malcolm Saunders, 'The ALP's Response to the Anti-Vietnam War Movement: 1965–73' (1983) 44 *Labour History* 75 ('ALP's Response').

[41] See James Hagan, *The ACTU: A Short History on the Occasion of the 50th Anniversary 1927–1977* (Reed, 1977); 'ACTU Opposes Strikes to Stop Troops', *The Australian* (Sydney, 7 May 1965) 4.

[42] Saunders, 'Trade Unions in Australia' (n 11) 65.

[43] Ibid., 66.

[44] Ibid., 73–76. See also 'ACTU Is Silent on Vietnam and the Call-Up', *The Australian* (Sydney, 14 November 1966) 1; Hagan (n 41).

federal election.[45] More than 100 different groups opposed to the Vietnam War or to conscription – or to both – were established in this period.[46] They formed a 'loose federation', maintaining their own philosophies and methods of protest while also revealing the diversity of people opposed to the government's policies.[47] Some of the more prominent anti-war groups included the 'moderate' Association for International Co-operation and Disarmament ('AICD'), with a membership of mostly older middle-class Australians, and the 'radical' Vietnam Action Committee (later the Vietnam Action Campaign or 'VAC'), which had arisen out of the Campaign for Nuclear Disarmament and had a predominantly youthful membership.[48] These groups built on the momentum of the existing Australian peace movement, which had been associated with the Communist Party of Australia ('CPA') through the 1950s and early 1960s.[49] They staged protests

---

[45] Ann Curthoys, 'Mobilising Dissent: The Later Stages of Protest' in Gregory Pemberton (ed), *Vietnam Remembered* (Weldon, 1990) 138, 146.

[46] Ann Mari Jordens counted at least 146 anti-war organisations, not including the churches, unions and political parties. See Ann Mari Jordens, 'Conscription and Dissent: The Genesis of Anti War Protest' in Gregory Pemberton (ed.), *Vietnam Remembered* (Weldon, 1990) 60, 74. See also York (n 11).

[47] Jordens (n 46) 74–75.

[48] Malcolm Saunders and Ralph Summy, 'One Hundred Years of an Australian Peace Movement, 1885–1984: Part II: From the Second World War to Vietnam and Beyond' (1984) 10 *Peace & Change* 57, 65 ('Peace Movement: Part II'); Alec Robertson, 'CPA in the Anti-War Movement' (October–November 1970) *Australian Left Review* 39, 47. On what it meant to be 'radical' in 1960s Australia, see Richard Gordon and Warren Osmond, 'An Overview of the Australian New Left' in Richard Gordon (ed.), *The Australian New Left: Critical Essays and Strategy* (William Heinemann, 1970) 3. See also Jon Piccini, Evan Smith and Matthew Worley (eds.), *The Far Left In Australia since 1945* (Routledge, 2018).

[49] For different views on the extent of communist influence in the Australian peace movement, see Robertson (n 48); Chris Guyatt, 'The Anti-Conscription Movement' in Roy Forward and Bob Reece (eds.), *Conscription in Australia* (University of Queensland Press, 1968) 178; Fred Wells, 'A Comment on Mr Guyatt's Chapter' in Roy Forward and Bob Reece (eds.), *Conscription in Australia* (University of Queensland Press, 1968) 191; Ralph V Summy, 'A Reply to Fred Wells' in Roy Forward and Bob Reece (eds.), *Conscription in Australia* (University of Queensland Press, 1968) 200. The Australian peace movement remains relatively unexplored in published research. Most of the published research is by Malcolm Saunders and Ralph Summy: see especially Malcolm Saunders and Ralph Summy, 'One Hundred Years of an Australian Peace Movement, 1885–1984: Part I: From the Sudan Campaign to the Outbreak of the Second World War' (1984) 10 *Peace & Change* 39; Saunders and Summy, 'Peace Movement: Part II' (n 48). See also John Murphy (n 11); Ann Curthoys, 'The Anti-War Movements' in Jeffrey Grey and Jeff Doyle (eds.), *Vietnam: War, Myth and Memory: Comparative Perspectives on Australia's War in Vietnam* (Allen & Unwin, 1992) 81 ('Anti-War Movements'); PT Findlay, *Protest Politics and Psychological Warfare: The Communist Role in the Anti-Vietnam War and Anti-Conscription Movement in Australia* (The Hawthorn Press, 1968).

against the war in the months after April 1965. Between April and December 1965, anti-war groups gradually attracted wider public support and contributed to a gathering of momentum for the Vietnam protest movement. One meeting in December 1965 included more than 3,000 participants, and a Sydney rally in October 1965 saw 50 people arrested after staging a sit-down protest at peak hour in a busy Sydney street.[50]

Opposition to the war came from other places too. The only newspaper to oppose Menzies' decision was the relatively new *The Australian*, owned by Rupert Murdoch, which called Australia's participation 'reckless' and 'wrong'.[51] Some Anglican bishops had made their opposition plain through two open letters sent to Menzies in the month before the troop announcement.[52] Despite the significant publicity given to the Anglican bishops' views, they represented a minority view among the mainstream Christian churches.[53] The leaders of the Presbyterian and Catholic churches, for example, supported Australia's intervention in Vietnam. Presbyterian representatives said that 'to support our allies and nations under threat of aggression, there is a moral obligation on every Australian to contribute'.[54] The deeply anti-communist and powerful Catholic National Civic Council dismissed the Anglican bishops' objections as 'naïve' in the face of communist aggression.[55] There was dissent fomenting too on university campuses, although this was initially marginal among a largely 'conservative' student body.[56] The President of the University of Melbourne's Students' Representative Council, Gareth Evans (later a Minister in two Labor Party governments), issued a letter supporting the Menzies government's decision to send troops.[57] And an open letter from academics from Melbourne and

---

[50] Saunders, 'Law and Order' (n 28) 368; Ralph Summy, 'Militancy and the Australian Peace Movement 1960–67' (1970) 5 *Australian Journal of Political Science* 148, 155 ('Militancy'). See also Curthoys, 'Mobilising Dissent' (n 45) 140–41.
[51] Editorial, 'The War that Can't Be Won', *The Australian* (Sydney, 30 April 1965) 8.
[52] The correspondence was reprinted in: Prime Minister's Department, *Exchange of Letters Between the Prime Minister The Rt Hon Sir Robert Menzies and The Rt Rev JS Moyes and Certain Archbishops and Bishops* (Prime Minister's Department Pamphlet, Canberra, 20 April 1965) ('*Exchange of Letters*'). See section 4.4.1.1 of this chapter for a detailed discussion of this correspondence.
[53] Jordens (n 46) 76.
[54] 'Presbyterian Statement: Former Leaders Support Call-Up', *The Sydney Morning Herald* (Sydney, 18 April 1966) 4.
[55] Quoted in Val Noone, *Disturbing the War: Melbourne Catholics and Vietnam* (Spectrum, 1993) 117.
[56] Jordens (n 46) 75; Curthoys, 'Mobilising Dissent' (n 45) 138; Russell (n 9) 105–09.
[57] Gareth Evans, 'Support for United States', letter printed in *The Age* (Melbourne, 7 May 1965).

Monash universities advocated a peaceful solution in Vietnam while assuring its audience of their support for Australia's alliance with the US.[58]

After Menzies' retirement in January 1966, Harold Holt was elected leader of the Liberal Party and became the new Prime Minister. Holt later cemented his position as Prime Minister with a landslide win for the Liberal–Country Coalition at the November 1966 election. That election was fought primarily on Australia's policies on Vietnam, and it provided a focus for public debate and protest on those issues. Holt prosecuted Australia's policies on Vietnam even more vigorously than Menzies had. In his first speech to Parliament in March 1966, Holt announced the commitment of a second Australian battalion to Vietnam, requiring the inclusion of conscripted national servicemen in order to make up the necessary numbers.[59] Holt also had a good relationship with US President Lyndon Johnson; and famously echoed Johnson's own campaign slogan when telling an American audience in June 1966 that Australia would go 'all the way with LBJ!'[60] The Australian public's majority support for the Holt government's policies was emphatically illustrated in June 1966 when an estimated half a million people turned out for a ticker-tape parade in Sydney to welcome home the first battalion sent to Vietnam.[61]

Over the course of 1966, Holt and his Coalition colleagues defended their Vietnam policies via public speeches, television advertisements and the release of a series of public pamphlets explaining the government's position. Such pamphlets were commonly used during 1965–66 by participants in the debates – such as the Liberal Party, the Communist Party and Jim Cairns – all aimed at convincing the public about the merits of their positions on Vietnam.[62] The pamphlets illustrate the types of

---

[58] W Macmahon Ball et al., 'American Policy in Vietnam War', letter printed in *The Age* (Melbourne, 25 May 1965).

[59] Commonwealth, *Parliamentary Debates*, House of Representatives, 8 March 1966, 27–28 (Harold Holt); Edwards, *Vietnam War* (n 13) 136–38.

[60] John Murphy (n 11) 155; Edwards, *Vietnam War* (n 13) 156.

[61] '500,000 Welcome Heroes', *The Australian* (Sydney, 9 June 1966) 1. This parade is usually remembered for the protestor who smeared red paint on the returning battalion's commander: see, for example, Michael Caulfield, *The Vietnam Years: From the Jungle to the Australian Suburbs* (Hachette Australia, 2007) 358–60.

[62] Department of External Affairs, *Viet Nam Recent Statements of Australian Policy* (Commonwealth Government Printer, 1965); Minister for External Affairs, *Viet Nam Questions and Answers* (Commonwealth Government Printer, 1966) ('*Viet Nam Questions and Answers*'); Minister for External Affairs, *Viet Nam and SEATO* (Commonwealth Government Printer, 1966) ('*Viet Nam and SEATO*'); Liberal Party of Australia, *Communist China's Objectives* (Liberal Party Publication, 1965); Liberal

4.3 THE CONTEXTS

questions that were of concern, and perceived to be of concern, to the public. All the pamphlets were widely distributed, and Menzies defended the distribution of the government pamphlets as part of the government's right and duty to explain in detail to the public the reasons for its Vietnam actions.[63] Historian John Murphy has referred to this flurry of pamphlets as 'Australia's last controversy using the pamphlet form'.[64]

Three government pamphlets are of particular interest. The first of the three was a collection of public correspondence between Menzies and a group of Anglican bishops shortly before Menzies announced Australia's intervention in Vietnam in April 1965 ('Bishops' pamphlet').[65] The second pamphlet – *Viet Nam Questions and Answers* – was issued by the Holt government in May 1966 as a means of answering 'frequent questions' about Australia's role in Vietnam.[66] These two general pamphlets were supplemented in June 1966 by a pamphlet on a specific international legal question – whether Australia's decision to intervene in Vietnam had been based on its obligations under the SEATO treaty ('SEATO pamphlet').[67] The government printed 100,000 copies of the *Viet Nam Questions and*

Party of Australia, *The Stake is Freedom. The Aims of Australian Foreign Policy* (Liberal Party Publication, 1966); Liberal Party of Australia, *The Facts About South Vietnam* (Liberal Party Publication, 1966); Communist Party of Australia, *Vietnam, The Answers: A Reply to the Holt Government's Pamphlet 'Vietnam, Questions and Answers'* (DB Young, 1966) ('*Vietnam, The Answers*'); Communist Party of Australia, *The Real Facts about South Vietnam: A Reply to the Liberal Party* (DB Young, 1966) ('*The Real Facts*'); Jim Cairns, *Vietnam: Is it Truth We Want?* (Victorian Branch of the Australian Labor Party, 1965). Some of the pamphlets had a print run of more than 70,000 copies: see Jonathan Gaul, 'Holt, the Public and Vietnam', *The Canberra Times* (Canberra, 5 April 1966) 2.

[63] Commonwealth, *Parliamentary Debates*, House of Representatives, 2 December 1965, 3482, 3478, 3480 (Robert Menzies). The statistics for the government pamphlets were as follows: *Viet Nam Recent Statements of Australian Policy*: 75,000 copies printed and distributed; *Viet Nam Questions and Answers*: 100,000 copies printed, 91,000 copies distributed; *Viet Nam and SEATO*: 30,000 copies printed, 22,000 copies distributed. Copies of all three pamphlets were distributed to members of Commonwealth and state parliaments, the Commonwealth press gallery, newspaper editors and Australian diplomatic missions. Copies of the first two pamphlets were also distributed to 'businessmen, clergymen, trade unions, political parties, university and public libraries, headmasters of secondary schools and foreign diplomatic missions in Australia'. The SEATO pamphlet did not receive the latter wider distribution. See Commonwealth, *Parliamentary Debates*, House of Representatives, 20 September 1966, 505–06 (John Gorton).

[64] John Murphy (n 11) 153.

[65] Prime Minister's Department ('*Exchange of Letters*') (n 52).

[66] Minister for External Affairs, *Viet Nam Questions and Answers* (n 62).

[67] *Viet Nam and SEATO* (n 62).

Answers pamphlet and 30,000 of the SEATO pamphlet.[68] Copies of all three pamphlets were sent to Commonwealth and state parliaments, journalists and media organisations, and Australian diplomatic missions overseas.[69] Copies of the *Viet Nam Questions and Answers* pamphlet were also sent to 'businessmen, clergymen, trade unions, political parties, university and public libraries, headmasters of secondary schools, and foreign diplomatic missions in Australia'.[70]

The Holt government's case was also boosted by Lyndon Johnson's visit to Australia one month before the election in October 1966 – the first visit by an incumbent US President in Australia's history.[71] Johnson's visit attracted large crowds and was given positive coverage in the major newspapers.[72] Johnson's visit was a catalysing force for the Vietnam protest movement. Although often outnumbered by supportive crowds, anti-war demonstrators were able to stage protests that garnered wide national coverage.[73] At one event in Sydney, protestors were particularly effective and famously caused the then Premier of New South Wales to instruct his driver to 'drive over the bastards'.[74]

The Labor Party responded to this government activity by focusing its 1966 election campaign on ending conscription and bringing conscripts home from Vietnam.[75] Calwell declared in April 1966 that he was willing to 'live or perish, politically' on the question of conscription.[76] A few days later, he called for 'protests and demonstrations from one end of the country to the other against conscription for overseas service – right up to the next federal elections'.[77] Anti-conscription and anti-war groups, in particular the groups organised under the VAC banner, took up Calwell's

---

[68] See Commonwealth, *Parliamentary Debates*, House of Representatives, 20 September 1966, 505–06 (John Gorton). I have not been able to find a record of the number printed or the distribution of the *Exchange of Letters* pamphlet, but its contents had been widely disseminated in the mainstream newspapers before the collation into a pamphlet.

[69] Ibid.

[70] Ibid.

[71] For an assessment of the impact of Johnson's visit, see Paul D Williams, 'Holt, Johnson and the 1966 Federal Election: A Question of Causality' (2001) 47 *Australian Journal of Politics and History* 366.

[72] See the summary of newspaper headlines in Williams (n 71) 375. See also, for example, 'LBJ is with Australia All the Way', *The Australian* (Sydney, 22 October 1966) 1; 'Melbourne Mobs the Johnsons', *The Canberra Times* (Canberra, 22 October 1966) 1.

[73] Curthoys, 'Mobilising Dissent' (n 45) 146.

[74] Edwards, *Vietnam War* (n 13) 157–58; 'Strong Police Action Sought', *The Australian* (Sydney, 24 October 1966) 3; Williams (n 71) 375.

[75] John Murphy (n 11) 149–50.

[76] 'Labor Will Bring the Boys Home', *The Australian* (Sydney, 14 April 1966) 3.

[77] 'Peace Before We Quit', *The Australian* (Sydney, 10 May 1966).

call and threw their support behind the Labor Party.[78] The 1966 election became the focus of Vietnam protest energies. Anti-war groups organised public meetings, rallies, marches, and 'teach-in' and 'preach-in' debates, and they issued responses to the series of government pamphlets on Australia's Vietnam policies. All this activity contributed to a significant revival of public debate on government policy in Australia, which had been effectively paralysed by the bipartisan consensus on the Cold War.[79] In the words of Humphrey McQueen, a leader of the youth movement,

> In 1966, the young left looked forward to a Labor victory. . . . They felt a tremendous sense of purpose and looked forward to great achievements. The defeat that followed either shocked them into apathy or slowly gave rise to undirected militancy.[80]

The scale of the Labor Party's loss in the 1966 election was astonishing, even to the Liberal Party.[81] During the campaign, the divisions within the Labor Party on both Vietnam policy and the general direction of the election campaign had been apparent.[82] These had combined with other factors, including deputy leader Gough Whitlam's undermining of Calwell's leadership and the 70-year-old Calwell's non-telegenic presence in a newly televisual age (especially in comparison with the younger, urbane Holt), to alienate many voters.[83] The size of the loss brought on

---

[78] See accounts of these groups' activities in, for example, Hamel-Green (n 30) 106–11; Pauline Armstrong, 'A History of the Save Our Sons Movement of Victoria: 1965–1973' (Master's Thesis, Monash University, 1991); Russell (n 9).

[79] John Murphy (n 11) 145–46. See also Summy, 'Militancy' (n 50); Payne (n 34) 60–64. Peter Cochrane places the public demonstrations of the Vietnam era in a wider social context in Peter Cochrane, 'At War at Home: Australian Attitudes during the Vietnam Years' in Gregory Pemberton (ed.), *Vietnam Remembered* (Weldon, 1990) 165.

[80] Humphrey McQueen, 'A Single Spark' (1968) *Arena* 16, 51, quoted in Gordon and Osmond (n 48) 25–26.

[81] For a summary of Australian election results, see, for example, Stephen Barber, 'Federal Election Results 1901–2010' (Research Paper No 6 2011–12, Parliamentary Library, Parliament of Australia, 7 August 2015) www.aph.gov.au/About_Parliament/Parliamentary_Departments/Parliamentary_Library/pubs/rp/rp1112/12rp06#comments. See also the website of the Australian Electoral Commission www.aec.gov.au/.

[82] Beazley (n 40) 46–51; Saunders, 'ALP's Response' (n 40); Williams (n 71) 377; Freudenberg (n 40). See also Editorial, 'Conflicting Policies on Vietnam', *The Australian* (Sydney, 11 May 1966) 2; 'Whitlam Invited by the Left Wing', *The Australian* (Sydney, 11 May 1966) 1; 'Holt Hits Labor Split on Vietnam', *The Australian* (Sydney, 23 November 1966) 3; 'Labor Leaders Move to Heal Split', *The Australian* (Sydney, 24 November 1966) 1.

[83] See, for example, 'ALP Puts Calwell in Background', *The Australian* (Sydney, 6 October 1966) 3; Williams (n 71) 376–77. Excerpts of some televised advertisements from the 1966 campaign featuring Calwell and Whitlam are available at 'ALP Federal Election 1966', *Australian Screen* (Video) http://aso.gov.au/titles/ads/alp-federal-election-1966/.

Calwell's retirement and saw the ascension of Gough Whitlam to the leadership of the Labor Party. It also influenced the Labor Party's policy towards Vietnam. Having tied itself closely to the anti-war and anti-conscription movements in 1966, the Labor Party under Whitlam then dissociated itself both from movements and from uncompromising policies on Vietnam.[84] The Labor Party's dramatic loss also signalled an end, of sorts, for the belief held by many protestors that parliamentary processes were the means to achieve change. Murphy characterised the period immediately after the 1966 election as a 'pause' in the anti-war and anti-conscription movement in Australia.[85] In this sense, the 1966 election acted as a rupture between the traditional sensibilities and modes of anti-Vietnam War protestors before the election and the more radical forms of protest that gained ascendance after 1967.[86]

Support for Australia's retaining troops in Vietnam fell from 62 per cent in May 1967 to 39 per cent in October 1969, with the August 1969 Gallup Poll recording the first majority (55 per cent) in favour of bringing Australian troops home.[87] Australia's system of conscription remained a primary cause of dissent. The individual acts of civil disobedience in protest of the *National Service Act 1964* (Cth) in 1966 became systematic acts of mass resistance during 1968 and 1969.[88] In just one example, 500 academics deliberately attempted to commit an offence under the *Crimes Act 1914* (Cth) by signing an open statement 'inciting' individuals not to register for the draft.[89] Building on this momentum, a conference of Australian peace groups was held in Canberra in November 1969 to create

[84] Saunders, 'ALP's Response' (n 40) 87–88; Beazley (n 40) 51–55; Ashley Lavelle, 'Labor and Vietnam: A Reappraisal' (2006) 90 *Labor History* 119.
[85] John Murphy (n 11) 197. An SOS member reflected that they had been convinced of victory, but in most cases, it turns out they had been 'talking to the converted': Armstrong (n 78) 88.
[86] This is not an argument that there was a clear division between the periods before and after the election, but that the sensibilities of the anti-war movement in the periods before and after the 1966 election were different. See, for example, John Murphy (n 11) 219–37; Russell Marks, 'Towards an Intellectual History of the Australian New Left: Some Definitional Problems' (2009) 34 *Melbourne Journal of Politics* 82; Russell (n 9) 116–21; Kate Murphy (n 9) 260; Jon Piccini, *Transnational Protest, Australia and the 1960s* (Palgrave McMillan, 2016); Curthoys, 'Mobilising Dissent' (n 45).
[87] Goot and Tiffen (n 28) 135. See also Russell Marks, '"1968" in Australia: The Student Movement and the New Left' in Piccini, Smith and Worley (eds.), *The Far Left In Australia since 1945* (Routledge, 2018) 134.
[88] Hamel-Green (n 30) 111–17.
[89] 'Academics Join Critics', *The Canberra Times* (Canberra, 5 July 1969) 1; 'Act of Defiance', *The Canberra Times* (Canberra, 10 December 1969) 8. See also Hamel-Green (n 30) 111–17; John Murphy (n 11) 211–18.

a national movement against the war. This meeting borrowed from the US protests to initiate a moratorium movement in Australia with the twin aims of stopping the war and ending conscription.[90] Led by Jim Cairns, among others, the moratorium movement gained mass support remarkably quickly. When Prime Minister John Gorton announced the first withdrawal of Australian troops from Vietnam in April 1970, public sentiment had already shifted dramatically against the war.[91] In May 1970, when the First Moratorium was staged in Australia, hundreds of thousands of people across the country participated.[92]

The moratorium movement staged further days of mass protest in September 1970 and June 1971. In August 1971, Prime Minister William McMahon announced that most of Australia's combat troops would be home by Christmas of that year.[93] When Gough Whitlam was elected as the Prime Minister of Australia in December 1972 – leading the first Labor Party government in Australia since 1949 – only 128 Australian military instructors remained in Vietnam.[94] The withdrawal of these instructors and the end of Australia's conscription programme were among the first acts of the Whitlam government.[95] Australia's participation in the Vietnam War eventually formally concluded after eleven years in January 1973.

4.4 The Public Debate

Nearly all of Australia's public debate about the Vietnam War was framed by its two foreign policy concerns: the domino theory and the insurance policy. For most speakers, the debate over Australia's international legal obligations was inseparable from a consideration of the contours of the US–Australia alliance and the perceived threat from communism. Although speakers used international legal language that arose out of the UN Charter system, there are few examples of speakers relying on explicit claims of legality or illegality to underpin their uses of international law. Most participants who spoke international legal language used it as a measure of moral judgment or as inseparable from

---

[90] Langley (n 8) 127.
[91] Edwards, *Vietnam War* (n 13) 220–22; Goot and Tiffen (n 28) 140–42.
[92] For a full account of the moratorium movement in Australia, see Saunders, 'Vietnam Moratorium Movement' (n 11).
[93] For an account of this period, see, for example, Edwards, *Nation At War* (n 13) 292–317; John Murphy (n 11) 241–58; Saunders, 'Vietnam Moratorium Movement' (n 11) 309–27.
[94] Edwards, *Nation at War* (n 13) 318–20.
[95] Ibid.

Australia's alliance interests with the US. In the examples that follow, speakers expressed concerns about a range of issues, including the nature of the invitation from the government of South Vietnam; whether there was aggression from North Vietnam; how South Vietnam could be assisted to exercise its right to self-determination; what further action, if any, could be taken by the UN or the Security Council to resolve the conflict; and Australia's obligations as a member of both SEATO and ANZUS. In these examples, international law acted as both an autonomous standard of justification and as a proxy for other justifications, in particular morality and alliance.

4.4.1 International Legal Language and Legality

4.4.1.1 Morality and Legality: Exchange of Letters between the Anglican Bishops and Robert Menzies, March and April 1965

Between 12 March and 20 April 1965, a group of Anglican bishops, led by the retired bishop of Armidale in New South Wales, the Reverend John Moyes, engaged in open correspondence with Prime Minister Menzies about the war in Vietnam. Moyes was an old foe of Menzies'. Along with other religious leaders, Moyes had been at the forefront of a campaign in 1950 and 1951 against the Menzies government's attempt to ban the Communist Party in Australia.[96] Moyes's biographer suggests that his past as a public opponent of Menzies may have been one reason for Menzies' sharp responses to Moyes's and the bishops' letters.[97] There were four letters in total; the text of each was published in the major metropolitan newspapers.[98] This correspondence, described by *The*

---

[96] Paul Terracini, 'Moyes, Menzies, and the Vietnam War: New Insights into the Public Correspondence between the Prime Minister and the Bishops' (2012) 36 *Journal of Religious History* 70, 73 ('Moyes, Menzies, and the Vietnam War').

[97] Ibid., 73.

[98] The bishops' first letter was published as follows: *The Age* (Melbourne, 15 March 1965); *The Sydney Morning Herald* (Sydney, 16 March 1965); *The Australian* (Sydney, 15 March 1965); *The Canberra Times* (Canberra, 12 March 1965). Menzies' first reply was published in these newspapers on 26 March 1965. The bishops' second letter was published in these newspapers on 12 April 1965. Menzies' final reply was published in these newspapers on 22 April 1965. For accounts of the background to and writing of this correspondence, see, for example, Terracini, 'Moyes, Menzies and the Vietnam War' (n 96); Paul Terracini, *John Stoward Moyes and the Social Gospel: A Study in Christian Social Engagement* (Xlibris AU, 2015) Chapter 4; Edwards, *Crises and Commitments* (n 13) 355–66.

Australian as 'unprecedented',[99] received extensive newspaper coverage and even greater public dissemination after the Department of the Prime Minister published it as a pamphlet for general distribution.[100] The timing of the exchange of letters allowed Menzies to prepare the Australian public for his government's announcement of troops for Vietnam. Menzies concluded the final letter of the exchange with an assessment that the correspondence had served 'a valuable public purpose'.[101]

International legal language was a key element of the bishops' objections to the Vietnam War. They focused on whether the terms of the Geneva Accords had been breached, who held responsibility for any breaches and what the possible consequences would be of such breaches. The bishops' letters urged the parties to the Vietnam conflict to negotiate a settlement. In building a case for a negotiated peace, the bishops relied on two arguments. The first was the need for all parties to adhere to the terms of the Geneva Accords of 1954, and the second was the need for the US to maintain its commitment to refrain from the 'threat of the use of force' in relation to Vietnam.[102] These arguments were stated briefly in the first letter and developed more extensively in the second. In their longer argument, the bishops quoted specific terms of the Geneva Accords and drew an equivalence between 'the illegal activities of North Viet Nam' and the 'serious breaches of the spirit and the letter of the Geneva agreements' by South Vietnam.[103] The bishops rejected Menzies' argument that the war in Vietnam was to protect 'local freedom and self-government', arguing that the South Vietnamese government had no basis in 'popular or democratic support'.[104] The bishops also objected to Menzies' characterisation

---

[99] Editorial, 'PM Shows Contempt for Public', *The Australian* (Sydney, 1 May 1965) 8.
[100] *Exchange of Letters* (n 52). See also 'Bishops Rally to Hit Back at Menzies', *The Australian* (Sydney, 26 March 1965) 3; Editorial, 'The Prime Minister and the Bishops', *The Sydney Morning Herald* (Sydney, 27 March 1965) 2; 'Bishops Hit Menzies', *The Australian* (Sydney, 12 April 1965) 1; 'Bishop Writes to PM', *The Canberra Times* (Canberra, 12 April 1965) 1, 4; 'Bishops Urge Vietnam Talks as Aust Policy', *The Sydney Morning Herald* (Sydney, 12 April 1965) 4; 'Bishop Hits at PM', *The Canberra Times* (Canberra, 12 April 1965) 1; 'Menzies Hits Back', *The Australian* (Sydney, 13 April 1965) 1; 'Menzies Replies to Bishops', *The Sydney Morning Herald* (Sydney, 22 April 1965) 10; Editorial, 'Sir Robert Menzies and the Bishops', *The Sydney Morning Herald* (Sydney, 23 April 1965) 2; 'Bishop Urges Support for Peace Talks', *The Canberra Times* (Canberra, 27 April 1965) 8.
[101] *Exchange of Letters* (n 52) 17.
[102] Ibid., 1.
[103] Ibid., 7.
[104] Ibid., 9.

of the moral and religious aspects of the conflict, instead stating they found themselves unable to agree with Menzies' view that a moral and religious distinction existed between the Christian forces of South Vietnam, the US and Australia, and the communist 'atheistic and materialistic' forces of North Vietnam and China.[105]

The bishops' letters suggested a deep engagement with the political and legal justifications for military intervention in Vietnam. They resisted general claims of morality or religion as justifications for war, preferring, they said, not to 'misuse' such calls to 'bolster one side of the case or the other'.[106] The bishops considered Menzies' characterisation of the moralities of the Vietnam War to be 'open to grave moral question' itself.[107] With this view that the moralities of the Vietnam War were complex, international legal language provided the bishops with the primary vocabulary to challenge Menzies' decision-making on the Vietnam War. Their letters suggest that they regarded the international legal arguments as self-evidently opposed to Australia's choice to send troops to Vietnam. The bishops used international legal language in the mode of experts: they constructed arguments that were coherent with principles of international law, and they made no suggestion that their views depended on those of professional international lawyers for support. International law as the bishops constructed it had the power to prevent a state's participation in a war.

In response, Menzies' first letter focused on the 'merits' of the Vietnam issues, arguing that the consistent violations of the Geneva Accords and the 'imperialist aggression' by the communist North Vietnamese justified the actions of South Vietnam and the US.[108] Furthermore, Menzies argued, negotiation with North Vietnam was impossible without an assurance that the people of South Vietnam would be allowed to exercise their right to self-determination to ensure 'independence and freedom'.[109] Menzies further developed these themes in his second letter. He defended the actions of the US as 'in strict conformity with the *Charter* of the United Nations' because the US had been invited by the government of South Vietnam to assist it in its 'defence against unprovoked aggression'.[110] Nine days before announcing Australia's military

[105] Ibid., 8.
[106] Ibid., 9.
[107] Ibid., 8.
[108] Ibid., 5.
[109] Ibid., 6.
[110] Ibid., 13.

4.4 THE PUBLIC DEBATE

commitment and in anticipation of arguments he would later give in Parliament, Menzies defended Australia's role in Vietnam. Australia, he said, would

> observe our obligations under SEATO and ANZUS not only because Australia has pledged its word – a reason compelling enough, in all conscience – but because those obligations have been accepted on behalf of our own free future.[111]

Menzies thus used international legal language too, but it was not the primary source of his justification for Australia's actions. Instead, he constructed Australia's international obligations as arising from a commitment to the US alliance that went beyond the mere terms of the treaties. For Menzies, these obligations were not just legal obligations – they were obligations to conscience, to freedom, to the security of Australia.[112] International law here was not important as a way to justify military action but as a manifestation of an alliance with the US that was vital to Australia's security interests. In Menzies' argument, the bishops' objections were both misguided and mistaken, and they would not achieve peace in the face of the 'aggressive imperialism' of North Vietnam.[113]

Menzies' second letter described the arguments it presented as 'fortified again ... by close consultation with the Minister and Department of External Affairs'.[114] This was a foregrounding of bureaucratic expertise but not of the legal kind. The reference signalled Menzies' belief in the superiority of his view over those of the bishops, reinforced as they were by experts in the area. Menzies' reliance on a generalised expertise over a specifically legal one was consistent with his view of the international legal arguments as secondary (and sometimes peripheral) to matters of strategy, alliance and the fight against communism. Evidence from the circumstances surrounding this correspondence indicates that the Department of External Affairs ('DEA') was also keen to defuse the tensions that the correspondence, and in particular the tone of Menzies' first reply, had inflamed.[115] Unlike the first letter, which Menzies himself had written, the second letter was drafted within the DEA,[116] and it appears to be an attempt to create public awareness of the department's views. Menzies, then,

---

[111] Ibid., 16.
[112] Ibid., 15–16.
[113] Ibid., 5.
[114] Ibid., 11.
[115] Ibid., 81–83.
[116] Terracini, 'Moyes, Menzies and the Vietnam War' (n 96) 74–75, 80–83.

did not rely on expertise in the same sense as Howard did in 2003, when expertise worked to distance politicians from the responsibility for a legal judgment. In 1965, the reference to the DEA was used to support Menzies' view while implying that within the department there were people whose perspectives were ostensibly more measured than Menzies' were. This was also a distancing function, but one designed to encourage a sense of public assurance in the decisions of both the politicians and the bureaucrats.

4.4.1.2 The Vibe of the Treaty: Speeches by Prime Minister Robert Menzies to Parliament, 29 April and 4 May 1965

On the evening of 29 April 1965, Prime Minister Menzies announced to an almost empty Parliament that Australia had decided to send an infantry battalion to South Vietnam. Menzies described this decision as a response to an invitation from South Vietnam. His government, he said, was 'now in receipt of a request from the Government of South Vietnam for further military assistance'.[117] Menzies did not mention either of the SEATO or ANZUS treaties but instead relied on the invitation from South Vietnam – proof of which he did not produce to Parliament – as the legal basis for Australia's increased military intervention in South Vietnam. He noted that the decision to commit troops had been taken 'after close consultation with the Government of the United States' and quoted a letter from President Lyndon Johnson thanking the Menzies government for responding 'to the needs brought about by the aggression being carried on from North Vietnam' and 'assisting South Vietnam to maintain its independence'.[118]

Parliamentary debate on Menzies' announcement did not occur until 4 May 1965. On that date, Menzies elaborated on his government's justifications for intervention in Vietnam. He characterised their position as consistent with Australia's obligations under the UN *Charter* and its membership of both SEATO and ANZUS. Menzies described his government's view that there had been aggression on the part of North Vietnam, which was 'a threat to international peace and security ... a breach of international law and a violation of Charter of the United Nations'.[119] On that basis, the Menzies government had informed the

---

[117] Commonwealth, *Parliamentary Debates*, House of Representatives, 29 April 1965, 1060 (Robert Menzies).
[118] Ibid., 1060, 1061.
[119] Commonwealth, *Parliamentary Debates*, House of Representatives, 4 May 1965, 1110 (Robert Menzies).

4.4 THE PUBLIC DEBATE

Security Council of its decision to act, and Menzies related to Parliament the terms of that notification:

> The decision has been made at the request of the Government of Republic of Vietnam and it is in accordance with Australia's international obligations.[120]

While Menzies maintained that his government's decision complied with the requirements of international law, Menzies made clear that he considered these to be technical necessities that were not important enough to justify military action on their own. Menzies described his government's Security Council notification as 'formalities', and, he continued, 'this is not a matter that lends itself to decision with reference to formalities only'.[121] Menzies viewed the substantive reasons for sending troops to Vietnam as the 'merits' of the situation, and he characterised Australia's 'commitments' and 'responsibilities' as a member of SEATO and ANZUS as among these merits.[122]

Menzies did not argue at this point that Australia had specific obligations under either of the ANZUS or SEATO treaties. Indeed, he noted that each of the treaties 'imported some contingency that may or may not arise'.[123] However, Menzies did reiterate an argument he had used when describing Australia's earlier commitment of military instructors to Vietnam – an argument that was subsequently maintained by Hasluck, Holt and many other government members.[124] This argument was that Australia's membership of SEATO (and ANZUS, although this was cited less frequently) created a relationship of mutual obligation between Australia and its SEATO partners, in particular the US. This relationship meant that, even absent a formal invocation of obligations under the SEATO treaty, Australia had an alliance obligation with the US that 'flowed from' the treaties and required Australia to act to support its partner.[125] 'Does [Calwell] really believe', asked Menzies, 'that the United States of America ... ought to be allowed to continue to carry this burden [of war] and that we, as one of the SEATO powers, with South Vietnam

---

[120] Ibid.
[121] Ibid.
[122] Ibid., 1108, 1110.
[123] Ibid., 1108.
[124] See Commonwealth, *Parliamentary Debates*, House of Representatives, 13 August 1964, 185–87 (Robert Menzies); Commonwealth, *Parliamentary Debates*, House of Representatives, 20 October 1964, 2131 (Paul Hasluck).
[125] Commonwealth, *Parliamentary Debates*, House of Representatives, 20 October 1964, 2131 (Paul Hasluck).

requesting our help, should say: "Sorry; there is nothing we can do about it?"[126]

Menzies' argument was, in effect, that the treaties created an alliance, and his government intended to abide by that alliance, whether or not it was technically required by one of the treaties. For Menzies, Australia's security relationship with the US was paramount and the regional treaty security arrangements of SEATO and ANZUS were a manifestation of that alliance. On this view, Australia's obligations to the US did not arise because of the treaties; the treaties arose because of the alliance. Australia's obligations to the alliance existed prior to and imported obligations that were larger than the mere terms of the treaties. This was international law and treaty obligation creating a 'vibe' of alliance, and it was in the spirit of this vibe that Menzies acted.[127]

Debates over Australia's participation in the Vietnam War continued through until the election of November 1966. The question of Australia's obligations under the SEATO and ANZUS treaties in particular was taken up by Labor Party Members of Parliament. In each of the instances when the government was questioned, the relevant Labor Party member sought a precise clarification around whether or not Australia was acting under the SEATO or ANZUS treaties.[128] According to Gough Whitlam, if SEATO had been properly invoked, the Labor Party would have supported Menzies' actions, but Australia's treaty obligations had not been formally enlivened.[129] The Labor Party aimed to undermine the government's argument – that it was acting with the authority of the

---

[126] Commonwealth, *Parliamentary Debates*, House of Representatives, 4 May 1965, 1110 (Robert Menzies).

[127] I borrow 'vibe' here from a famous Australian film, *The Castle*, where a hapless lawyer, when asked by a judge to identify the section of the Constitution on which argument relied, replied that his argument relied on the 'vibe of the whole thing'.

[128] See, for example, Commonwealth, *Parliamentary Debates*, House of Representatives, 6 May 1965, 1247 (Malcolm Fraser); Commonwealth, *Parliamentary Debates*, House of Representatives, 6 May 1965, 1252 (Gough Whitlam); Commonwealth, *Parliamentary Debates*, House of Representatives, 28 September 1965, 1366 (Bill Hayden and Paul Hasluck); Commonwealth, *Parliamentary Debates*, House of Representatives, 28 April 1966, 1268 (Arthur Calwell and Paul Hasluck); Commonwealth, *Parliamentary Debates*, House of Representatives, 4 May 1966, 1429–30 (Paul Hasluck and Jim Cairns); Commonwealth, *Parliamentary Debates*, House of Representatives, 5 May 1966 (Nigel Bowen and Paul Hasluck) 1502.

[129] Commonwealth, *Parliamentary Debates*, House of Representatives, 19 August 1965, 242 (William Aston, quoting Gough Whitlam). Whitlam also noted in May 1965 that formal invocation of the SEATO treaty would have enlivened Australian action 'legally as well as morally': Commonwealth, *Parliamentary Debates*, House of Representatives, 6 May 1965, 1252 (Gough Whitlam).

regional security arrangements – by forcing the government to state that neither the SEATO nor ANZUS treaties had been invoked by any of the parties in relation to Australia's action in South Vietnam. In response, government members maintained that Australia's support for the US in South Vietnam was consistent with its obligations under both SEATO and ANZUS, although no government member ever actually stated that either treaty had been formally invoked.

In August 1965, Menzies dismissed a detailed engagement with the terms of the SEATO treaty as a 'parlour game' but continued, nevertheless, to outline his view of what each of those treaties meant.[130] He described failure to support the US military intervention in Vietnam as tantamount to repudiation of Australia's obligations because each of SEATO and ANZUS 'involves mutuality of obligations'.[131] Menzies also relied on US Secretary of State Dean Rusk's view that the US had a commitment under the SEATO treaty and that there was 'no need to parse these commitments in great detail'.[132] Gough Whitlam rejected Menzies' conclusion by arguing that, as neither Vietnam nor the US had explicitly requested Australia's assistance under the treaty, Australia could not be said to be acting under it. Further, if Australia were acting under SEATO's terms, it would be obliged to also provide social, economic and political assistance, which it was not doing.[133] Whitlam also engaged with the argument that intervening on the side of South Vietnam was akin to intervening to support one side in a civil war, which was prohibited under international law.[134] He accused members who used phrases such as 'sovereign independence' and 'territorial integrity' to describe North and South Vietnam of adopting 'traditional and legalist' attitudes,[135] neither of which seemed to Whitlam to be useful or desirable.

Two perspectives on international legal language emerge from Menzies' speech and the subsequent 1965 debates. The first is that international law, rather than being a substantive reason in itself to go

---

[130] Commonwealth, *Parliamentary Debates*, House of Representatives, 19 August 1965, 282 (Robert Menzies).
[131] Ibid.
[132] Ibid., 288.
[133] Commonwealth, *Parliamentary Debates*, House of Representatives, 19 August 1965, 290, 294 (Gough Whitlam).
[134] For an account of the state of the law on the use of force in this period, see Ian Brownlie, *International Law and the Use of Force by States* (Oxford University Press, 1963).
[135] Commonwealth, *Parliamentary Debates*, House of Representatives, 19 August 1965, 293 (Gough Whitlam).

to war, was a necessary but irksome requirement in grounding a military intervention. In the minds of Menzies and the other parliamentary speakers, the ability to describe Australia's intervention in Vietnam as 'legal' provided authority but not justification for that action. Menzies' preference for debating the 'merits' of a situation, and Whitlam's dismissal of 'legalist' approaches suggest that, for them, a concern for process and for the requirements of positive law were quaint views, ill-suited to the realities of 1965 and evidence of a speaker's unhealthy obsession with process over substance. Here, then, was international legal language as a symbol of an older fashion, of the nineteenth-century prioritising of technicality, the dangers of which had been laid bare by the two world wars of the twentieth century.

The second perspective on international law, which flowed from the first, is that international legality was not enough on its own to justify war. Instead, international legality was measured in combination with another, external, reason for war. In this case, that reason was the maintenance of an alliance relationship. In his speech of 4 May 1965, Menzies' reliance on Australia's obligations under the SEATO and ANZUS treaties as justification for intervention in Vietnam depended on the broader foundation of Australia's alliance relationship with the US. The treaties' functions were to ground Australia's ability to intervene in Southeast Asia but as a corollary to the much more important relationship that Australia had with the US. For Menzies, the power of the SEATO and ANZUS treaties came not from the legal support they could provide for Australia's actions but from the way the treaties manifested a strong relationship with Australia's most powerful ally.

4.4.1.3 Formal Treaty Obligations: Speech by Jim Cairns to Parliament, 26 April 1966

In April–May 1966, a year after Menzies' initial infantry commitment, and in the wake of new Prime Minister's Holt's announcement of a second Australian battalion for Vietnam, Jim Cairns challenged the legal justifications of an invitation from South Vietnam and a treaty obligation under SEATO on two new grounds. First, Cairns argued that, in April 1965, the then government of Vietnam had had no right to invite Australia to assist it because that government had had 'no basis in law, no constitutional practice, no claim in democracy'.[136] Cairns

---

[136] Commonwealth, *Parliamentary Debates*, House of Representatives, 26 April 1966, 1170 (Jim Cairns).

4.4 THE PUBLIC DEBATE

relied on the terms of the 1954 Geneva Accords to argue that the 'group of people' who had issued the invitation to Australia had no claim to be the government of South Vietnam and, indeed, had 'no legal basis at all'.[137] Cairns's second argument extended the Labor Party argument that the SEATO treaty had not been invoked. Cairns reiterated the claim that the Australian Government had not and could not have invoked Article IV of the SEATO treaty because the process required under that Article had not occurred. Furthermore, the Menzies government's notification to the Security Council in 1965 had not included a reference to SEATO. The reason for this could only have been, said Cairns, because the government was not acting under SEATO. 'Those persons who know the legal position', he continued, 'know very well that the government was not so acting'.[138] In the absence of a Security Council authorisation for Australia's regional military action, Cairns argued that Australia had allowed its obligations under a regional agreement to prevail over its obligations under the UN *Charter*, in violation of Article 103 of the *Charter*.[139] 'There is no basis', Cairns concluded, 'in law or constitutional practice for the position the Government claims to have taken'.[140]

Cairns's emphasis on the need for a legal justification was a shift from his response to the April 1965 announcement. At that time, Cairns had characterised the legal question of assisting a self-determination movement as a matter of morality. '[W]hether the Government's course of action is right, proper and justified', Cairns had said, 'we have a right to come to the aid of other people if questions of self-determination are involved.'[141] This right, he had insisted, was a 'moral' one.[142] In this 1966 speech, however, Cairns chose to make two carefully woven legal arguments; both were designed to undermine in precise terms the legal justifications for Australia's intervention in Vietnam. Cairns's arguments presented international law as an expert practice, something known only to '[t]hose persons who know the legal position'. Cairns seemed to consider himself someone with access to international legal knowledge – he did not attempt to portray himself as relying on the expert advice of others in forming his view of the law. Cairns's speech also portrayed

---

[137] Ibid.
[138] Ibid., 1172.
[139] Ibid., 1173.
[140] Ibid.
[141] Commonwealth, *Parliamentary Debates*, House of Representatives, 4 May 1965, 1112 (Jim Cairns).
[142] Ibid.

international law as a force that could constrain government decision-making and a force whose violation would concern at least some Australians.

It is difficult to measure how much weight the parliamentary arguments about SEATO carried in the broader public debate. In April 1965, in opposing Australia's commitment of troops to Vietnam, the editors of *The Australian* had noted that SEATO did not apply,[143] but the bulk of the SEATO debate had occurred thereafter in Parliament. The publication of the SEATO pamphlet in June 1966 suggests that at least some within the Australian Government were worried about the wider impact of the persistent questioning in Parliament about SEATO.[144] Attributed to Paul Hasluck in his role as External Affairs Minister, the SEATO pamphlet set out in detail the government's case that its actions in Vietnam were justified under the SEATO treaty. This case was, in essence, that South Vietnam, as a Protocol state under the treaty, was entitled to the assistance of other SEATO members in the event of external aggression against it. The joint and several obligations of members under the treaty meant that they could act collectively or individually in assisting other SEATO states who were the subjects of international aggression. Australia's military intervention in South Vietnam was justified under the treaty because, first, Australia had made an individual determination that South Vietnam was the victim of external aggression and, second, the government of South Vietnam had requested Australia's assistance. The pamphlet included the full text of the SEATO treaty as an appendix.

Hasluck had been making these arguments in Parliament as part of the back-and-forth of debate over Vietnam, but the release of these arguments as a pamphlet disseminated the arguments in an accessible form to a broader audience. Sir Alan Watt – an Australian diplomat, writer and former head of the DEA – considered the SEATO pamphlet a response to the 'increasingly embarrassing' questions being asked in Parliament.[145] Writing in 1966, Watt considered the DEA's relatively new practice of issuing these pamphlets to be a useful means of explaining government policy, even if it did have a 'propagandist' flavour.[146] Even so, in Watt's view, the dissemination of the government's case via a pamphlet was

---

[143] Editorial, 'The War that Can't Be Won', *The Australian* (Sydney, 30 April 1965) 8.
[144] *Viet Nam and SEATO* (n 62). See earlier discussion in section 4.3 of this chapter.
[145] Sir Alan Watt, 'Australia and the War in Vietnam', *The Canberra Times* (Canberra, 4 October 1966) 2, 17.
[146] Ibid.

4.4 THE PUBLIC DEBATE

likely to be futile because its intended audience – the Australian people – were, Watt argued, rarely moved by questions of international law and policy. The debates about SEATO by politicians and others were unlikely to have had 'any deep or lasting effect upon the ordinary Australian citizen', Watt wrote, because their outlook 'is based upon a certain pragmatic consideration rather than upon ideology or a close analysis of international documents and political trends'.[147] The more limited distribution that the SEATO pamphlet received compared with the earlier pamphlets suggests that Watt's view was shared by the government.[148]

4.4.1.4 The Limitations of 'International Legality' 1965–66

In debating Australia's obligations under SEATO in the vocabulary of international law and in a manner coherent with international legal principles, the parliamentary and pamphlet-based exchanges prefigured the 2003 debate on the interpretation of Security Council resolutions. The focus on the invocation of SEATO raised a similar question to the 2003 question about whether a second Security Council resolution was necessary to authorise intervention in Iraq. The 1965–66 parliamentary exchanges on SEATO contained the kinds of detailed expert argument in which some politicians, trade unionists and journalists engaged in 2003. In 2003, however, many speakers attributed their interpretations of the law to the advice of legal experts. For example, as described in Chapter 3, to address the persistent criticisms from protestors and other parliamentarians that the proposed invasion of Iraq was illegal, the Howard government released legal advice that supported the proposed action. This advice was authored and signed by the government's senior advisers on international law – both highly regarded international lawyers among Australia's international law profession. Howard's separation of his own decision-making from the advice on which he relied had the double effect of allowing him to distance himself from it while simultaneously claiming that the advice was spoken in an expert voice that was superior to other voices. The release of this legal advice was unprecedented in Australian

---

[147] Ibid. Watt reiterated this view in his book published in 1968. In a chapter assessing the strengths and weaknesses of the legal case for the Vietnam War, Watt observed, 'The ordinary citizen, preoccupied with his own affairs, has neither the time nor the training to ... judge between conflicting arguments on issues of international law advanced by eminent specialists on both sides': Watt (n 20) 118.

[148] See above nn 65–70 and accompanying text.

decision-making about war – no Australian government had previously given the public access to advice in this form.

The events of 1965–66, and in particular Hasluck's SEATO pamphlet, are another example of an Australian government providing legal justifications for war to the public and parliamentarians. The form of these justifications was different from those in 2003, however. In 1965–66, the parliamentarians who spoke using the vocabulary and grammar of international legal language did not separate themselves from the opinions on the law that they were presenting. Hasluck, as the Minister for External Affairs, spoke international legal language with assumed authority, and the SEATO pamphlet was drafted in the same tone. Cairns, too, used international legal language in his own voice. For Cairns and Hasluck, specialised legal expertise was not necessary in order to use international legal language, and both men assumed responsibility for the legal views they were expressing.

The debate over the invocation of the SEATO treaty underlines the limits of legal language. It is impossible to know whether the Labor Party would have supported Australia's participation in Vietnam if it had been strictly invoked under the SEATO treaty. Whitlam suggested that it would have, but he was not yet the leader of the Labor Party. It is unlikely that an authorisation under SEATO would have overcome the various Labor Party objections to the Vietnam War. An unambiguous SEATO authorisation would not have remedied the objections to the undemocratic leadership of South Vietnam, nor would it have resolved the dispute over whether the events in Vietnam constituted a civil or international war. A clear SEATO authorisation also would have contributed nothing to the debate over whether Australia needed to fight in Vietnam in order to prevent Chinese communism from spreading through South East Asia and to Australia. Even engaging in this counterfactual emphasises the difficulties of thinking about war through the language of international law. It exemplifies indeed the limitations that James Boyd White identified when he described legal language as an 'imperfect medium of speech, that ... does not permit one to say all that needs to be said about an event', particularly when that event is a question of life and death.[149] The Labor Party had many objections to the Menzies government's policy in relation to Vietnam and, in particular, to the decision to send a battalion to fight there. It is implausible that these

---

[149] James Boyd White, *The Legal Imagination: Studies in the Nature of Legal Thought and Expression* (University of Chicago Press, abridged ed., 1973) 73.

objections would have been swept away by a clear invocation of a treaty obligation.

It nevertheless seems from these exchanges that the institutional structures of the post-1945 international regime had an impact on Australian deliberations about international action. International legal language was used by many speakers in the public debate, most of them within Parliament and a small number outside. These contributions did not depend, however, on naming 'legality' itself in order to hold persuasive power. Indeed, to be relying only on a claim to legality was viewed as limited and limiting: a 'parlour game' in which only those who were 'legalistic' would engage. Only Jim Cairns consistently pursued arguments that relied solely on international legality. And although Cairns was determined in this pursuit, his tactic of challenging the government's policy by interrogating its approach to international legal standards was not adopted by many of his Labor Party colleagues. In 1965–66, the power of international legal language did not depend on an explicit claim to legality but on its close association with other forms of justification – in particular, arguments based on morality and on alliance.

4.4.2 International Law as a Standard of Morality

The vocabulary of morality was ubiquitous in Australia's 1965–66 public debates over the Vietnam War. Sometimes this language was used in conjunction with legal, security or alliance justifications that were also characterised as arguments about sovereignty or self-determination. At other times, international legal obligations were constructed as moral rather than legal imperatives. In these cases, the power of international legal language came not from any assertions of authority for legality in itself but from the claims that international law represented a standard of morality. These different uses are illustrated in the three examples that follow.

4.4.2.1 Self-Determination as a Moral Obligation: *Viet Nam Questions and Answers*, Australian Government Pamphlet 1966

Issued in May 1966, the *Viet Nam Questions and Answers* pamphlet was designed to directly address the questions that had been circulating in the press and Parliament about Australia's intervention in Vietnam. The pamphlet provided answers to 25 different questions, including 'Why is Viet Nam divided?'; 'Does our involvement arise more from our commitment to the United States than from our wish to help defend South Viet Nam?' and 'Are allied forces in South Viet Nam using poisonous gas against the Viet Cong?'[150] Some of the questions concerned international legal issues, including, for example, 'Do Australian actions in Vietnam constitute a breach of the Geneva Agreements of 1954?'; 'What right have we to interfere in the domestic affairs of Viet Nam?' and 'Is it not correct to describe the struggle between North and South as a civil war?'[151] The pamphlet did not address Australia's obligations under either of the SEATO or ANZUS treaties. Jim Cairns's persistent questioning in Parliament on Australia's SEATO obligations occurred in late April 1966, probably too late for inclusion in this pamphlet. These issues were then addressed in the *Viet Nam and SEATO* pamphlet issued a month later as a 'supplement' to the *Viet Nam Questions and Answers* pamphlet.

The answers in the *Viet Nam Questions and Answers* pamphlet illustrate the multiple ways legal language was used within a single text in the 1965–66 debates. The answer to the question about whether the Geneva Accords had been breached, for example, was a claim expressed in unambiguous international legal language: South Vietnam was exercising 'its right of self-defence' and Australia's actions were in response to South Vietnam's 'appeal for help'.[152] In contrast, the question about whether Australia was intervening in a civil war in Vietnam was answered with the language of morality. There was 'no moral equation', the pamphlet insisted, between assisting South Vietnam 'to defend itself', as Australia was doing, and assisting North Vietnam 'to wipe out another state by military force'.[153] The pamphlet adopted similarly moralistic language in other answers, claiming a 'collective responsibility among nations to resist aggression' and calling Australia's assistance to South Vietnam a 'just cause'.[154] On these constructions, the legality of Australia's role in South Vietnam was secondary to a moral need to assist South Vietnam in its quest for self-determination. International legality here was only one part – and a relatively minor part – of the totality of the collective claims to self-defence, self-determination and resisting aggression. In the *Questions and Answers* pamphlet, it was the moral aspect of these claims that was the dominant basis for public justification.

[150] Minister for External Affairs, *Viet Nam Questions and Answers* (n 62) 7, 19, 28.
[151] Ibid., 9, 10.
[152] Ibid., 10.
[153] Ibid., 11.
[154] Ibid., 14, 19.

4.4.2.2 Aggression, Self-Defence and Treaty Obligations as Moral Standards: Open Letters, October and November 1966

Many group and individual objections to the Vietnam War were expressed through the form of open letters printed in newspapers. They are examples of the views held by elite members of Australian society who were not Members of Parliament but who had either sufficient influence or finances to have their views published in the form of an open letter or statement in major metropolitan newspapers. These letters were often short and expressed succinct objections to Australia's participation in the Vietnam War. The necessity of brevity in their form makes the letters a useful indication of the issues that were both most urgent for their authors and perceived to be most persuasive with their audiences. In this section, I examine several of the open letters printed by newspapers in 1966. Some of these were joint letters with signatories numbering in the hundreds; some were published by individuals. Although most of the letters opposed Australia's participation in the Vietnam War, they did so for different reasons. Notwithstanding these differences, each of the letters also characterised as matters of moral reckoning issues that in 2003, and today, would have been considered international legal questions. For all these speakers, deliberations over issues such as self-defence, sovereignty, and the means and methods of warfare were moral issues first, and legal issues second, if at all.

The catalysts for the outpouring of open letters in October and November 1966 were President Johnson's visit to Australia in late October and the Australian federal election at the end of November. Several open letters from 1966 were directly addressed to President Johnson. In its open letter to President Johnson titled 'All the Way to Where?', the AICD invoked the 'solemn international undertakings' of the parties, and in particular the US, under the Geneva Accords.[155] Capturing the moral underpinnings as well as the legal status of those obligations, the AICD constructed the Geneva Accords as a collective justification that relied on both morality and legality for its power. A letter authored by Gordon Barton, founder of the Liberal Reform Group – a splinter group of the Liberal Party that ran in the 1966 election on an anti-Vietnam War platform – described international law explicitly as a measure of morality. Barton's letter accused Australia and the US of 'moral bankruptcy' for 'killing people in a remote country which has

---

[155] 'All the Way to Where? An Open Letter to President Johnson', *The Sydney Morning Herald* (Sydney, 20 October 1966) 10.

offered us no provocation'.[156] He described Australia as having participated to 'protect our interests', irrespective of the 'moral issues' involved.[157] These violations of international legal standards of aggression and self-defence were, for Barton, moral transgressions.

The sense of international law as both moral and legal standard was also evident in a letter signed by more than 280 individual Australians and published in *The Australian* during Johnson's visit.[158] In that letter, the individuals disavowed the Menzies government's 'unconditional support' for US policy in Vietnam in favour of 'peace' and 'honour' through 'strict adherence to the principles of the Geneva Convention'.[159] On the eve of the 1966 election, an open letter that had been previously published in American newspapers was published in *The Australian* but with the additional signatures of more than 6,400 Australian academics, clergy and other professionals (and notably no one who identified as a lawyer – international or otherwise). This letter characterised US action in Vietnam as interfering with the South Vietnamese right to self-determination and argued that to 'escalate militarily while our position disintegrates politically is immoral, futile and perilous'.[160] Here, again, international law was law, but more importantly for the letter writers, it functioned as a touchstone against which a higher standard of moral behaviour could be measured.

Australia's religious leaders, who identified as the public custodians of moral standards, had continued to play an active role in the Vietnam debate after the initial intervention of the bishops' letters in 1965. Much of this debate also took place via open letters and statements to the press. The leaders of Australia's major Christian churches were divided on the justifiability of Australia's actions in Vietnam. Nevertheless, all of them deliberated on questions of aggression, self-defence and alliance as primarily moral, not legal, considerations.

---

[156] 'An Open Letter to the President of the United States of America', *The Sydney Morning Herald* (Sydney, 22 October 1966) 11 ('Open Letter to the President'). For a contextualisation of the role of the Liberal Reform Group in Australia's Vietnam War debates, see, for example, John Murphy (n 11) 150.

[157] 'Open Letter to the President' (n 156).

[158] 'Mr President', letter printed in *The Australian* (Sydney, 21 October 1966) 8. These individuals included some well-known opponents to the Vietnam War, including the academics Max Charlesworth and Max Teichmann, and a future Labor Party Member of Parliament and Minister in the Whitlam government, Moss Cass.

[159] Ibid.

[160] 'On Vietnam', *The Australian* (Sydney, 24 November 1966) 10 ('On Vietnam').

Guided by the standards of the 'just war', these religious leaders came to different conclusions on the justness of the Vietnam War, but they were consistent in claiming morality as the measure they applied to make their assessments. Three Anglican bishops from Sydney, for example, supported Australia's role in Vietnam and conscription. They declared that this was 'much more than a civil war' with a 'well-established pattern of active interference by [North Vietnam]'.[161] Responding against North Vietnamese actions was justified, according to these bishops, because the Church of England 'has always taught that it is lawful for Christian men to engage in war for a just cause and that it is their duty to do so when the Government of their country calls upon them'.[162] Leaders of the Presbyterian Church supported the government's policy, saying that 'to support our allies and nations under threat of aggression, there is a moral obligation on every Australian to [contribute]'.[163] In contrast, Bishop Moyes kept up his anti-war campaign, insisting that the Vietnam War was not a just war because it was not a war of self-defence, and 'preventive wars and pre-emptive nuclear strikes' could not be justified under 'either of Christian or of secular morality'.[164] Other Christian leaders agreed about the moral ambiguities of the war. In a letter published in *The Australian* during President Johnson's visit, over 100 Christian ministers declared themselves to be 'deeply distressed in conscience' over the Vietnam War and asked for a de-escalation of the war and a resumption of peace negotiations.[165]

In one sense, it is unsurprising that religious leaders would characterise their interventions in debates about war as based on moral standards and particularly on the requirements of the Christian just war.[166] The overlap between some of the requirements for a just war and the UN *Charter* seems to have given some of the religious leaders a level of

---

[161] 'Three Anglican Bishops Back Vietnam Policy, Conscription', *The Sydney Morning Herald* (Sydney, 7 April 1966) 1.
[162] Ibid.
[163] 'Presbyterian Statement: Former Leaders Support Call-Up', *The Sydney Morning Herald* (Sydney, 18 April 1966) 4.
[164] 'Bishop Attacks Conscription', *The Sydney Morning Herald* (Sydney, 4 April 1966) 5.
[165] 'At the Time of the Visit of President Johnson to Australia', letter printed in *The Australian* (Sydney, 21 October 1966) 8.
[166] For an introduction to the relationship between the just war tradition and international law, see, for example, John F Coverdale, 'An Introduction to the Just War Tradition' (2004) 16 *Pace International Law Review* 221; Thomas H Lee, 'The Just War Tradition and Natural Law: A Discussion' (2005) 28 *Fordham International Law Journal* 756; Joseph C Sweeney, 'The Just War Ethic in International Law' (2004) 27 *Fordham International Law Journal* 1865; Alex J Bellamy, *Just Wars: From Cicero to Iraq* (Polity Press, 2006).

confidence with the language of international law, evidenced, for example, in references to the characteristics of civil wars and the identity of the aggressor. It is striking that, in 1965–66, the language of moral justification was not limited to religious leaders. In contrast with the debates of 2003, the international legal language of aggression, self-defence and provocation was used in the Vietnam War debates to condemn the government's actions as immoral, not illegal. It was casting the failure to comply with international law as moral transgression rather than as the failure to meet a legal requirement that was more persuasive in the debates of 1965–66.

4.4.2.3 Immorality and Illegality in the Means and Methods of Warfare: Editorial, *The Australian*, 26 March 1966

One other set of legal standards was featured in the public debate about the Vietnam War. These were the laws in relation to *jus in bello*, or the means and methods of warfare. Protestors, religious leaders and political parties decried the atrocities being committed by the US forces in Vietnam, calling them 'genocide' and 'crimes against humanity'.[167] Such was the extent of the public outcry that the methods of warfare were addressed in the Holt government's *Viet Nam Questions and Answers* pamphlet, which included answers to the questions 'Are allied forces in South Viet Nam using poisonous gas against the Viet Cong?' and 'While the Viet Cong must be resisted, is it necessary to use methods such as the bombing and burning of villages?'[168]

Consistent with the emphasis on morality during the Vietnam War debates, questions of *jus in bello* were characterised as moral questions more than legal ones. An editorial in *The Australian* in March 1966 typified this view when it condemned the US methods of war as moral atrocity. Titled 'Beyond the Debate on Vietnam', the editorial argued that, whatever the ends of the war might be, they were 'being corrupted by the immorality of the means we are using to achieve it'.[169] After listing some of the American and South Vietnamese atrocities, including torturing captured troops and dropping napalm bombs on civilian villages, the editorial continued:

---

[167] See, for example, Communist Party of Australia, *The Real Facts* (n 62) 11–12; Communist Party of Australia, *Vietnam: The Answers* (n 62) 8–11; 'More Viet Protests', *The Australian* (Sydney, 1 April 1966) 1; 'LBJ: A View from the Crowd', *The Australian* (Sydney, 22 October 1966) 9.

[168] Minister for External Affairs, *Viet Nam Questions and Answers* (n 62) 28, 29.

[169] Editorial, 'Beyond the Debate on Vietnam', *The Australian* (Sydney, 26 March 1966) 2.

> If we claim the right to fight wrong with wrong, how can we insist that our reason for being in Vietnam lies in the superiority of our standards and our morality? Evil cannot justify evil. When supporters of our commitment talk about 'moral responsibility', they forget what is being done in our name.[170]

The editorial constructed the immorality and the illegality of the US conduct in Vietnam as equivalent. Just as the purported immorality of the North Vietnamese could not excuse immoral behaviour by the US or Australia, so, too, Australia could not justify 'illegal means to achieve the rule of law in Vietnam'. Doing so, the editorial opined, demonstrated the same 'perverted logic' of the Nazi treatment of the Jews and the South African policy of apartheid.[171] *The Australian* editorial gestured to the necessity of conducting war in legal ways, but the bulk of the text was a critique of the immorality of the methods of warfare and the double standards of the US and Australian policies in Vietnam. The moral standards established by the vocabularies of war crimes and crimes against humanity were cast by the speakers of that language as more important than the legal ones.

The interest in *jus in bello* exemplified by this editorial seems to support an argument made by Samuel Moyn that there was 'a relative but palpable shift from a legal concern with aggression to one with atrocity' in the period between the debates over the Vietnam War and those conducted over the war on terror.[172] Moyn has argued that the US debate over methods of warfare in Vietnam did not centre on potential war crimes in the way that the parallel debate did during the later war on terror. According to Moyn, even when a small number of participants in the Vietnam debates turned their attention to atrocity after the My Lai massacre, it was to condemn both illegal means of warfare and illegal warfare itself.[173] This editorial published in *The Australian*, and the other examples discussed in this chapter, suggest a similar pattern during the Australian debates of 1965–66. Most of the contributions were concerned with *jus ad bellum* but those who wrote, as this *Australian* editor did, about *jus in bello* did not exclude arguments about the legality of the war itself, rather they wove together the two forms of argument. And, in most cases, these writings subordinated the legal aspects of the laws to their

---

[170] Ibid.
[171] Ibid.
[172] Samuel Moyn, 'From Antiwar Politics to Antitorture Politics' in Austin Sarat et al. (eds.), *Law and War* (Stanford University Press, 2014) 154, 156–57.
[173] Moyn focuses on the role of Richard Falk in this debate in particular, ibid., 171–76.

role as moral standards. In the Vietnam War debates in Australia, concerns about legality were consistently expressed as one element of a collective of justifications, in which legality itself did not assume priority.

4.4.3 International Law as Alliance

International legal language represented alliance in 1965 and 1966 in two ways. First, it was used to underpin the vitality and necessity of Australia's relationship with the US. Second, in a different form of language, Australia's alliance relationships were recast as empire and employed by protestors against Australian policy.

The Australian governments of 1965 and 1966 were committed to the US alliance. Menzies called it a relationship of 'the deepest friendship, the deepest co-operation, the deepest mutual understanding'.[174] It was not, however, an alliance of equals. Evident in all the justifications made for Australia's presence in Vietnam was a consciousness, even a celebration, of the superior power of the US and its ability to protect Australia. Indeed, it was Australia's interests in ensuring that the US would continue to provide security to the region that drove both Menzies' and Holt's commitments to the alliance.[175] The 'deepest' friendship that Menzies treasured so greatly was therefore precious because, as Menzies confirmed in that same speech, the friendship was with one of the 'the greatest nations of the world'.[176] In a speech during Johnson's visit to Australia in October 1966, Holt described the two countries as 'allies. ... You are the powerful ally, we are a staunch ally. ... We see our destinies being linked together for as long as our two countries survive'.[177]

The alliance with the US, underpinned by a series of treaty obligations, was the Menzies and Holt governments' insurance form of defence policy for Australia.[178] In section 4.4.1 of this chapter, I argue that Menzies used

---

[174] Robert Menzies, 'Speech by the Prime Minister' (Speech, Federal Council of the Liberal Party of Australia, Canberra, 12 April 1965).
[175] See, for example, text accompanying footnotes 20–26. See also McLean (n 20); Bongiorno (n 12); Laura Stanley and Phillip Deery, 'The Menzies Government, the American Alliance and the Cuban Missile Crisis' (2013) *Australian Journal of Politics and History* 178.
[176] Robert Menzies, 'Speech by the Prime Minister' (n 174).
[177] Harold Holt, 'President Johnson's Visit to Australia 1966' (Speech, Parliament House, Canberra, 21 October 1966).
[178] Commonwealth, *Parliamentary Debates*, House of Representatives, 31 March 1966, 866 (Harold Holt).

international legal language only if he could reinforce or subordinate the argument to another primary justification. In many cases, international law as evidence and manifestation of alliance constituted this other primary justification. One example is the debate over Australia's SEATO and ANZUS obligations, which Menzies characterised as a relationship of mutual obligation that was larger than the terms of the treaties themselves. As argued in section 4.4.1.1, the treaties did not give rise to the alliance; rather, the alliance gave rise to the treaties. Thus, even absent a formal invocation of obligations under the SEATO treaty, Australia had obligations with the US that 'flowed from' the treaties and required it to act to support its partner.[179]

Those opposed to Australia's participation in the Vietnam War constructed Australia's relationship with the US differently. Many protestors celebrated a different kind of US–Australia alliance – that between Australian and US objectors to the war. 'We stand beside those American citizens who themselves are opposed to the war' stated one open letter sponsored by the Youth Campaign Against Conscription Committee.[180] The hundreds of people who signed the Australian version of an American mass protest letter also did so because they were convinced that demanding the right to self-determination for the people of South Vietnam was 'in accord with the mood of increasing numbers of Americans'.[181] Here was international law as alliance at a sub-state level, bringing together individuals and groups with the same aims in the same language.

The links between Australian and American projections of power were the foundation of the accusations of imperialism that were sometimes made against Australia. In these cases, Australia was portrayed either as an outpost of the US and thus complicit in American imperialism or as acting as an imperial power itself – or as both. For example, Professor CP Fitzgerald,[182] speaking at a teach-in at the Australian National University, suggested that Australia's military action in Vietnam 'would be indistinguishable from colonial rule reimposed, except that it would be worse than any colonial rule ever was'.[183] Gordon Barton, too, based his description of

---

[179] Commonwealth, *Parliamentary Debates*, House of Representatives, 20 October 1964, 2131 (Paul Hasluck).

[180] 'We Oppose Overseas Conscription', *The Australian* (Sydney, 19 June 1965) 5.

[181] 'On Vietnam' (n 160) 10.

[182] Fitzgerald was a historian of China and the first Chair of Far Eastern Studies at the Australian National University. See Wang Gungwu, 'In Memoriam: Professor C. P. Fitzgerald 1902–1992' (1993) 29 *The Australian Journal of Chinese Affairs* 161.

[183] 'Problem "One for the UN": ANU Teach-In on Vietnam', *The Canberra Times* (Canberra, 24 July 1965) 8.

the Vietnam War as a 'dirty war' on his assessment that, in part, 'it retains much of its original character of a colonial war'.[184] Bishop Moyes made a similar argument in one of his speeches against the war, protesting that Australia had no right to 'indulge in war that is killing thousands of innocent people in the hope that their deaths will save us'.[185]

The vocabularies of international law as alliance and as imperialism were employed differently by the speakers and were used both in defence of and in opposition to Australia's Vietnam policy. Their common feature, however, was their claim to solidarity with people beyond Australia's borders. For the government members, this was a solidarity with a powerful partner whose friendship Australia's leaders needed to cultivate. For the protestors, the links of language with American protestors were part of what historian and activist Ann Curthoys has called 'a conscious internationalism' of the anti-war movement.[186] Australian anti-war activists did not only share languages with their American counterparts, but they also borrowed techniques, such as civil disobedience, and practices, including the teach-in and the moratorium. These choices helped the Australian protest movement to situate itself as part of the worldwide anti-war movement and to claim solidarity with anti-war activists in the US and around the world.[187] Making these links of language and technique meant Australian anti-war activists could position their protests not as the particular objections of people within Australia but as part of a wider international movement against the Vietnam War.

4.5 Conclusion

The international legal vocabulary and grammar of the 1965–66 debates resembled in many ways the language of professional international lawyers. The Anglican bishops urged Menzies to adhere to the terms of the Geneva Accords, Jim Cairns asked questions about the specifics of Australia's obligations under the SEATO and ANZUS treaties, and the government released public pamphlets that attempted to answer those objections. In all these cases, the public and political speakers made arguments that sought to cohere with existing principles of international law. Their arguments demonstrated an awareness of and facility with the

---

[184] 'Open Letter to the President' (n 156).
[185] 'Viet War Call to Bishops', *The Australian* (Sydney, 8 June 1966) 4.
[186] Curthoys, 'Anti-War Movements' (n 49) 98.
[187] Ibid.

4.5 CONCLUSION

grammars of international law, in particular the oscillations between law and politics, justice and consent. The success of international legal arguments in the public debates did not, however, depend on the ability of the speaker to characterise an argument as a 'legal' one. Indeed, when Cairns did so in relation to Australia's SEATO obligations, Menzies dismissed his claims as a 'parlour game'.

One example suggests that international law as an autonomous justification had at least some influence in 1965–66: the Holt government's response to the persistent questions on Australia's SEATO obligations. In debating Australia's obligations under SEATO, the parliamentary and pamphlet-based exchanges resemble the debates over Security Council resolutions in 2003. While they were not presented as formal 'legal advice', the *Viet Nam Questions and Answers* and *SEATO* pamphlets resemble the legal advice that was released by the Howard government in 2003. They were certainly crafted in a way that would perform the same function – which was to quell the questions that were being asked in Parliament and in the public sphere about the legal justifications for Australia's actions. Nevertheless, while the SEATO discussions were significant, they remained largely confined to parliamentary debate. The uses of international legal language by public and political speakers relied more often on a different kind of competence.

Competent use of international legal language in the 1965–66 debates turned predominantly on the ability of the speaker to cast international law as something more than merely law – as a standard of morality or as a manifestation of alliance, with the US or with protestors around the world. The examples in this chapter suggest that Menzies saw the international legal issues as part of a larger commitment to the alliance with the US; that the signatories to the series of open letters regarded international law as a moral standard rather than a legal one; and that many anti-war activists sought solidarity for their actions with similar groups around the world. The legality or illegality of Australia's actions was not enough, on its own, to provide a persuasive public justification for war in 1965–66. International law worked only when it was one justification use in collection with others. It was international law in combination with other factors – such as morality, alliance and power – that made international law persuasive in the Vietnam War debates. For the public and political speakers in the 1965–66 debates, to treat morality, law, alliance and power as separate would have been both artificial and futile.

One consequence of this form of competence in the use of international law during the Vietnam War debates was that professional international lawyers did not have a foregrounded role in the public debates of 1965–66. Their opinions were not sought by the media, nor were there prominent examples of international lawyers intervening in the public debate to give an expert view. With the professional international lawyers in the background, politicians such as Menzies and Cairns presented their international legal views as their own, not as the advice of unnamed experts. For Cairns, Hasluck and the others who argued about the SEATO treaty, no special expertise was needed in order for them to speak international legal language with authority. This non-separation of government decision-making from the advice on which those decisions relied allowed what David Kennedy has called the 'moment of responsible political discretion' to rest publicly on the politicians themselves.[188] In the 1965–66 debates, there was not the same form of ventriloquy that political speakers, such as John Howard, had used in 2003, where politicians had relied on international legal language while simultaneously distancing themselves from it.

International law as a measure of morality appears also to have functioned as a language through which public and political speakers could express solidarity across national borders. For those who objected to the Vietnam War, the moral wrongs of Australian action in Vietnam had an international character – they were violations of an international code that objectors regarded as moral rather than legal. On this view, Australia had failed to respect South Vietnamese autonomy, it had acted aggressively in participating in military action in South Vietnam, and it was complicit in the use of immoral methods of warfare. Characterising Australia's actions as moral wrongs allowed speakers to express solidarity, both with the Vietnamese victims of those wrongs and with the other anti-war activists across the world.

The Menzies and Holt governments expressed solidarity too, but their form of solidarity combined international law with their alliance with the US in order to defend their decision to intervene in Vietnam. In this justification, international law was the expression of a strong alliance relationship, rather than the basis of that relationship. The requirements of the alliance were broader and deeper than the terms of any international legal obligations alone. In 2003, the Howard government displayed a similarly strong commitment to the US–Australia alliance. In that case, international legal language provided the way for the Howard government to demonstrate that it shared the Bush administration's defiant attitude

---

[188] David Kennedy, *Of War and Law* (Princeton University Press, 2006) 12.

towards the international legal system. In both 1965–66 and 2003, international legal language in the form of a combined justification with alliance was key in allowing the Australian governments to publicly confirm the strength of their relationship with their US counterparts.

The studies of 2003 and 1965–66 suggest some surprising similarities in the forms of the international legal language that were used. The regulation of the use of force under the UN *Charter* appears to have influenced public debate about war into adopting particular patterns. In the next chapter, I examine the roles that were available for international law in public debate about war before the Charter system was in place.

5

Public Debate in 1916: The First World War

5.1 Introduction

In this chapter, I examine debates surrounding the conscription referenda of First World War Australia, before the international legal institutions of the twentieth century had been established.[1] Histories of international law traditionally position the First World War as the break – or the 'hinge'[2] – between the imperialism of the nineteenth century and the modernity of the twentieth century. War, at the turn of the twentieth century, was still an element of statecraft: a choice for a sovereign to make, along with diplomacy or other measures short of war.[3] International legal rules did not attempt to prevent war, although they did establish the distinction between a state of war and a state of peace, and regulate the conduct of belligerents in a state of war (*jus in bello*).[4] The rise of dedicated peace movements in the nineteenth century,

---

[1] Under the Australian constitutional system, the conscription 'referenda' were plebiscites rather than referenda because no change to the Australian Constitution was proposed. However, because the conscription plebiscites are referred to as 'referenda' in nearly all scholarly and popular literature, I adopt the same terminology here.

[2] See Rose Parfitt, 'The Anti-Neutral Suit: International Legal Futurists, 1914–2017' (2017) 5 *London Review of International Law* 87.

[3] For examples of nineteenth-century state practice on measures short of war, see, for example, Ian Brownlie, *International Law and the Use of Force by States* (Oxford University Press, 1963) 28–38. For a general overview of the development of the laws on the use of force, see, for example, Stephen C Neff, *War and the Law of Nations: A General History* (Cambridge University Press, 2005); Randall Lesaffer, 'Too Much History: From War as Sanction to the Sanctioning of War' in Marc Weller (ed.), *The Oxford Handbook of the Use of Force in International Law* (Oxford University Press, 2015) 35; Mary Ellen O'Connell, 'Peace and War' in Bardo Fassbender and Anne Peters (eds.), *The Oxford Handbook of the History of International Law* (Oxford University Press, 2012) 272; David Kennedy, *Of War and Law* (Princeton University Press, 2006); Yoram Dinstein, *War, Aggression and Self-Defence* (Cambridge University Press, 5th ed., 2011).

[4] See generally Neff (n 3) 167–214. For a detailed examination of the role of international law in relation to the First World War, see Isabel V Hull, *A Scrap of Paper:*

5.1 INTRODUCTION

The Hague Peace Conferences of 1899 and 1907, and the proliferation of bilateral arbitration treaties had encouraged states to first attempt to resolve disputes peacefully and to regard war as a last resort.[5] Those developments, however, had not curtailed the sovereign ability to engage in war as a means of dispute resolution. Thus, for participants in public debates about war in 1916, international law supported the use of war as an element of statecraft. There was no institutionalised international legal system within which individuals could judge the decision of their sovereigns to engage in war. The public debates about war in 1916 provide, then, a counterpoint to the public debates of the Vietnam War and the 2003 Iraq War, both of which were conducted under the system to control war established by the *Charter of the United Nations* ('UN Charter').

The 1916 debates also differed from the debates of 2003 and 1965–66 in that they centred on the question of conscription for Australia, rather than on whether Australia should have participated in the war. As a dominion of the British Empire, Australia did not have an independent capacity to declare war and peace. When Britain declared war in 1914, Australia, as a consequence of that declaration, was also at war. The 1916 conscription debates were much more than proxies for disputes over Australia's participation in the war, however. The Australian people overall trusted the initiator of the conscription referenda, Prime Minister Billy Hughes, to lead Australia in wartime. This trust was made clear when Hughes's Nationalist Party won a significant majority in the election of 1917 on an explicit 'Win the War' ticket.[6] The 1916 debates were also more than a straightforward vote about conscription. Australia had had a system of conscription for home defence since the passage of the *Defence Act 1903* (Cth) in 1903. The question put to the Australian people in 1916 was about extending this system of conscription to include compulsory service *overseas*. Asking this question – whether Australians supported conscription for the British Empire's wars in lands that were far from the territory of Australia – tapped into

---

Breaking and Making International Law during the Great War (Cornell University Press, 2014).

[5] See the examples given in Brownlie (n 3) 22–25.
[6] Ernest Scott, *Official History of Australia in the War of 1914–18: Australia during the War* (Angus and Robertson, 1936) vol 11, 392–96. See also Joan Beaumont, '"Unitedly We Have Fought": Imperial Loyalty and the Australian War Effort' (2014) 90 *International Affairs* 397, 404; Margaret Levi, 'The Institution of Conscription' (Spring 1996) 20 *Social Science History* 133, 157–58.

simmering tensions around class, race, religion and loyalty to the Empire. The conscription debates enabled Australians to deliberate the extent of their contribution to Britain's wars and the manner in which these contributions were made. They were the scene of passionate, sometimes violent, disputes about what it meant to be the dominion and nation-in-waiting that was Australia.

These differences between the 1916 debates and the later debates in 1965–66 and 2003 make the analysis of the public debates of 1916 different from those in Chapters 3 and 4. First, the language analysed is different. For the Dominion of Australia, and thus for this chapter, 'international law' consisted of the law of nations, and the dominion and constitutional law that governed Australia's relationships beyond its territorial borders.[7] These combined legal languages make the vocabulary, grammar and competences of the 1916 debates distinctive when compared with the debates of 1965–66 and 2003. The combined legal languages also broaden the category of the professional speakers of those languages to include individuals with legal qualifications who worked for the Australian Government or within academia primarily in the field of dominion or constitutional law. The second difference arises from the different internationalisms that were still in competition in 1916, offering alternative visions of internationalist futures. Without the settlement on the form of liberal internationalism embodied by the League of Nations and the United Nations ('UN'), multiple internationalisms abounded in 1916.[8] In this chapter, I examine the influence of one of these internationalisms – a radical socialist internationalism – through an analysis of the role of the language of class in the debates. The prominence of the language of class in the 1916 debates points to some of what has been lost in the later debates of 1965–66 and 2003.

---

[7] For arguments on how the relationships within and beyond the British Empire framed visions of the global legal order and provided models for inter-polity relations, see, for example, Lauren Benton and Lisa Ford, *Rage for Order: The British Empire and the Origins of International Law* (Harvard University Press, 2016).

[8] For a detailed study of these different internationalisms, see Glenda Sluga, *Internationalism in the Age of Nationalism* (University of Pennsylvania Press, 2013) 11–44. For studies of other internationalisms, see, for example, Rose Parfitt, *The Process of International Legal Reproduction: Inequality, Historiography, Resistance* (Cambridge University Press, 2019) ('*Process of International Legal Reproduction*'); Christopher Gevers, 'To seek with beauty to set the world right: Cold War international law and the radical "imaginative geography" of Pan-Africanism' in Matthew Craven, Sundhya Pahuja and Gerry Simpson (eds.), *International Law and the Cold War* (Cambridge University Press, 2020); Adom Getachew, *Worldmaking after Empire: The Rise and Fall of Self-Determination* (Princeton University Press, 2019).

In section 5.2 of this chapter, I explain my choices regarding timing and sources for the 1916 debates. Section 5.3 sets out the context of 1915 and 1916 Australia. In Section 5.4, I examine the public debates through an analysis of a series of texts.

5.2 Timing and Sources

The push to establish a system of conscription for overseas service in Australia had begun in earnest in 1915, with the formation of the Universal Service League (USL), a group whose manifesto called for 'compulsory and universal war service for all classes'.[9] Prime Minister Hughes called the first conscription referendum for October 1916 and, following the loss of that referendum vote, called a second for December 1917. Although the two referenda are usually discussed together, the question put in 1916 differed from that in 1917, and the conscription eligibility criteria for men were different. In 1916, the question was 'Are you in favour of the Government having, in this grave emergency, the same compulsory powers over citizens in regard to requiring their military service, for the term of this war, outside the Commonwealth, as it now has in regard to military service within the Commonwealth?'[10] This question had the dual effect of minimising the nature of the change (casting it as a simple extension to existing government powers) while also emphasising that the change would introduce compulsory service *outside* the Commonwealth. Following the loss of the 1916 referendum, the 1917 referendum asked a simpler question: 'Are you in favour of the proposal of the Commonwealth Government for reinforcing the Australian Imperial Force overseas?'[11] While still referring to the need for overseas service, this question adjusted the nature of the change to emphasise that Australian troops were already serving overseas and the change would further support those troops.

In this chapter, I examine material that dates from the inception of the USL in mid-1915 to the conclusion of the first conscription referendum in November 1916. For political speakers, I focus on Prime Minister Billy Hughes. Conscription was Hughes's initiative. He attached his own political future to the success of the referenda and led the public campaigns to promote the government's 'Yes' case. Opposition to conscription was spearheaded by the labour movement and the trade unions. The

---

[9] Universal Service League, *A Manifesto* (Sydney, 1915). See text accompanying nn 74–77 in this chapter for a more detailed discussion of the Universal Service League.
[10] *Military Service Referendum Act 1916* (Cth) s 5.
[11] *War Precautions Act 1914–1916* (Cth), Statutory Rules 1917, No 290, reg 6.

labour movement was a powerful force in 1916 Australia. At that time, the unions had made major gains for working-class Australians, and the support for unions was such that Australia had a government led by a labour-affiliated party.[12] For public speakers, I thus take a wide view of trade union representatives and include texts that were produced by the broader labour movement. For representation from religious groups, I concentrate on statements by the Irish Catholic Archbishop Daniel Mannix, on the writings of Tighe Ryan, the editor of *The Catholic Press*, and on key publications of the Protestant denominations.

In 1916, individuals relied on public meetings, printed pamphlets and newspaper accounts of meetings and speeches for an airing of the conscription arguments. Strict wartime censorship rules meant that mainstream newspaper reporting was almost exclusively in favour of conscription.[13] In addition, a decision from Hughes not to issue formal material that canvassed the 'Yes' and 'No' cases for the referendum question meant that printed material promulgating the 'No' case was produced only by labour publications and a small number of independent newspapers.[14] I use in this chapter readings of a selection of these sources as a way to analyse the language of public debate in 1916 Australia. The themes that emerge from these readings are law as a 'quibble', White Australia, civil liberties, Australia's relationship with the British Empire, and the lost possibilities of internationalisms built on considerations of class. These themes are discussed below.

5.3 The Context

The federation of Australia established on 1 January 1901 was not a fully independent state. Rather, it was a dominion of the British Empire, a status that allowed Australia a significant measure of self-government while preserving certain powers for the Imperial Parliament.[15] Being part of the

---

[12] See, for example, Vere Gordon Childe, *How Labour Governs: A Study of Workers' Representation in Australia* (Melbourne University Press, 1965); Frank Cain, The Wobblies at War: A History of the IWW and the Great War in Australia (Spectrum Publications, 1993) 81–122; Frank Farrell, 'Socialism, Internationalism and the Australian Labour Movement' (1985) 15 *Labour/Le Travail* 125, 128–29.

[13] Bertha Walker, *How to Defeat Conscription: A Story of the 1916 and 1917 Campaigns in Victoria* (Anti-Conscription Jubilee Committee Melbourne, 1968) 10; Scott (n 6) 347–49.

[14] Walker (n 13) 10; EJ Holloway, *The Australian Victory Over Conscription in 1916–17* (Anti-Conscription Jubilee Committee Melbourne, 1966) 6–8; Scott (n 6) 353–54.

[15] The uncertainty around precisely which territories were 'dominions' was settled in section 1 of the *Statute of Westminster 1931* (Imp), in which the dominions were

Empire was a key part of the evolving Australian identity. Indeed, many Australians in 1916 defined themselves by race, in particular as white Britishers.[16] At the same time, Australian politicians and civilians recognised that their interests diverged from those of the Imperial government in important ways, especially in foreign relations.[17] Australians' relationship with the Empire in 1916 was defined by the tension between loyalty to the Empire and the desire to protect the developing sense of Australian sovereignty – to the extent that this was possible as a dominion. This 'colonial nationalism' or 'empire nationalism'[18] was at once for Australia and for the Empire – even though it was sometimes difficult to reconcile the interests of the two.

From the perspective of the law of nations, the dominions did not have independent international legal personality. For Lassa Oppenheim, the dominions, although appearing to have the characteristics of independent states, effectively retained colonial status because the Imperial Parliament retained key powers over the dominions. In the 1912 edition of his international law treatise, Oppenheim described the dominions as having

identified as the Dominion of Canada, the Commonwealth of Australia, the Dominion of New Zealand, the Union of South Africa, the Irish Free State and Newfoundland. I use 'dominion' here in this sense.

[16] The 'race patriotism' of Australians had been described by Sir Henry Parkes, one of the founding fathers of the Australian Federation, as 'the crimson thread of kinship' between Australia and Britain, in a speech Parkes delivered to the Federation Conference in Melbourne on 6 February 1890: see 'The Crimson Thread Speech (1890)', *Foundation 1901* (Web Page) http://foundation1901.org.au/the-crimson-thread-speech/.

[17] I draw here in particular on Neville Meaney's study of Australia's defence policies of the period. See Neville Meaney, *The Search for Security in the Pacific 1901–14* (Sydney University Press, 1976). See also Neville Meaney, 'Britishness and Australian Identity: The Problem of Nationalism in Australian History and Historiography' (2001) 32 *Australian Historical Studies* 76; JB Hirst, 'Australian Defence and Conscription: A Re-Assessment Part I' (1993) 25 *Australian Historical Studies* 608; Joan Beaumont, *Broken Nation: Australians in the Great War* (Allen & Unwin, 2013) ('*Broken Nation*'). Those who have disputed Meaney's construction include Marilyn Lake, 'British World or New World? Anglo-Saxonism and Australian Engagement with America' (2013) 10 *History Australia* 36; Christopher Waters, 'Nationalism, Britishness and Australian History: The Meaney Thesis Revisited' (2013) 10 *History Australia* 12. For a response to these critiques, see Neville Meaney, 'The Problem of Nationalism and Transnationalism in Australian History: A Reply to Marilyn Lake and Christopher Waters' (2015) 12 *History Australia* 209; Christopher Waters, 'A Reply to Neville Meaney' (2015) 12 *History Australia* 232.

[18] See Hirst (n 17) 611; Mark Hearn, 'Bound with the Empire: Narratives of Race, Nation and Empire in the Australian Labor Party's Defence Policy 1901–21' (2013) 32 *War & Society* 95, 95.

[N]o international position whatever; they are, from the standpoint of the Law of Nations, nothing else than colonial portions of the mother-country, although they enjoy perfect self-government, and may therefore in a sense be called States.[19]

Australia's relationship with the international system was thus governed by Australia's dominion status. Dominion law determined Australia's relations with the Imperial Parliament, with other dominions and colonies and with states outside the British Empire. The limited foreign affairs power held by dominions allowed them to conclude commercial and technical treaties with other dominions and, in certain circumstances, independent states. Representatives of the dominions were empowered, for example, to sign the *International Telegraphic Convention* and the *International Convention on the Safety of Life at Sea*.[20] The dominions' powers excluded, however, the powers to conclude 'political' treaties and to declare war and peace.[21] This exclusion was justified on the basis that 'colonial "freedom" in respect of political matters struck at the roots of Empire solidarity'.[22] In 1911, British Prime Minister Asquith had insisted that, in the case of 'grave matters' such as the power to declare war and peace, authority rested with the Imperial Parliament and it 'could not be shared'.[23] Representatives of the dominions were not content with their constitutional positions on foreign affairs.[24] This dissatisfaction saw the 1911 Imperial Conference adopt a resolution under which the dominions would be consulted in

---

[19] Lassa Oppenheim, *International Law: A Treatise* (Longmans, 1912) vol 1, 110. Another view was that the dominions were more like the components of a federation. See Malcolm M Lewis, 'The International Status of the British Self-Governing Dominions' (1922–23) 3 *British Yearbook of International Law* 21, 39–40.

[20] Sir Kenneth Roberts-Wray, *Commonwealth and Colonial Law* (Stevens & Sons, 1966) 250. Australia acceded to the *International Telegraphic Convention* (1903) ATS 6 on 1 January 1903; the 1914 version of the *International Convention on the Safety of Life at Sea* never entered into force due to the outbreak of the First World War.

[21] For detailed accounts of these powers, see MHM Kidwai, 'International Personality and the British Dominions: Evolution and Accomplishment' (1975–76) 9 *University of Queensland Law Journal* 76; DP O'Connell, 'The Evolution of Australia's International Personality' in DP O'Connell (ed.), *International Law in Australia* (Lawbook, 1965) 1; Anne Twomey, 'International Law and the Executive' in Brian R Opeskin and Donald R Rothwell (eds.), *International Law and Australian Federalism* (Melbourne University Press, 1997) 69; Leslie Zines, 'The Growth of Australian Nationhood and Its Effect on the Powers of the Commonwealth' in Leslie Zines (ed.), *Commentaries on the Australian Constitution* (Butterworths, 1977) 1.

[22] O'Connell (n 21) 3.

[23] Quoted in Zines (n 21) 26.

[24] Representatives of Canada were particularly active in seeking greater autonomy. See, for example, Roberts-Wray (n 20) 251.

relation to international treaties affecting the dominions.[25] The dominions also secured a greater formal role during the First World War. The leaders of all the dominions participated in the Imperial War Cabinet sessions of 1917 and 1918, although they were excluded from substantive decision-making.[26]

The Australian Constitution, passed as a statute of the Imperial Parliament in 1900, elaborated the powers of the Australian federal government.[27] Australia's dominion status meant that these powers did not – and could not – include the power to make war. The Australian Government did not therefore make an autonomous decision to participate in the First World War. Australia considered itself to be at war because Britain was at war. Indeed, Australian Prime Minister Joseph Cook had announced in August 1914, 'when the Empire is at war, so is Australia at war'.[28] After war had been declared, however, there was general agreement that the dominions had the power to determine the extent of their contribution to the war efforts.[29] The commitment of all sides of Australian politics to the war was made clear by Andrew Fisher, who succeeded Cook as Prime Minister after the elections of September 1914. During the election campaign, Fisher had famously declared that Australia would support Britain's war effort 'to the last man and the last shilling'.[30]

By 1916, the stream of volunteer forces from Australia had diminished.[31] The recently installed new Prime Minister Billy Hughes, a 'bellicose ... union organiser turned politician with an authoritarian streak',[32] had spent the first six months of 1916 in England at the invitation of the Asquith government. Before he left Australia, Hughes had insisted there would be no conscription for the First World War. 'In no circumstances would I agree to send men out of this country to fight against their will', Hughes told

---

[25] Roberts-Wray (n 20) 251.
[26] Billy Hughes called the process 'a farce': see Neville Meaney, *A History of Australian Defence and Foreign Policy 1901–23* (Sydney University Press, 2009) vol 2, 238.
[27] *Commonwealth of Australia Constitution Act 1900* (Imp).
[28] *The Argus* (Melbourne, 1 August 1914). See also *Farey v Buvett* (1916) 21 CLR 433, at 452 (Isaacs J). Justice Isaacs made the same point more explicitly in a decision later in 1916 in relation to the power to restrict 'trading with the enemy'. See *Welsbach Light Co of Australasia v Commonwealth of Australia* (1916) 22 CLR 268, 277–83 (Isaacs J).
[29] See, for example, Roberts-Wray (n 20) 252; Twomey (n 21) 74–75.
[30] Fisher made this statement on 31 July 1914 in an election speech in country Victoria: see Jonathan Curtis, 'To the Last Man: Australia's Entry to War in 1914' (Research Paper, Parliamentary Library, Parliament of Australia, 31 July 2014).
[31] Scott (n 6) 338–39.
[32] Stuart Macintyre, *A Concise History of Australia* (Cambridge University Press, 1999) 160.

Parliament in July 1915.[33] Hughes, however, had long been a supporter of compulsory military training, and his experiences in England made him determined to introduce conscription for overseas service in order to maintain Australian troop numbers.[34] Australia's existing system of compulsory call-up for home defence had been introduced with the passage of the *Defence Act 1903* (Cth), only two years after Federation.[35] The system had then been extended in amendments to the *Defence Act 1903* (Cth) in 1909 to include compulsory military training for all eligible men, including young men and boys up to the age of 25.[36] The idea of compulsion for military service was then endorsed by both major political parties and was accepted, if not universally supported, by the Australian population.[37]

The distinction between compulsion for home defence and compulsion for overseas service was an important one. During the drafting of the *Defence Act 1903* (Cth), the Australian Parliament had rejected a proposal to allow for a small permanent armed force that could serve outside Australia.[38] Parliamentarians had been keen to prevent Australians from being forced to serve in Britain's wars.[39] Historian John Hirst has argued that the home-defence/foreign-service distinction was part of Australia's colonial nationalism, under which the nation-in-the-making sought to establish its independence from the colonial power.[40] Thus, the

---

[33] Commonwealth, *Parliamentary Debates*, House of Representatives, 16 July 1915, 5066 (Billy Hughes).

[34] LF Fitzhardinge, *The Little Digger 1914–52: William Morris Hughes, A Political Biography* (Angus & Robertson, 1979) vol. 2, 171–92; 'The Speech', *The Sydney Morning Herald* (Sydney, 2 September 1916) 17–18. See also Manning Clark, *A History of Australia, Volume 6: 'The Old Dead Tree and the Young Tree Green' 1916–1935* (Melbourne University Press, 1991) 1–46.

[35] *Defence Act 1903* (Cth) ss 59–62. See discussion in Hirst (n 17) 612–16.

[36] *Defence Act 1909* (Cth) s 62. On this system of 'boy conscription', see especially John Barrett, *Falling In: Australians and 'Boy Conscription', 1911–15* (Hale & Iremonger, 1979). See also JM Main, *Conscription: The Australian Debate, 1901–70* (Cassell Australia, 1970) 7–30; Hearn (n 18) 107.

[37] For some examples of objections to the system under the *Defence Act* of 1909, see Main (n 36) 7–30.

[38] Hirst (n 17) 612. See also Ann Mari Jordens, 'Conscription and Dissent: The Genesis of Anti War Protest' in Gregory Pemberton (ed.), *Vietnam Remembered* (Weldon Publishing, 1990) 60, 60–65.

[39] See, for example, Main (n 36) 7–30; Hirst (n 17) 612.

[40] See Hirst (n 17) 613. On 'colonial nationalism', see also John Fitzgerald, 'Who Cares What They Think? John Winston Howard, William Morris Hughes and the Pragmatic Vision of Australian National Sovereignty' in A Broinowski (ed.), *Double Vision: Asian Accounts of Australia* (ANU E-Press, 2010) 15; Meany, *Search for Security* (n 17). The dichotomy between inside and outside – Australian and foreign – remains one of the defining characteristics of Australia's relationship with international law. See, for example,

Australian landmass could be protected by compulsorily trained military men, but those same men would not be available for compulsory service beyond that border; in particular, they would not be available to serve in Britain's wars. Allowing men to be compulsorily available for wars beyond Australia's borders would, on this thinking, potentially allow the colonial power the ability to 'seduce or stifle' a young nation.[41]

Hughes, however, was determined to introduce conscription for overseas service. Faced with a Senate that would not pass the necessary legislation, he judged that a plebiscite demonstrating majority public support for conscription would give him the political suasion he needed for his conscription plan to succeed.[42] In August 1916, Hughes announced the first conscription referendum, to take place on 28 October 1916. Anticipating victory, at the end of September 1916, Hughes issued a pre-emptive call-up of men under the government's existing *Defence Act 1903* (Cth) powers. Under the Act, such a call-up could only be for home defence, but Hughes's proclamation was widely understood to be in preparation for overseas deployment, which caused consternation among the many who were opposed to Hughes's referendum.[43] Hughes also relied on the *Defence Act 1903* (Cth) when constructing the referendum question, styling it as an extension to the Australian Government's existing powers.[44] He opened his conscription campaign in Sydney by pointing out that the principle of compulsion for military service already existed in Australian law. It was, he said, 'no new principle with us'.[45] The conscription referendum, Hughes argued, merely sought an extension to that law to allow conscription for foreign service.

Hilary Charlesworth et al., *No Country Is an Island: Australia and International Law* (UNSW Press, 2006).

[41] Hirst (n 17) 614.

[42] Hughes's party – the Labor Party – had a majority in the Senate, but most of the Labor Senators were anti-conscription and had made it clear they would not support conscription legislation. For Hughes's justification of this decision, see 'The Speech' (n 34). For contemporary commentary on this decision, see, for example, 'The Conscription Issue: Government's Decision, Feeling in Launceston' *Examiner* (Launceston, 1 September 1916) 3; 'Conscription and the Referendum: Why Mr Hughes Should Be Supported' (n 42). For a secondary discussion, see, for example, Fitzhardinge (n 34) 179–80; Inglis, 'Conscription in Peace and War, 1911–1945' in Roy Forward and Bob Reece (eds.), *Conscription in Australia* (University of Queensland Press, 1968) 22, 33–35; Childe (n 12).

[43] See, for example, Commonwealth, *Parliamentary Debates*, House of Representatives, 29 September 1916, 9148–50 (Frank Brennan), 9151–53 (Frank Anstey); John McQuilton, 'Doing the "Back Block Boys Some Good": The Exemption Court Hearings in North-Eastern Victoria, 1916' (2000) 115 *Australian Historical Studies* 237.

[44] See above text accompanying nn 10–11.

[45] 'The Prime Minister's Manifesto on Conscription', *Chronicle and North Coast Advertiser* (Queensland, 22 September 1916) 5.

And once the law was extended, the Australian state would have 'the right to compel the individual citizen to obey the laws'.[46]

Even before Hughes had left Australia in 1916, the question of conscription had been canvassed by politicians and the public. By the time he formally announced the first conscription referendum at the end of August 1916, the pro- and anti-conscription forces had been working for more than a year. In the pro-conscription camp were Hughes, some members of the Labor Party, the members of the Opposition Liberal Party, and groups, including the USL and the Australian Natives' Association. The USL was the most prominent and established pro-conscription group, with branches in all the Australian states and a membership that included professors, archbishops and members of state parliaments.[47] The USL's manifesto and its pamphlet *The Case for Universal Service* were two of the pro-conscription movement's key documents.[48] Also in favour of conscription was the Anglican Church of Australia, whose leaders formally declared their support via a declaration of the Anglican General Synod in October 1916.[49]

Opposed to conscription were the remaining members of the Labor Party; the labour movement in general, including most trade unions;[50] labour newspapers; and a small number of newspaper editors. The Catholic Church did not take a formal position in the 1916 referendum, preferring to leave the question to the individual consciences of Australian Catholics.[51] Despite the lack of an official stance, individual Catholic leaders adopted public positions. Archbishop Kelly of Sydney,

---

[46] 'Mr Hughes at the Town Hall', *The Sydney Morning Herald* (Sydney, 19 September 1916) 6 ('Mr Hughes at the Town Hall'). See also 'Compulsion. Mr Hughes' Words', *The Sydney Morning Herald* (Sydney, 9 August 1916) 12 ('Compulsion'); 'The Campaign for Conscription', *Mudgee Guardian and North-Western Representative* (New South Wales, 12 October 1916) 28 ('The Campaign for Conscription').

[47] Scott (n 6) 333.

[48] Universal Service League, *A Manifesto* (n 9); Universal Service League, *The Case for Universal Service* (William Brooks, Sydney, 1915) ('*The Case*').

[49] 'For "Yes". Anglican Synod. Unanimous Vote', *The Sydney Morning Herald* (Sydney, 17 October 1916) 6. See also Michael McKernan, *Australian Churches at War: Attitudes and Activities of the Major Churches 1914–18* (Catholic Theological Faculty, 1980) ('*Australian Churches at War*'); John A Moses, 'Australian Anglican Leaders and the Great War 1914–18: The "Prussian Menace", Conscription and National Solidarity' (2001) 25 *The Journal of Religious History* 306.

[50] Unlike the other unions, the Engine Drivers' Union supported conscription: Scott (n 6) 335.

[51] 'The Attitude of the Church', *The Catholic Press* (Sydney, 5 October 1916) 25. See also Jeff Kildea, 'Australian Catholics and Conscription in the Great War' (2002) 26 *The Journal of Religious History* 298 ('Australian Catholics'); McKernan (n 49).

for example, supported conscription and was a member of the executive branch of the USL in 1916.[52] Perhaps most famously in opposition was the Irish Catholic Archbishop of Melbourne, Daniel Mannix. Mannix made only two speeches opposing conscription in the 1916 debates, but three days after his first speech in September 1916, he launched an appeal for the victims of the Easter Rising in Ireland.[53] Mannix was accused of treachery and disloyalty for his stance, and the lack of an official position from the Catholic Church brought the sectarian tensions of 1916 Australia to the foreground of the debates.[54]

All the participants in the debates conducted their campaigns using pamphlets, speeches at public meetings or demonstrations, and reports in newspapers. The public meetings and demonstrations were usually rowdy, and sometimes violent, affairs. Missiles – most often eggs, but occasionally chairs, stones or even cabbages – were regularly thrown at speakers or other members of the crowd.[55] The attendees at meetings also persistently interrupted speakers.[56] One meeting, organised by conscription groups in the Collingwood Town Hall in Melbourne, Victoria, unfolded thus:

---

[52] This position had changed by the time of the 1917 referendum, however, when the same Archbishop Kelly of Sydney declared the Catholic Church to be opposed to conscription: see Kildea, 'Australian Catholics' (n 51) 303–12.

[53] Clark (n 34) 18–19, 33–34. Mannix was a divisive figure, and he took a far more active role in the 1917 conscription debates. See, for example, BA Santamaria, *Daniel Mannix: The Quality of Leadership* (Melbourne University Press, 1984) 74–94.

[54] See, for example, Jeff Kildea, *Tearing the Fabric: Sectarianism in Australia 1910–1925* (Citadel Books, 2002).

[55] See, for example, 'Botanic Park Speeches: Excitement and Enthusiasm', *The Register* (Adelaide, 25 September 1916) 5, 7 (describing egg-throwing and a broken nose); 'Anti-Conscription Meeting', *Great Southern Star* (Leongatha, 13 October 1916) (detailing a cabbage thrown at a speaker in Ballarat); 'The Conscription Campaign', *Southern Cross* (Adelaide, 13 October 1916) 7 (describing multiple 'hostile' meetings); 'A Town Hall Scene', *The Advertiser* (Adelaide, 21 October 1916) 18 (describing the forced ejection of a soldier); 'Meeting at Fawkner', *The Age* (Melbourne, 25 October 1916) 8 ('Eggs were thrown in all directions, the supply being apparently unlimited'). See also Marilyn Lake, *A Divided Society: Tasmania during World War I* (Melbourne University Press, 1975) 64–83 ('*Divided Society*').

[56] See, for example, 'No-Conscription Fellowship', *Labor Call* (Melbourne, 22 June 1916) 8; 'Anti-Conscriptionist Meeting at North Fremantle', *Western Mail* (Perth, 25 August 1916) 16–17; 'Anti-Conscription. Meeting in the Exhibition Hall', *The Brisbane Courier* (Brisbane, 29 September 1916) 8; 'Big "Anti" Meeting At Exhibition Building', *The Register* (Adelaide, 9 October 1916) 5, 7; 'The Campaign for Conscription', *Mudgee Guardian and North-Western Representative* (Mudgee, 12 October 1916) 28; 'Howling Down Tactics Introduced in Sydney', *The Argus* (Melbourne, 12 October 1916) 8; 'Mixed Feeling. Meeting at Parkside', *Daily Herald* (Adelaide, 13 October 1916) 6. See also Judith Smart, 'The Right to Speak and the Right to Be Heard: The Popular Disruption of Conscriptionist Meetings in Melbourne 1916' (1989) 23 *Australian Historical Studies* 203.

> The meeting opened with groans, cat-calls and other hostile sounds, and when the Minister rose the scene was indescribable. Men shouted and women screamed with rage. The uproar was simply deafening, and [Defence Minister] Senator Pearce was counted out. One woman walked up to the Minister and, shaking her umbrella, screamed a dozen times 'Traitor'.[57]

The rowdy meetings occurred on both sides of the debate – 'antis' disrupted conscription meetings, and supporters disrupted anti-conscription meetings. Melbourne crowds were especially vocal. Thirty thousand people were reported to have marched, and some rioted, in an anti-conscription demonstration in Melbourne on 22 October 1916.[58] Other mass meetings in Melbourne and Sydney drew similar-sized crowds,[59] including one in Melbourne attended by an estimated 50,000 people, and requiring 10 different platforms to allow the speakers to address the entire crowd.[60]

During the debates, accusations of treachery and disloyalty on both sides were standard. By the time of the 1917 debates, class and sectarian bitterness were rife. Some of the most widely distributed materials from the campaigns were poems with names such as 'The Blood Vote' and 'The Anti's Creed'. As a form, these poems were especially emotive. 'The Blood Vote' for example characterised the ballot paper as 'the grim death warrant of doom' and the ballot box as 'the Box of Blood' and warned mothers not to '[doom] a man to death'. 'The Anti's Creed', conversely, accused anti-conscriptionists of being 'worms' who believed in 'the murder of women and baby killing' and of 'handing Australia over to Germany'.[61] EJ Holloway, Secretary of the Melbourne Trades Hall Council during the conscription debates and later a Cabinet Minister in three Australian governments, described 'The Blood Vote' as 'the most effective single piece of propaganda for our side'.[62]

Hughes's 'Yes' case ultimately lost the 1916 referendum by a narrow margin of just over 72,000 votes.[63] After the loss of the referendum, on which Hughes had staked his reputation, his Labor Party colleagues

---

[57] 'The Conscription Campaign' (n 55).
[58] 'Riot in Melbourne during Anti Procession', *Sunday Times* (Sydney, 22 October 1916) 9.
[59] See, for example, Holloway (n 14) 10–11.
[60] Ibid., 11.
[61] Both poems are in the online collection of the Australian War Memorial. 'The Blood Vote' is reproduced at www.awm.gov.au/collection/RC00337/. 'The Anti's Creed' is reproduced at www.awm.gov.au/collection/RC00317/.
[62] Holloway (n 15) 14.
[63] There were 1,087,557 'Yes' votes and 1,160,033 'No' votes. See Scott (n 6) 352.

attempted to force his resignation as party leader (and thus as Prime Minister). Hughes pre-empted this move by leaving the party entirely, taking twenty-three other party members with him. Hughes remained Prime Minister by forming a new party, the Nationalist Labor Party, through a merger with the Commonwealth Liberal Party. This Nationalist Party then won a comprehensive victory in the election of May 1917. That victory, combined with continuing falls in recruitment numbers and setbacks in the progress of the war, convinced Hughes to put the conscription issue to a second referendum in December 1917.[64] The 'Yes' case lost the December referendum by 166,588 votes – a larger margin than in 1916. The loss of both referenda made Australia the only participant in the war not to have had a programme of conscription.[65]

Writing in the 1930s, Ernest Scott, the author of the official history of the Australian home front 1914–18, underscored the extraordinary divisiveness of the conscription debates. In his otherwise sober account of Australian society during the First World War, Scott described the conscription debates as follows:

> Heated political controversy was no stranger to Australian public life. . . . But if all the bitterness, abuse, misrepresentation, anger and hatred pertaining to the whole of these former disputes could have been pooled, the volume thereof would not perhaps have equalled the fury of the storm which burst upon Australia when the conscription issue was brought before the people for decision.[66]

The 1916 public debates were not only an avenue for the Australian population to express their strong feelings about conscription for the First World War; the debates became a site in which profound questions about Australian society were contested.[67] These included, for example, the obligations of being 'Australian', the direction of the Australian labour movement, the place of Catholics in Australian society, and the tensions between Australianness and Britishness. The complexities of these debates mean that there is no simple explanation for the failure of

---

[64] For accounts of this episode, see, for example, Clark (n 34) 63–79; Scott (n 6) 363–96; LC Jauncey, *The Story of Conscription in Australia* (MacMillan of Australia, re-issue, 1968) 266–335.
[65] Macintyre (n 32) 163.
[66] Scott (n 6) 341–42.
[67] See, for example, Beaumont, *Broken Nation* (n 17) 219–44; Joan Beaumont, 'Going to War 1914–18: The View from the Australian Parliament' (Strategic and Defence Studies Centre, ANU College of Asia and the Pacific, Australian National University, 2014) 7 ('Going to War'); Patrick O'Farrell, 'Foreword' in LC Jauncey, *The Story of Conscription in Australia* (MacMillan of Australia, re-issue, 1968) xiii.

both conscription referenda. In his official history, Scott considered the failure of the 1916 referendum to be a consequence of not only Hughes's decision to issue the pre-emptive call-up of men but also the inconsistencies in Hughes's claims over the required troop numbers, which allowed anti-conscriptionists to argue that Hughes was exaggerating the need for more recruits.[68] Subsequent analyses have put the failures of the referenda down to a range of factors, including farmers' reluctance to lose their remaining able labour, the desire of Australian Catholics to punish the English for their repression of the Irish Catholics in the 1916 Easter Rising, and the sheer impossibility of securing a public vote in favour of a policy that was a life-or-death question.[69] Whatever the reasons for the failure of the conscription referenda, the debates they generated bitterly divided Australians. Reflecting on the experience of Australia during the First World War, historian Joan Beaumont has concluded that the war left Australians 'inward-looking, almost xenophobic, traumatised by grief and deeply divided by the political rancour over conscription and the inequality of sacrifice'.[70]

5.4 The Public Debate

As already noted, the 1916 debates did not look, and could not have looked, like the debates of 1965–66 and 2003. There were two main reasons for this. The first was the difference in the international law on the use of force. In 1916, there was no Charter, of either the League of Nations or the UN, purporting to regulate a state's ability to wage war. Under the international law of 1916, legality as a concept did not attach to decisions to go to war. Instead, states could resort to war 'for a good reason, a bad reason or no reason at all'.[71] Naming a justification as 'legal'

---

[68] As it turned out, Scott explained, 'they were right': Scott (n 6) 356–60, 359. For an example of Hughes's claims in relation to troop numbers, see, for example, Commonwealth, *Parliamentary Debates*, House of Representatives, 1 September 1916, 8421–27 (Billy Hughes).

[69] See, for example, Jauncey (n 64) 215–44; Beaumont, 'Going to War' (n 67); Hearn (n 18); Levi (n 6); Jenny Tilby Stock, 'Farmers and the Rural Vote in South Australia in World War I: The 1916 Conscription Referendum' (1985) 21 *Historical Studies* 391; Glenn Withers, 'The 1916–17 Conscription Referenda: A Cliometric Re-Appraisal' (1982) 20 *Historical Studies* 36. So many factors influenced the outcome of the 1916 referendum that KS Inglis concluded 'any one of a number of things can be said to have been decisive ... and historians can choose, according to taste and interest': Inglis (n 42) 39.

[70] Beaumont, 'Going to War' (n 67) 9.

[71] HW Briggs, *The Law of Nations* (Appleton-Century-Crofts, 2nd ed., 1952) 976, quoted in Dinstein (n 3) 78.

or 'illegal' could not have happened in 1916 in the ways that it did in 1965–66 and 2003. Even if it could have, that language would have had limited use in a dominion such as Australia, which did not have an independent power to declare war and peace. Australia's lack of independent status relates to the other key difference between the debates of 1916 and those of 2003 and 1965–66. The dominions' decisions to wage war were governed by the laws of the Empire and mediated through the Imperial Parliament. Australia's relationship with Britain in 1916 was an alliance but it was underpinned by legal structures that had no equivalent in the later alliance between Australia and the United States ('US'). The relationship between empire and dominion thus defined Australia's relationships with all other states, both within and outside the Empire. That relationship gave rise to tensions that manifested, among other things, in a colonial nationalism that was, at once, for Australia and for empire and that underpinned the 1916 debates about conscription and war.

In the following sections, I describe four forms of international legal language as understood for 1916 Australia. These are expressed in the vocabularies of a 'legal quibble', 'White Australia', 'freedoms' or 'civil liberties', and 'empire'. The argument characterised as the legal quibble was presented in language where legality was an autonomous form. This argument gained little traction in the public debates. The debates were dominated by the vocabularies of White Australia, freedoms and civil liberties, and empire, all of which carried implications about one or more of law, nationalism, race, alliance and morality. In the following sections, I describe how the grammar of these vocabularies worked and argue that the key competence for speakers of these languages was the ability to construct arguments that straddled the tensions within Australia's colonial nationalism. I conclude this section by considering the arguments constructed around the idea of equality of sacrifice, which foregrounded considerations of national and international relations of class in the public debates.

5.4.1 The Legal Quibble

Even without a measure for the legality of war in 1916, two arguments were used that relied on the explicit language of 'legality'. The first claim, which was not widely made, arose from Australia's lack of international legal status. The second claim arose under a combination of international, dominion and constitutional law and received greater attention, although it was still not a major part of the public debates.

The editor of *The Catholic Press*, Tighe Ryan, used Australia's lack of independent international legal status as a reason to reject conscription. As 'merely a dependency of England, without a voice in international affairs', Ryan argued, Australia lost control of its troops as soon as they left Australian shores.[72] For Ryan, it was unthinkable that Australia should agree to compel men into becoming part of an army over which it lacked ultimate control. On this reasoning, international law was relevant to the conscription debate because it evidenced an absence – of international legal status – that in turn supported an anti-conscription stance. Ryan's was an influential voice in the 1916 debates, but this particular argument was not adopted by many others.

The second question of legality concerned the authority of the Australian federal government to conscript men for overseas service. As discussed earlier, the government's power to conscript men for home service, established under the *Defence Act 1903* (Cth), had depended on the compulsion for military service being limited to home defence.[73] Hughes's characterisation of the referendum question as an extension of an existing government power was in part a response to questions that had been circulating since at least 1915 about the government's legal authority to conscript men for overseas service. In the second half of 1915, the USL published a 29-page pamphlet that included an exhortation to join the USL, an extract from a letter written by a soldier at Gallipoli, and a short bibliography. The substance of the pamphlet outlined what it titled 'The Issues in General', before setting out arguments in favour of compulsory service and rebutting the arguments against compulsion. The overall tenor of the pamphlet was captured in the opening lines of its substantive parts, in which the interests of the Empire and of Australia were presented as identical. 'In the present struggle', the pamphlet said, 'the British Empire, the Australian Commonwealth, and the ideals of both are threatened. In respect of each, our duty is clear'.[74]

The final paragraph of the pamphlet was titled 'The Legal Quibble'.[75] According to the pamphlet, a 'legal question' had been raised over whether the federal government had the power to compel men to serve 'outside the territorial limits of Australia'.[76] The authors of the pamphlet

[72] 'God Help Australia', *The Catholic Press* (Sydney, 5 October 1916) 24.
[73] See text accompanying above notes 38–41.
[74] Universal Service League, *The Case* (n 48) 3.
[75] Ibid., 18.
[76] Ibid.

expressed the view that such a power 'probably' existed under the Australian Constitution and that, if it did not, it would be 'quite absurd' if a 'legal technicality' of this kind could hamper the Australian Government's attempts to serve the Empire. Indeed, the authors of the pamphlet argued that, if there were any doubt about the authority of the federal government in this matter, the Imperial Parliament could address it by the passage of legislation granting such power. 'The whole thing could be done in a few hours', the authors concluded.[77] And so, for the USL, the 'legal quibble' was resolved.

This USL discussion is a rare example of legal language in its autonomous form in the 1916 debates, and it captures the complexities that Australia's colonial nationalism created. As a dominion, Australia did not have independent status under international law. Australia was bound to participate in the Empire's war, even though it was being fought far from Australian territory. Defending Australia could mean defending Australia's physical borders at home, or stopping the enemies of the British Empire (and therefore of Australia) from ever reaching Australian shores by fighting them on foreign territory, or both. The Australian Government was independent enough to determine the number and method of its contributions to the war effort but not so independent that its authority to do so was unassailable. Further, if assurance of the federal government's power was needed, that assurance was not to be found in the Australian Constitution but in the ability of the Imperial Parliament to confirm the powers of the Australian Government. The specific legal question raised by the USL – the federal government's power to legislate to compel men to serve overseas – was of enough concern that the USL included a rebuttal of the argument in its manifesto. The USL's characterisation of the question over the government's authority as a legal quibble may have reflected genuinely held views of the USL members, but it also suggests a deliberate attempt to minimise the role of the legal issue. USL members could not conceive that a question about legality would stand in the way of Australia's duty to the Empire.

The issue underpinning the USL's so-called legal quibble was raised in different ways in the public debates. Labor politicians, for example, raised questions in Parliament about the ability of Hughes's government to issue the pre-emptive compulsory call-up of men under the *Defence Act 1903* (Cth). These men argued that the Act only authorised compulsion

[77] Ibid.

for home service but that Hughes had made it clear that the call-up was in anticipation of a victory for foreign service in the 1916 referendum. Hughes, these politicians argued, did not yet have the requisite authority for the call-up. Frank Brennan, a lawyer and future Attorney-General of Australia,[78] called the call-up 'wholly illegal'.[79] He argued that any 'public man' who had suggested at the time of its passage that the *Defence Act 1903* (Cth) authorised 'compulsion of Australian citizens to go 13,000 miles outside the Commonwealth to fight in a foreign country' would have been 'hooted off the platform'.[80] The Australian Trades Union Anti-Conscription Congress issued a manifesto that called the proposal 'despotic and unlawful' and 'destructive of the basic principles of civil liberty and democratic rule'.[81] The Central Executive of the Political Labor Council of Victoria called Hughes's call-up 'a fraud upon the Defence Act' because the men were called up 'for use at the other end of the world'.[82]

These arguments drew on a combination of dominion, constitutional and domestic law in order to constrain the government's powers of conscription for overseas service. The reliance on these arguments, and their rebuttal, suggest there was probably some public purchase in claims that the government's proposed actions were illegal, but it was limited. Among those opposed to conscription, only a small number chose to challenge Australia's alliance with the Empire by relying on arguments that framed legality in its autonomous form. Overall, arguments in the language of legality played a minor role in the public debate.

5.4.2 White Australia, Civil Liberties and Empire

Three sets of prominent arguments in the 1916 public debates are used in this chapter as examples of international legal language in its collective

---

[78] Kevin Ryan, 'Brennan, Francis (Frank) (1873–1950)', *Australian Dictionary of Biography*, National Centre of Biography, Australian National University http://adb.anu.edu.au/biography/brennan-francis-frank-5347.
[79] Commonwealth, *Parliamentary Debates*, House of Representatives, 29 September 1916, 9150 (Frank Brennan).
[80] Commonwealth, *Parliamentary Debates*, House of Representatives, 29 September 1916, 9149 (Frank Brennan). See discussion in Scott (n 6) 356–57. See also 'The Campaign for Conscription' (n 46).
[81] Australian Trades Union Anti-Conscription Congress, *Manifesto No 2* (Melbourne, 29 September 1916).
[82] Political Labor Council of Victoria, *Anti-Conscription Manifesto* (Melbourne, October 1916).

form because all three arguments are related to Australia's relationships beyond its physical borders and relied on varying combinations of international, dominion or constitutional law. These were debates about the White Australia policy, the preservation of civil liberties in Australia, and Australia's relationship with the British Empire. While many public and political speakers presented a combination of these arguments in their contributions to the public debate, in this section I separate the three arguments for analytical purposes.

5.4.2.1 White Australia: No-Conscription Council of New South Wales, Anti-Conscription Manifesto

Australia in 1916 was a White Australia. One of the earliest pieces of legislation passed by the new Australian Parliament was the *Immigration Restriction Act 1901* (Cth). This Act – with its dictation test that enabled the exclusion of non-European immigrants – was part of a broader legislative architecture designed to preserve Australia's status as a white nation. By the time of the First World War, White Australia was 'a key element in the narrative identity embraced by most Australians'.[83] White Australia was not simply about maintaining biological racial purity, however. In early twentieth-century Australia, 'whiteness' was a question of domestic, imperial and international identity; a 'mode of subjective identification that crossed national borders and shaped global politics'.[84] The identity of being 'white' was interchangeable with British, Anglo-Saxon and European, and the laws of White Australia shared a legacy with the other white settler colonies.[85] For the promoters of White Australia, the key shared element of whiteness was a 'common loyalty to common ideals ... to preserve the unity of their national life'.[86] This sense of national life was tied to the ideals of British standards of political, social and economic organisation, as much as it was tied to the

---

[83] Hearn (n 18) 97.
[84] Marilyn Lake and Henry Reynolds, *Drawing the Global Colour Line: White Men's Countries and the International Challenge of Racial Equality* (Cambridge University Press, 2008) 2. See also Marilyn Lake, 'From Mississippi to Melbourne via Natal: The Invention of the Literacy Test as a Technology of Racial Exclusion' in Ann Curthoys and Marilyn Lake (eds.), *Connected Worlds: History in Transnational Perspective* (ANU Press, 2005) 209.
[85] Ann Curthoys, 'White, British and European: Historicising Identity in Settler Societies' in Jane Carey and Claire McLisky (eds.), *Creating White Australia* (Sydney University Press, 2009) 3, 9 ('White, British and European'). See also Lake and Reynolds (n 84).
[86] Myra Willard, *History of the White Australia Policy to 1920* (Psychology Press, 1967, first published 1923), quoted in Curthoys, 'White, British and European' (n 85) 9.

need to maintain racial purity.[87] Appeals to White Australia in public debate thus carried multiple meanings and linked the identity of many Australians as white British Australians living in a legal and political system that upheld the ideals of British parliamentary democracy. The multiple meanings that arguments about White Australia held meant that, in the 1916 debates, conscription for overseas service was characterised both as posing an existential threat to Australia and White Australian identity on the one hand, and as crucial for the preservation of Australia and Australian democracy on the other.

The No-Conscription Council of New South Wales placed the risks posed to White Australia by conscription at the forefront of its manifesto, issued on 26 September 1916. Consisting of representatives from various New South Wales Labor branches and executives, the No-Conscription Council was the formal voice of the New South Wales branch of the Labor Party.[88] In its opening paragraph, the manifesto contended that, if the proposal for conscription were successful, 'the great masses ... in Asia ... are left untouched and ... this lonely outpost of the white man's civilisation [is deprived] of its scanty garrison'.[89] Draining Australia of its 'virile' manhood in this way would then place Australia 'at the mercy of any power that might choose to attack her'.[90] Further, the manifesto argued, beyond the introduction of conscription lay Australia's financial ruin:

> The people of Australia have therefore to ask themselves the question whether after all the sacrifices they have made to build up a white man's civilisation in this part of the world we shall ... throw all to the winds by sacrificing (by conscription) our adult male population in a foreign war, thereby reducing ourselves to the social and economic level of Paraguay or some other semi-barbarous country.[91]

The language of the manifesto captured the multiple claims that appeals to White Australia carried. For the No-Conscription Council, the White Australia policy was not just a bulwark against external threats to

---

[87] See, for example, Jeremy Sammut, 'The Long Demise of the White Australia Policy' (November 2005) 49(11) *Quadrant* 34, where he critiques (in part) Keith Windschuttle's revisionist argument that the White Australia policy was not about biological racial purity: see Keith Windschuttle, *The White Australia Policy* (Macleay Press, 2004).
[88] 'Anti-Conscription Manifesto. Issued from Sydney', *The Age* (Melbourne, 27 September 1916) 11.
[89] Ibid.
[90] Ibid.
[91] Ibid.

5.4 THE PUBLIC DEBATE

Australia's racial purity; it protected Australia's security, its economic stability and, ultimately, the existence of a white and British civilisation in Australia. The manifesto positioned the laws of White Australia as enabling the preservation of democracy and the Australian way of life by excluding those non-whites who would undermine both whiteness and Britishness. It was unthinkable for the No-Conscription Council that such laws would then be undermined by the introduction of conscription for overseas service.

The No-Conscription Council's position was echoed by other contributors to the public debates. For these other speakers, conscription posed a threat to White Australia because it would open the physical borders of Australia to foreign workers and foreign capital. The places of white Australian workers would be filled by cheap labour from China or Malta, and it would be the capitalists, not the workers, who would then profit from conscription.[92] Conscription also threatened the existential borders of whiteness protected by the White Australia policy. It was to preserve Australia from this external threat that voters should reject conscription. Only in this way would the industries and the (white) people of Australia be safe.[93]

Supporters of conscription also argued in the language of White Australia. Billy Hughes, an architect of the White Australia regime, had spoken during his 1916 tour of England of his commitment to creating circumstances in the dominions in which the British race could 'rapidly increase and multiply'.[94] Hughes contended that the real risks to White Australia came from rejecting conscription for this war. Australia, Hughes claimed, was an isolated white nation surrounded by potential enemies in Asia. Australia's white status did not thus depend only on the legal architecture of White Australia but also on the existence of military security to protect it. For Australia, that security came from the British navy. It was in order to support Britain and its navy that Australia needed conscription for this war. '[O]n our very borders', said Hughes,

> there are teeming millions who envy our land and our wealth. Yet they make no move. They are held in check not by our White Australia law ... but by the might of the British navy. Let that navy be defeated or Great

---

[92] See, for example, 'The Referendum Campaign. An Anti-Conscription Meeting', *Border Watch* (Mount Gambier, 25 October 1916) 4; 'Final Protest', *National Advocate* (Bathurst, 28 October 1916) 2; 'Against Conscription. Leeton Laborites Advance Their Arguments', *The Murrumbidgee Irrigator* (Leeton, 6 October 1916) 7; 'The Referendum', *The Bathurst Times* (Bathurst, 23 October 1916) 1.
[93] Ibid.
[94] 'Mr Hughes's Speech', *Daily Telegraph* (Launceston, 20 April 1916) 5.

Britain cease to lend us its protection, and the Commonwealth straightaway becomes Asiatic, the possession of a people who would inflict on our women and children sufferings more cruel than ... the Hun.[95]

In another speech, Hughes had referred to the White Australia laws as 'a scrap of paper' protected only by the British navy that 'stands behind that law and behind the people of Australia'.[96] For Hughes then, law meant little if there was no force to protect it. It was not only the multiple characteristics of White Australia that mattered but also the ability of Australia to call on the power of the British navy to preserve Australia's whiteness, and ensuring the protection of the British navy meant that Australians had to fight for Britain in this war. Only by sending conscripted men to the battlefields of Europe would White Australia be saved.

These conflicting arguments in the language of White Australia manifested again the complex role of Australia's colonial nationalism in the 1916 debates. Nearly all Australians agreed on the importance of preserving a White Australia and everything that it signified. The divergences in their techniques for ensuring this protection were expressed in existential arguments about the contours of Australian identity and arose from differing views on how domestic and imperial interests should be prioritised. If the *Defence Act 1903* (Cth) marked Australia's attempt to protect its physical borders, the White Australia policy was Australia's way of protecting its borders of national (white) identity. For the No-Conscription Council, the possibility that taking men out of Australia would open the doors to cheap foreign labourers who might also dilute the British race meant that the greatest protections for Australia had to happen within the Australian territory. The laws of White Australia that preserved Australians from threats from the outside needed to be protected, and at least for some anti-conscriptionists, this protection could only be achieved by ensuring that a mass of white men remained in Australia. Conscription for foreign service would make this impossible. For Billy Hughes, the only way to guarantee a White Australia was to maintain a relationship of trust and admiration with the Empire and in particular with Britain. The laws of White Australia relied for their preservation on the military power of the Empire; they meant nothing, Hughes maintained, without the power of Britain's navy to enforce them.

---

[95] 'The Federal Arena', *Barrier Miner* (Broken Hill, 21 October 1916) 3. See also 'Mr Hughes at the Town Hall' (n 46).

[96] 'The Referendum. Australia's Peril'. *Barrier Miner* (Broken Hill, 12 October 1916) 4.

Australians therefore had to fight on foreign shores, by conscription if necessary, to ensure that both the British race and the British civilisation were secure in Australia.

5.4.2.2 Civil Liberties: Political Labor Council of Victoria, Anti-Conscription Manifesto

The vocabulary of freedom and civil liberties was also prominent in the 1916 debates. The overarching claim of anti-conscription groups was that conscription was the antithesis of an unelaborated 'freedom', which was assumed to be good in itself. Tighe Ryan, for example, wrote in *The Catholic Press*, 'Where there is compulsion there is no freedom',[97] and the opening statement of the manifesto of the Anti-Conscription League was 'The Rights and Liberties of the Australian People tremble in the balance'.[98] When speakers elaborated on these freedoms, they generally characterised them as having two aspects. First, conscription was characterised as a threat to specific civil liberties – the freedoms of speech, association and conscience – that were central to Australian democracy and were the hard-won victories of the labour movement in particular. Second, the potential loss of these civil liberties threatened to transform Australia's precious democracy into the same despotic militarist regime embodied by Germany.

The Political Labor Council (PLC) – the Executive of the Labor Party in Victoria – put these arguments at the centre of its crusade. The Central Executive of the Council issued its *Anti-Conscription Manifesto* in October 1916. The manifesto opened by comparing the Australian Government to a military tyranny. Addressed to 'Fellow Citizens', the manifesto began

> Two years ago Australia engaged in the war with Germany because she loved Civil Liberty and loathed tyranny. . . . In those two years our country has seen that military tyranny, against which she fought, imitated by her own rulers. She has no longer free speech; she has no longer a free press.[99]

The PLC drew here a distinction between the reasons for entering the war – helping the Empire in a justified fight against the 'tyranny' of Germany – and the ways in which Australia had chosen to participate in the war, which the PLC argued were themselves creating a situation of tyranny. In asserting that Australia no longer had free speech or a free

---

[97] '"The Curse of Billy Hughes"', *The Catholic Press* (Sydney, 21 September 1916) 25.
[98] 'Manifesto of the Anti-Conscription League', *People* (Sydney, 4 November 1915) 2.
[99] Political Labor Council of Victoria (n 82).

press, the PLC highlighted both the censorship measures and the pre-emptive call-up of men under the terms of the *Defence Act 1903* (Cth). Conscription, however, was the primary target of the manifesto. The PLC's arguments on conscription's effects on civil liberties are illustrated by the manifesto's final call to arms, which implored:

> You prize freedom of conscience. Conscription is the enemy of freedom of conscience.
>
> You prize civil liberty. Remember that Conscription is the enemy of civil liberty. It has destroyed civil liberty in Germany, and is destroying it in England.
>
> ...
>
> Australians, All! In the name of LABOR, of LIBERTY, of CONSCIENCE, and of our COMMON HUMANITY, we urge you to answer NO.[100]

For the PLC, conscription had to be resisted because it heralded the arrival of militarism in Australia. The PLC used the language of freedom and liberty to emphasise the loss of civil liberties that Australia was already suffering as a result of its participation in the war. These losses, the PLC argued, would only be compounded by a vote for conscription. In this argument, Australia's ongoing participation in the war imperilled the hard-won civil liberty victories of the labour movement that were central to Australian democracy. The potential loss of these civil liberties threatened to transform Australia's democracy into the same despotic militarist regime that Germany embodied. The PLC feared the threat that conscription posed to those precious civil liberties that were established and protected by Australia's laws. Under this argument, the continued erosion of those liberties would inevitably lead to militarism.

Billy Hughes agreed that Australia's democracy had to be protected, but he argued that only through conscription could these precious rights be protected. Fundamental to a man's right to live in a free society, Hughes argued, was his willingness to fight for that society. 'No man has a place in a free society who is not prepared to fight for freedom', Hughes told a meeting in Sydney in August 1916.[101] Hughes returned to this theme consistently across his campaigning.[102] While Hughes agreed

---

[100] Ibid.
[101] 'Compulsion' (n 46).
[102] See, for example, 'The Referendum: Victorian Campaign Opened', *The Argus* (Melbourne, 22 September 1916) 6, 7; 'The Prime Minister's Manifesto on Conscription' (n 45); 'Manifesto to Organised Labour', *The Sydney Morning Herald* (Sydney, 25 October 1916) 11, 12.

5.4 THE PUBLIC DEBATE

that despotism was the great danger, for him despotism was embodied by Germany, not by conscription. Indeed, Germany posed such a great threat to Australia's liberties and democracy that Australia had to do whatever was necessary, including conscript men, in order to defeat Germany. 'The great enemy of Australia, of labour, of liberty', Hughes wrote in his final appeal, 'is military despotism, of which Germany is the living embodiment. If we defeat her, the future of Australia, free and white, is secured'.[103] The Anglican Synod echoed Hughes's position on freedom. For the Synod, preserving Australia's liberties required sacrificing some of those liberties, at least temporarily. 'Only by sacrifice and service, by the abandonment of liberty for a time can we hope to possess it forever', the Synod proclaimed.[104] The Anglican Primate also shared Hughes's position that a man who enjoys the privileges of Australia's freedoms should also be willing to fight to protect them. To do otherwise would be a 'strange liberty', maintained the Primate.[105]

The debate in the language of civil liberties created a distinction between Germany's militaristic system of government and Australia's young democracy. Speakers used the language of civil liberties to argue for Australia's freedom to determine its own legal and political system and, in particular, to resist militarism. As with the language of White Australia, this language was used by both supporters and opponents of conscription. For the PLC of Victoria, conscription drew Australia's democratic system too close to German despotism. Emphasising the risks posed to civil liberties by conscription was an attempt to protect individual rights from being assailed from within by the Australian Government and from outside by Germany. This language was used to assert claims against the government in order to preserve both the liberties of the individual and the form of government of the Australian state as a whole. For Hughes, Australia's democratic constitutional system was endangered by an outside threat – German despotism – and it could be maintained only by a temporary sacrifice of some of the liberties otherwise protected by that system. This, then, was the language of civil liberties as collective sacrifice. Hughes maintained that the protection of the whole – the Empire, and Australia within it – required the sacrifice of a part – civil liberties – if only for a limited time. This was sacrifice of

---

[103] 'The Great Issue: Mr Hughes' Final Appeal', *The Argus* (Melbourne, 27 October 1916) 7.
[104] 'For "Yes". Anglican Synod. Unanimous Vote' (n 49).
[105] 'The Church's Duty. General Synod', *The Sydney Morning Herald* (Sydney, 11 October 1916) 9. See also 'Conscription Referendum', *Hamilton Spectator* (Victoria, 19 October 1916) 3; '"Yes"', *The Sydney Morning Herald* (Sydney, 27 October 1916) 6.

rights protected through law for the greater good of the nation and the Empire.

5.4.2.3 Duty to Empire: Billy Hughes, 'Manifesto for Conscription', and Archbishop Mannix, 'Against Conscription', September 1916

Australia's loyalty to the British Empire was at the core of the case for conscription. In its 'A Manifesto for Conscription', for example, the USL had placed duty to the Empire at the forefront of its case:

> The existence of the British Empire and all that it stands for ... is in danger. If the Empire should fall, the rights and liberties which, to a British community, are as necessary and natural as the air they breathe, will fall with it. There is not a man, woman or child in the Empire whose interests are not directly at stake.[106]

On this construction, all the other matters raised in the public debates – White Australia, civil liberties, 'legal quibbles' – were subsidiary to protect the Empire. If the Empire fell, all the other concerns would fall too. In this way, Australians were the Empire, and the Empire was Australians. 'Loyalty to the Empire, to the Commonwealth, and to our own flesh and blood', wrote the editor of *The Sydney Morning Herald* the day before the 1916 vote, 'is loyalty to ourselves'.[107]

Duty was a consistent theme in Billy Hughes's 1916 speeches: duty to the Empire, which was Australia's protector, and duty to Australia, whose continued existence was at stake in this war. In his 'Manifesto on Conscription' of September 1916, Hughes said, 'This is a war to the death. The future of Australia, and the hopes of Australian democracy, hang upon victory'.[108] Having established the stakes, Hughes exhorted Australians to do their duty – to Australia, to the Empire and to Australia's allies – by agreeing that Australia should send its share of troops to fight. Australia's duty, argued Hughes, was to do no more than its share, and this could only be achieved through conscription. Australia's obligation, the manifesto repeated, was to do 'whatever is necessary to be done to defend Australia, to enable her to do her share in this great war'.[109] This obligation to the Empire arose because it was

---

[106] Universal Service League, *A Manifesto* (n 9). See also '"Yes"' (n 105).
[107] '"Yes"' (n 105).
[108] 'The Prime Minister's Manifesto on Conscription' (n 45). See also 'The Speech' (n 34); 'The Referendum: Victorian Campaign Opened' (n 102) 7.
[109] 'The Prime Minister's Manifesto on Conscription' (n 45).

under the 'broad wings' of Britain's 'mighty navy' that Australia was sheltered. 'Duty and national honour' were at stake, and they commanded that Australians endorse conscription.[110] Hughes took this argument further in his final speech before the vote, when he argued that Australia's duty to the Empire arose not only because Australia was a part of the Empire or enjoyed the protection of the British navy but also because Australia owed its existence and continued prosperity to the Empire. 'The Empire', he said, 'has done its duty since the time we were born. It is now time for us to do our part. There rests with us the awful responsibility of keeping our great country for the Empire'.[111]

The language of duty to the Empire was also fundamental to the Protestant churches of Australia's position in favour of conscription. The Protestant churches were united in preaching that Christians had a moral duty to vote 'Yes' to conscription. Historian Michael McKernan has argued that this attitude stemmed from the Protestant belief that the war had religious significance.[112] The war was a moral crusade to resist the rise of Prussianism, which the Protestants regarded as a threatening alternative form of state religion.[113] Brisbane's archbishop had said not long after the outbreak of war in 1914 that 'We believe that God has called us in the British Empire to serve the world'.[114] Supporting conscription was thus essential to support the war, which in turn was crucial in ensuring the continuation of the great British Empire. 'We should think imperially and not locally', the Dean of Ballarat told the Anglican General Synod.[115]

For Hughes and other supporters of conscription, the legal, social and political ties of dominion meant that duty to Australia and duty to the Empire in this war coincided. In the words of a *Sydney Morning Herald* editorial, 'The State ... is the British Empire first, and Australia is integral with it'.[116] There was, in this sense, no separation between the Empire and dominion or within the laws that institutionalised that relationship. For some, the connection between Australia and the British Empire was more than just an alliance – it defined Australia's being. As Hughes

---

[110] Ibid.
[111] 'Mr Hughes at the Town Hall' (n 46).
[112] See McKernan (n 49).
[113] Ibid., 315–17.
[114] Quoted in Moses (n 49) 318.
[115] 'For "Yes". Anglican Synod. Unanimous Vote' (n 49). See also 'The Church's Duty. General Synod' (n 105).
[116] '"Yes"' (n 105).

constructed it, the very existence of Australia was at stake, and that meant Australia had to do whatever was necessary to support the Empire, including sending conscripted men to fight in the war.

For others, however, the interests of Australia and the Empire diverged. One of the most high-profile resisters of Hughes's arguments on empire was the Irish Catholic Archbishop Daniel Mannix. In the first of his two interventions in the 1916 debates, Mannix picked up in particular on the argument that conscription meant only that Australia would do its share in this war. Mannix rejected Hughes's conception of Australia's 'fair share'. Instead, he argued:

> Australia has done her full share – I am inclined to say more than her full share – in this war. Her loyalty to the Empire has been lauded to the skies, and the bravery of her sons has won the admiration of friend and foe alike.[117]

Mannix returned to the point later in the speech, assuring his audience that he 'honestly believe[d] that Australia has done her full share and more'.[118] Further, Mannix continued, he could not see how the addition of 100,000 or even 200,000 conscripted Australians could make any significant impact to the fifteen million men already fighting for the allies.[119]

The suggestion from an Irish Catholic Archbishop that Australia was already fulfilling its duties to the Empire aggravated the longstanding sectarian divide between Protestants and Catholics – and particularly Irish Catholics – in Australia. Hughes and his supporters interpreted Mannix's words as the ultimate in disloyalty to Australia.[120] Mannix had support within the Catholic population, however, and he reiterated these views in his second speech on conscription in October 1916.[121] It was possible, according to Mannix, to satisfy separate duties to both the Empire and Australia. Mannix's argument was not that Australia had

---

[117] 'Against Conscription. Archbishop Mannix', *The Catholic Press* (Sydney, 21 September 1916) 25.
[118] Ibid. Others made similar arguments: see, for example, 'Meeting at Ballarat', *The Age* (Melbourne, 5 October 1916) 6; 'Anti-Conscription Councils' Manifesto', *The Register* (Adelaide, 4 October 1916) 9; 'The Campaign Opens', *Worker* (Brisbane, 5 October 1916) 4, 5; 'The Referendum Campaign', *Border Watch* (Mount Gambier, 25 October 1916) 4; 'Final Words', *Worker* (Brisbane, 26 October 1916) 9.
[119] 'Against Conscription. Archbishop Mannix' (n 117).
[120] Clark (n 34) 34. See also DJ Murphy, 'Religion, Race and Conscription in World War I' (1974) 20 *Australian Journal of Politics and History* 155.
[121] 'Archbishop Mannix. Opposition to Conscription. His Views Unchanged', *The Argus* (Melbourne, 23 October 1916) 6.

no duties to the British Empire but that those duties had a limit, and that limit would be reached, in Mannix's argument, when supporting the Empire threatened Australia's freedom and democracy. For Mannix, conscription for foreign service represented the point at which Australia's own interests would be jeopardised in the service of the Empire.

Some speakers in the debates took the 'separate interests' argument even further, protesting that Australia should reject conscription not only to protect itself but because this was not Australia's war in the first place. The No-Conscription Council of New South Wales, for example, called this a 'foreign war'.[122] Frank Tudor, a Labor Member of Parliament, distinguished between the conscripted armies of Russia, which were fighting 'on their own soil', and the military contribution of Australia, which 'was not'.[123] Tighe Ryan extended this argument to suggest that conscription would not only undermine Australia's interests but would threaten the relationship between Australia and the Empire. Any attempt to introduce conscription for 'foreign conflicts' in the making of which the dominions had 'no voice', Ryan warned, would 'imperil the silver thread of kinship which links the dominions with the motherland'.[124]

For men like Mannix, Tudor and Ryan, the interests of Australia and the Empire may have been linked by a special bond of history and of race, but they did not coincide. In their view, Australia needed to consider the Empire's interests in determining its contributions to the war, but Australia need not also be compelled into actions that would put its continued survival and prosperity at risk. Conscription for foreign service would, on this view, constitute just such an action. In response, the USL called this a 'selfish argument', one that failed to see how much Australia was at risk of being 'Germanised' if the Empire lost the war.[125] The Anglican Synod, too, rejected this characterisation. This was Australia's war, not only because Australia was part of the Empire but also because, in this war, the boundaries of Australia had extended beyond its landmass to Europe. For the Synod, the need to fight this war on territories outside Australia did not make this a 'foreign' war but instead extended their understanding of how 'Australia' should be

---

[122] 'Anti-Conscription Manifesto. Issued from Sydney', *The Age* (Melbourne, 27 September 1916) 11.
[123] 'Anti-Conscription. Speech by Mr Tudor', *The Argus* (Melbourne, 12 October 1916) 8.
[124] 'The Case Against Conscription', *The Catholic Press* (Sydney, 21 September 1916) 24.
[125] Universal Service League, *The Case* (n 48).

imagined. The frontier of Australia in 1916 'and the one that required defending', claimed the Synod, 'was in France'.[126]

The language of duty to the British Empire illustrates again the complexities of the colonial nationalism that underpinned the public debates of this period. Australia's dominion status meant that all speakers acknowledged the connection – the thread of kinship – between Australia and the Empire. It also forced those same speakers to articulate what the resultant duty to the Empire meant, and whether and how this was different from or identical to the duty to Australia. The varied conceptions of Australia's duties to the Empire arose from speakers' different ideas about what the 'Australia' of 1916 was. Those, such as Mannix, who saw Australia as primarily defined by the people and government within its territorial boundaries, expressed a parochialism that manifested in their opposition to conscription. They resisted the totalising pull of the Empire and pushed for greater consideration of the needs of Australia and Australians at home. Those who constructed Australia's interests as inextricably bound to the British Empire – who thought imperially, as Hughes and the Anglican Synod did – had a more expansive view of Australia. For them, if Australia's interests were best protected by fighting alongside the Empire, then the boundaries of what it meant to be 'Australia' extended to the places where the Empire was fighting. And thus the commitments that Australia needed to make to the Empire included conscription.

In each of the examples of the 1916 public debates described thus far, the international element of the argument was directed at a construction of the fledgling nation that was Australia. The languages of the legal quibble, of White Australia, of civil liberties and of empire were constituted by a colonial nationalism defined by the simultaneous consideration of both national and international interests – of Australia and of the Empire. Although the speakers differed on how they understood Australia's duties and interests, all were concerned to protect the emerging Australian state. These, then, were languages that contained conceptions of the international that always returned in some way to the national and, in particular, to the preservation and development of the state. There was one form of language in the 1916 debates with a different idea of the international, and I conclude this chapter with a description of that language of class.

---

[126] 'For "Yes". Anglican Synod. Unanimous Vote' (n 49).

5.4.3 Equality of Sacrifice: A Different Internationalism

One set of arguments in the 1916 debates was constructed around the language of class. The uses of the language of class in the 1916 debates arose out of what was called the 'equality-of-sacrifice' argument. Speakers opposed to conscription used equality of sacrifice to condemn the war, the economic systems of Australia and the Empire, and the Hughes government. At its simplest, 'equality of sacrifice' meant an equal commitment of both labour and wealth to the war cause. The argument went as follows: this war was a capitalist war, entered into for profit by the capitalist forces of both Germany and the Empire. It was therefore not a war into which the worker should be conscripted unless there was also equality of sacrifice by the capitalist.[127] Equality of sacrifice in this case meant the conscription of wealth. Without the conscription of wealth, the labour movement was firmly against the 'conscription of human life to protect the wealth of the capitalistic class'.[128] One particularly vivid illustration of the equality-of-sacrifice argument was a widely distributed poster created in 1915 by Tom Barker of the Industrial Workers of the World (IWW).[129] A radical syndicalist labour group, the IWW had been one of the few groups within Australia to oppose the war from its beginning.[130] Tom Barker, the son of an English labourer, had joined

---

[127] See, for example, Nick Dyrenfurth, '"Conscription Is Not Abhorrent to Laborites and Socialists": Revisiting the Australian Labour Movement's Attitude towards Military Conscription during World War I' (2012) 103 *Labour History* 145; John Lack, 'Class or Nation? Worker Loyalties in Melbourne during the Great War' (2015) 86 *Victorian Historical Journal* 141.

[128] 'Last Sunday's Great Meeting', *Labor Call* (Melbourne, 7 September 1916) 4.

[129] I give a fuller account of Tom Barker and his poster in Madelaine Chiam, 'Tom Barker's "To Arms!" Poster: Internationalism and Resistance in First World War Australia' (2017) 5 *London Review of International Law* 125.

[130] The front page of the IWW newsletter *Direct Action* on 10 August 1914 asked the following: 'War! What For? For the workers and their dependents: death, starvation, poverty and untold misery. For the capitalist class: gold, stained with the blood of millions ... Send the capitalists to hell and wars are impossible.' The Women's Peace Army, whose executive included Vida Goldstein as president and Adela Pankhurst as secretary, also opposed the war, along with pacifist groups: see Jauncey (n 64) 105–06. The Australian IWW shared its anti-war stance with American socialist labour groups and with most European syndicalist groups: see, for example, Elizabeth McKillen, *Making the World Safe for Workers: Labor, the Left and Wilsonian Internationalism* (University of Illinois Press, 2013); Ralph Darlington, 'Re-Evaluating Syndicalist Opposition to the First World War' (2012) 53 *Labour History* 517; Wayne Thorpe, 'The European Syndicalists and War, 1914–1918' (2001) 10 *Contemporary European History* 1.

the IWW shortly after his arrival in Sydney in 1914 and he quickly became one of the leading figures of the movement.[131]

Barker's poster reversed the usual targets of a call to arms. 'To Arms!', it commanded. 'Capitalists, Parsons, Politicians, Landlords, Newspaper Editors and Other Stay-At-Home Patriots. Your country needs YOU in the trenches!! Workers Follow your Masters.'[132] Rather than appealing to the young working-class men who were the traditional objects of such calls, Barker set the poster's sights directly on the wealthy classes of Australia: capitalists, parsons, politicians, landlords, newspaper editors and other stay-at-home patriots. It was these people – representing the most powerful social and political figures within First World War Australian society – whom Barker's poster argued should volunteer for war service. The primary message of the poster was that the working and capitalist classes of Australia were making unequal sacrifices for the war. Where the working classes were giving their lives in the service of the Empire, the capitalist and other wealthy members of Australian society were seeing out the war from the safety of their homes. Barker's closing invocation to workers to 'follow your masters' emphasised that, just as the 'masters' should be the ones enlisting, so too the workers should be the ones resisting the calls to arms and remaining at home to look after themselves, their jobs and their families. The poster's argument was not that workers should follow their 'masters' to the war, but that they should follow the actions of their 'masters' in choosing not to enlist. Barker's poster called for equality, both in the sacrifice of lives from the different classes and the sacrifice of the wealth of the capitalist.

The equality-of-sacrifice argument was fundamental for Barker and the IWW. They believed in a working-class internationalism under which they identified themselves not horizontally with the hierarchy of the state, but vertically in solidarity across national borders with the workers of the world. For the IWW, the loyalty of Australian workers was with the working classes around the world, not with the capitalists of Australia: '[A] thousand times it is better to be a traitor to your country than a traitor to your class', proclaimed *Direct Action* in 1915.[133] Barker and the IWW also rejected White Australia and its exclusions. For them, the transformation of the world would come about only when the

---

[131] EC Fry, *Tom Barker and the IWW: Oral History* (Australian Society for the Study of Labour History and Industrial Workers of the World, 1965/1999) 5–6.

[132] This poster is reproduced at the website of the Industrial Workers of the World: see https://iww.org/history/biography/TomBarker/1.

[133] 'Patriotic ... Boneheads', *Direct Action* (Sydney, 1 January 1915) 2.

5.4 THE PUBLIC DEBATE

working classes of all nations and all races came together.[134] The Australian IWW subscribed to a Marxist internationalism that viewed capitalism as international and that required workers to organise internationally to defeat it. Discrimination among the working classes because of race was illogical and counterproductive to the larger project of destroying the capitalist system. Or, as editorialised in *Direct Action* in 1916, 'The IWW [opposes conscription] because it will deprive us of the right to educate and organise our class-brothers, be they black, white or brown, for the overthrow of the Capitalist system'.[135]

There was power in the claims for equality of sacrifice. When Barker's poster first appeared on Sydney buildings in July 1915, its message of working-class solidarity against the failure of the wealthier classes to do their duty caused consternation.[136] '[T]he placard', fumed Sir Joseph Harrington to the New South Wales Parliament, '[tries] to rouse class hatred and cause every working-man to avoid his obligation'.[137] The Honourable J Garland characterised the notion that the 'well-to-do' classes were not doing their duty as a 'gross and egregious falsehood' that should result in the most serious punishment possible for the 'disloyal ruffians' responsible for it.[138] The politicians recognised the poster's potential to undermine ties with the Empire. In this time of war, it was unimaginable for these men that any decent Australian would be so disloyal.

Prime Minister Billy Hughes also reacted strongly against the IWW argument during the conscription debates. While he conceded the need for equality between the classes in fighting the war, Hughes's personal commitment to conscription and his intolerance of opposing views meant that he regarded nearly every argument against conscription as shielding disloyalty and cowardice. In his 'Manifesto on Conscription' of September 1916, for example, while assuring his audience that 'we shall not hesitate to call upon wealth to bear an equality of sacrifice with

---

[134] See discussion in Verity Burgmann, *Revolutionary Industrial Unionism: The Industrial Workers of the World in Australia* (Cambridge University Press, 1995) 79–91.

[135] Editorial, *Direct Action* (Sydney, 28 October 1916). See also Burgmann (n 134) 197.

[136] 'The "To Arms" Poster', *Direct Action* (Sydney, 1 October 1915) 3. For full accounts of the story of Barker's poster, see Cain (n 12); Verity Burgmann (n 134); Ian Bedford, 'The Industrial Workers of the World in Australia' (1967) 13 *Labour History* 40; Ian Turner, *Sydney's Burning* (Alpha Books, 1967).

[137] New South Wales, *Parliamentary Debates*, Legislative Council, 11 August 1915, 1000 (J Carruthers).

[138] New South Wales, *Parliamentary Debates*, Legislative Council, 11 August 1915, 1002 (J Garland).

manhood', Hughes accused those making the class argument of cowardice – of being frightened of having to fight for their country.[139]

New South Wales authorities eventually prosecuted Barker in relation to the poster and charged him under the New South Wales War Precautions Regulations with making a statement likely to prejudice recruiting.[140] In his appearance before a magistrate, Barker protested that his poster was designed to encourage recruits, not deter them.[141] Barker's lawyer added that only those who were affected by war hysteria could find anything objectionable in Barker's poster.[142] The magistrate was not persuaded by Barker's arguments and convicted him. Rather than giving Barker the jail sentence that the prosecutor had sought, however, the magistrate ordered a fine of 50 pounds or six months' imprisonment in lieu. He also ordered that Barker enter a surety of 100 pounds to ensure that Barker complied for the remainder of the war with the regulations under the *War Precautions Act 1914* (Cth), in particular those that made it an offence to make statements likely to prejudice recruiting.[143] Barker's conviction was ultimately overturned on appeal, on the basis that the existence of regulations under the *War Precautions Act 1914* (Cth) rendered *ultra vires* the New South Wales regulation under which he had been charged.[144]

Barker's poster posed an explicit challenge to Australia's colonial nationalism. Protecting Australia's physical and metaphysical borders and maintaining the ties with the Empire may have been in tension, but few disagreed with their importance.[145] The IWW's internationalist orientation defied such nationalism and proved particularly provocative for Billy Hughes. As described earlier, in Hughes's view, Australia's status as a British dominion and as a preserve of whiteness depended on the protection of the British navy, which in turn required maintaining a strong British Empire.[146] Ensuring victory for the British in the war

---

[139] 'The Prime Minister's Manifesto on Conscription' (n 45); 'The Referendum: Victorian Campaign Opened' (n 102) 7.
[140] Cain (n 12) 232–33; 'The "To Arms" Poster' (n 136).
[141] 'The "To Arms" Poster' (n 136).
[142] Ibid.
[143] Ibid.
[144] Ibid.
[145] Fitzgerald (n 40) 15. See also Hirst (n 17) 608–27. In failing to recognise either the authority of the Australian state or the need for racial purity, the attitudes of the Australian IWW echoed the resistance of European syndicalists, who also challenged their countries' appeals to nationalism and the preservation of culture as justifications for war. See, for example, Thorpe (n 130); Darlington (n 130).
[146] 'The Federal Arena' (n 95).

was therefore not only an imperative of Australia's membership of the British Empire; it was also essential for the security and existence of Australia itself.[147] For Hughes, the revolutionary industrial unionism of the IWW did not simply fail to recognise the importance of Australia's national and imperial identities – it rested 'on the negation of nationality'.[148] The class-based internationalism and racial inclusion of the IWW were more than a threat to the government or to the war; they represented the ultimate threat – one to the very existence of the Australian state itself. The IWW, Hughes told Parliament, had 'declared war upon society'.[149]

Hughes saw in the agitation of the IWW an opportunity to undermine his most strident opponents in the conscription debates and in the labour movement more generally.[150] Hughes's reactions to the poster, to Barker and to the IWW underlined the importance of the preservation of national borders for Hughes's conceptions of Australia. Indeed, Hughes eventually took both of these priorities to the Paris Peace Conference where he advocated for the racial equality clause to be excluded from the League of Nations Covenant.[151] The deep antipathy, led by Hughes, towards the IWW led ultimately to the manufacture of evidence against twelve IWW members, who were then tried and convicted on charges that included treason and conspiracy to burn down Sydney buildings.[152] This trial and posters such as Barker's allowed Hughes and other conscriptionists to paint the IWW as friends of Germany and enemies of Britain. The pro-German portrayal of the IWW in turn enabled Hughes to tar the entire anti-conscription labour movement as disloyal.[153] Despite many protestations from within the labour movement and attempts to disassociate themselves from the IWW, the suggestions 'found a receptive audience'.[154] After a legislative attempt to ban membership of the IWW

---

[147] 'The Great Issue: Mr Hughes' Final Appeal' (n 103).
[148] Commonwealth, *Parliamentary Debates*, House of Representatives, 18 December 1916, 10100 (Billy Hughes).
[149] Ibid., 10099.
[150] For a detailed account of the state actions against the IWW, see Burgmann (n 134) 103–245.
[151] See, for example, Fitzhardinge (n 34) 370–418; Clark (n 34) 109–16.
[152] Turner (n 136); Cain (n 12) 201–25; Fitzhardinge (n 34) 201.
[153] See, for example, '"Trust Billy Hughes"', *The Mirror of Australia* (Sydney, 12 August 1916) 5; 'Conscription and the Referendum. Why Mr Hughes Should Be Supported' (n 42); Editorial, *The Argus* (Melbourne, 21 October 1916) 16; 'Nation's Choice: Speech by Mr Hughes', *The Sydney Morning Herald* (Sydney, 18 October 1916) 11. See also Burgmann (n 134) 181–202.
[154] Lake, *Divided Society* (n 55) 76.

in 1916, Hughes's government finally passed legislation in 1917 that suppressed the IWW and its activities entirely.[155] Members of the IWW were arrested and jailed, and those who were born outside Australia (even those born within the British Empire) were deported. Tom Barker was deported to Chile in 1918.

5.5 Conclusion

The 1916 conscription debate was conducted in languages that differed from those of 2003 and 1965–66. In 1916, the commitments to the Empire and the preservation of the White Australia policy were factors that were no longer an explicit part of the Australia of 1965–66 or 2003. Similarly, the debates about the different responsibilities of the classes of Australian society did not feature in the later debates as they had in 1916. An autonomous vocabulary of legality also had a minimal role in these debates, where the few examples of that language failed to gain traction. The USL's characterisation as a 'quibble' the question of the Australian Government's legal authority to conscript men for foreign service does suggest, however, an attitude towards legal argument that also emerged in the debates of 1965–66. This is the view that saw legal justifications as necessary but irksome, and it was evident, for example, in Robert Menzies' attitude in 1965–66 to the international legal arguments that threatened to undermine his government's proposed military actions.[156] On this approach, international legal language was wholly in the service of inter-state relationships, and any reasoning based on international law was secondary to the larger interests of maintaining those alliances.

Running through the languages of White Australia, civil liberties and empire was a strong desire to protect the hard-won rights of Australian workers, ensure that Australia remained white and preserve the freedoms that sprang from Australia's democratic system. These demands, aimed at protecting 'inside' Australia, competed with the calls of the world 'outside' Australia – particularly the call of duty to the Empire. If the vocabulary of the 1916 debates was the legal quibble, White Australia, civil liberties, empire and class, the grammar of those languages arose from the tensions between independence and loyalty, between inside and outside, and between Australian and other. The examples in this chapter underpin how false these dichotomies were and how the conception of

---

[155] *Unlawful Associations Act 1916* (Cth). See discussion in Cain (n 12) 251–73.
[156] See, for example, analysis in section 4.4.1.2 in Chapter 4.

5.5 CONCLUSION

each idea depended on, and was constructed by, the other. Arguments about White Australia, civil liberties and empire were characterised as simultaneously 'inside' and 'outside', 'independent' and 'loyal', 'Australian' and 'other', depending on the priorities of the speaker. Concerns to keep Australia white consistently looked to places outside Australia – in particular to the countries of Asia – as evidence of the threats to that whiteness. And Archbishop Mannix's calls to protect the interests of Australia were a rejection of empire built upon the fear that Britain's repression of the Irish Catholics might be repeated in Australia. And yet, in each of these cases, the places identified as 'other' were members of the British Empire – India, South Africa, Ireland – and could have been characterised as part of the inside of 1916 Australia, especially by those speakers who thought 'imperially and not locally'.[157]

Colonial nationalism was a complex construction – a nationalism that was at once for Australia and for the Empire. This nationalism meant that competence in the vocabulary and grammar of 1916 required participants in the debates to take into account the interests of both Australia and of Empire, rather than choosing one and ignoring the other. Thus, although they disagreed on method and on degree, most speakers claimed to be both for Australia and for Empire. Not even trenchant critics of the Empire, such as Mannix, argued that its interests should be ignored altogether, and nor did the Empire's most ardent supporters argue that Australia's interests were not also served by the critics' positions. The Empire was an overarching presence that Australia could not have rejected unilaterally, even if it had wanted to. Colonial nationalism seems to have forced the participants in the conscription debates into sophisticated thinking about how to accept and confront the tensions between Australia and Empire. Or, to put it differently, in the 1916 debates, competent arguments in the public debates constructed both Australia and the Empire as necessary factors in considering Australia's participation in the war. The outside represented by the Empire was thus very much inside the Australian debates of 1916.

The 1916 conscription debates were also a site of struggle over competing ideas of internationalism.[158] The arguments framed in the languages of class and of equality of sacrifice were not languages of international law in either the autonomous or collective forms. Rather,

---

[157] 'For "Yes". Anglican Synod. Unanimous Vote' (n 49).
[158] Rose Parfitt, for example, constructs the tensions between the internationalism of the League of Nations and that of Bolshevik Russia as a clash between two rival international orders. See Parfitt, *Process of International Legal Reproduction* (n 8).

they represented a wholly different conception of how an international system of relations could be organised – not on the basis of sovereignty of states, but on the basis of solidarity of the working class. In promoting a world where national borders were subordinate to the ties of class and of race, Tom Barker and the IWW championed the marginalised internationalism of their revolutionary industrial unionism.[159] This was an internationalism under which the working classes would triumph, the capitalist classes would be destroyed, and the nation-state would give way to a phenomenon called the 'One Big Union' over which the workers had direct control.[160] It was an internationalism abandoned by most European socialists in 1914 and rejected by the liberal internationalists who oversaw the move to institutions at the end of the war.[161] The League of Nations, and the international system it established, adopted an internationalism of a different kind – one in which sovereignty and the respect for national boundaries was foundational. The treatment of the public speakers who rejected the calls of empire and nation, as the IWW did, emphasises how powerful the needs of colonial nationalism were within mainstream Australian society. The internationalism of Barker and the IWW was too radical, too dangerous, for that world.

The particular internationalism of Barker's 'To Arms' poster illustrates too what has been lost from the public debates of 1965–66 and 2003. In First World War Australia, the language of equality of sacrifice kept the social and economic structures in the foreground of debates about war. The class challenges of Barker's poster made transparent the different expectations that Australians had of their world and demonstrated their awareness of the ways in which their society affected, and would be affected by, Australia's continued participation in the war. In the 1965–66 and 2003 public debates, the economic consequences of war

---

[159] Verity Burgmann, 'Cosmopolitanism and the Labour Movement' (2015) 34 *Social Alternatives* 39.

[160] Ibid.

[161] For a recent overview of the different theories on the collapse of the Second International, see Marc Mulholland, '"Marxists of Strict Observance?" The Second International, National Defence, and the Question of War' (2015) 58 *Historical Journal* 615. On the move to institutions, see David Kennedy, 'The Move to Institutions' (1987) 8 *Cardozo Law Review* 841. See also Sluga (n 8); Martti Koskenniemi, *The Gentle Civilizer of Nations: The Rise and Fall of International Law 1870–1960* (Cambridge University Press, 2001); Mark Mazower, *No Enchanted Palace: The End of Empire and the Ideological Origins of the United Nations* (Princeton University Press, 2013); Nathaniel Berman, *Passion and Ambivalence: Colonialism, Nationalism and International Law* (Martinus Nijhoff, 2012); Susan Pedersen, *The Guardians: The League of Nations and the Crisis of Empire* (Oxford University Press, 2015).

5.5 CONCLUSION

were secondary to arguments about Security Council authorisation, alliance priorities and national security.[162] Barker's poster prompts consideration of the consequences for international law of the role of a language of class in public debates about war.[163]

The constitutional aspects of the laws of Dominion and Empire bring the events of 1916 closest to the forms of lawmaking proposed by the popular constitutionalist literature discussed in Chapter 2. Billy Hughes staged two plebiscites in order to give political and popular credibility to a policy that he had long wished to introduce, and he was denied both times. Although the reasons underlying the conscription votes in both 1916 and 1917 are complex, the debates remain a powerful example of popular lawmaking, or perhaps un-making, in Australia. By refusing to allow Hughes and his governments' popular authority to introduce conscription, voters created – in the words of Robert Cover – their own world of 'valid and void'.[164] This was a world in which voters deliberated the tensions between loyalty to nation and empire and determined a pathway, which, depending on one's perspective, satisfied both, none or either. In the process, the debates unleashed campaigns that were relentlessly vituperative and that ultimately created a deeply divided Australian society that took decades to recover.

---

[162] See Chapters 3 and 4 of this book.

[163] 'Class' has been and continues to be a subject for some who work in public international law, primarily through Marxian analyses of international law. For an overview, see Robert Knox, 'Marxist Approaches to International Law' *Oxford Bibliographies in International Law Online* (28 March 2018). See also Robert Knox, 'Marxist Approaches to International Law' in Anne Orford and Florian Hoffman (eds.), *The Oxford Handbook of the Theory of International Law* (Oxford University Press, 2016) 306; BS Chimni, 'Prolegomena to a Class Approach to International Law' (2010) 21 *European Journal of International Law* 57; Akbar Rasulov, '"The Nameless Rapture of the Struggle": Towards a Marxist Class-Theoretic Approach to International Law' (2008) 19 *Finnish Yearbook of International Law* 243; Susan Marks (ed.), *International Law on the Left: Re-examining Marxist Legacies* (Cambridge University Press, 2008); China Mieville, *Between Equal Rights: A Marxist Theory of International Law* (Brill, 2005).

[164] Robert M Cover, 'The Supreme Court, 1982 Term: Foreword' (1983–84) 97 *Harvard Law Review* 4, 4.

6

Conclusion

I argue in this book that there is a long practice of speaking international legal language in public debate, at least in some places, and that this practice has produced a popular form of international law. In this concluding chapter, I reflect in two ways on the questions that have informed my analysis. First, I reiterate the argument for a popular international law and the characteristics that I have identified in this book. Second, I consider some of the implications of my argument for international legal practice.

6.1 A Popular International Law

My argument that international law in public debate has given rise to a popular form of international law rests on two bases. I argue first that two characteristics of public debate enable the generation of popular international law. These are that public debate is a process of argument and persuasion and that the state is a participant in almost all public debates about international law. And second, I argue that participants in public debates who are public, political and professional speakers of international law have used that language in debates across the twentieth and twenty-first centuries. In this section, I conclude with some further observations on the individuals who spoke international legal language in public debates, and the characteristics of popular international law that they spoke.

6.1.1 Who Spoke International Legal Language?

Nearly all of the people whose speech I examine in this book spoke international legal language. This does not, however, support a conclusion that everyone in the public debates used international law. My focus on the contributions to public debate from three groups – politicians, trade unionists and religious leaders – prevents a generalised conclusion of that kind.

6.1 A POPULAR INTERNATIONAL LAW

The answer to the question of 'who spoke international legal language?' then is not that everyone did. Rather, the answer is that, of the individuals and groups who were examined for this book, nearly all of them used international law in each of the three debates. Chapters 3, 4 and 5 argue that, in each of the public debates of 2003, 1965–66 and 1916, there were examples of politicians, trade unionists, religious leaders and others who articulated their arguments in the language of international law. These include the contributions of Rob Durbridge, Kerry O'Brien and John Howard in 2003; the Anglican Bishops, Robert Menzies and the multiple authors of the open letters in 1965–66; and the Political Labour Council of Victoria, Billy Hughes and Archbishop Mannix in 1916. In most cases, these speakers did not employ international legal language carelessly; rather, they used its vocabulary and grammar to construct sophisticated arguments for and against the different wars. Competent speakers directed these arguments at both the state and the wider Australian public in the hope that those audiences would be persuaded by the forms of international legal argument that the speakers made. Public and political speakers demonstrated a facility with international legal language that produced a popular international law.

Broadening the idea of who can speak international law, as I do in this book, underscores how there are speakers with privileged access to public debate. My decision to focus on the categories of politicians, trade unions and religious groups arose because they were consistent and prominent voices in the public debates of the three time periods. One result of this decision is that almost all of the speakers of this book are educated white men, speaking in their roles as Anglican and Catholic bishops, prime ministers and foreign ministers of Australia, leaders of the trade union movement, journalists and newspaper editors. The democratising move that I attempt to make in this book by pluralising the scope of people who speak international law has effectively reproduced a conception of the authorised speakers of international law as predominantly male and white. While I disagree with such a limited conception of international law, it does highlight the structural obstacles of class, race and gender that prevent residents of liberal democracies from full participation in public debates and, thus, from contributing to popular international law.[1]

The possibility that my argument contains both transformative and conservative consequences applies also to the ways in which the role of professional speakers unfolded in the debates. In 2003, the expertise of professional international lawyers was foregrounded, and the autonomous

---
[1] See the text accompanying nn 14–16 in Chapter 2.

form of international legal language dominated. Nevertheless, international law was not used in public debates as an exclusively professional language. Instead, the presence of professional speakers seemed also to sanction the use by political and public speakers of the autonomous form in the debates; international legality became something about which everyone could form a view, not just the experts. Casting international law in this way empowered speakers such as the trade unions to express firm views on the illegality of the Iraq War, and underpinned John Howard's description of the legal argument as 'commonsense'.[2] In this way, the prominence of the professional language of international law had a democratising effect.

At the same time, the March 2003 debate between Kerry O'Brien and John Howard over which professional international lawyers had the better expert view illustrates how the ability of a speaker to characterise the autonomous form of international legal language as authoritatively determinable by certain people limits the potential of that language.[3] In their debate over expertise to speak international law, Howard and O'Brien assumed that only narrow categories of experts could speak international legal language with authority. Their discussion suggests that, for some participants in the 2003 debates, public and political speakers could not give authoritative determinations of international legality, regardless of how coherent their arguments were with those of the professional speakers. The views expressed by the authors of the Iraq Inquiry, described in Chapter 1, suggest that, at least for some people, this formalist view of international law has become more entrenched since 2003.

The 2003 debates over authority to speak international law did not occur in the same way in either 1965–66 or 1916. In 1965–66, speakers characterised international law as consolidating an alliance with the US, or they prioritised what they considered to be the moral imperatives of the Vietnam War over the legal ones. There was no dispute in those debates over a speaker's capacity to use international legal language. It may be that the characterisation of international legal obligations as moral as well as legal opened that language to a wide range of speakers. A speaker's view on the morality of a war could not be dismissed on the grounds that they lacked professional training in the same way that arguments about legality could. In addition, the anti-formalism expressed by Menzies and others

---

[2] See text accompanying nn 89–94 and nn 101–03 in Chapter 3.
[3] See text accompanying nn 95–103 in Chapter 3.

6.1 A POPULAR INTERNATIONAL LAW 177

suggests that relying on international law as an autonomous justification for war simply lacked persuasive power in 1965–66. In 1916, the question of authority to speak international legal language did not arise in the same way. If speakers were critiqued for their background or qualifications, it was generally in relation to their class or their religious affiliation, rather than their training or expertise in law. The absence of foregrounded roles for professional speakers in both 1965–66 and 1916 seemed to allow public and political speakers to present their arguments in both the autonomous and the collective form with authority.

6.1.2 What Were the Characteristics of This Popular International Law?

If professional, political and public speakers of international law all used international law and, in many cases, considered their international legal arguments to be authoritative, what kind of international law did that generate? My argument is that popular international law has taken two main forms: it has appeared as a collective language of legality and as an autonomous language of legality. In these two forms, the vocabulary and grammar of popular international law cohered with that of the professional language and it was in the competences to speak international law that distinctions emerged. My claim is not that popular international law was the same as that of professional speakers, but rather that they were different yet complementary languages of international law.

As a collective language of legality, a number of different vocabularies of international law were used in the debates in this book, including self-defence, humanitarianism, aggression and the just war. Speakers who used this language to justify or challenge government decisions relied on the collective of implications that the concepts carried. Two collective justifications appeared most frequently – international law as a standard of morality and international law as evidence of an alliance relationship. The collective language of international law was the more prevalent form in the debates of 1965–66 and 1916, but it was present across all three periods. Speakers who deployed this collective form were able to deflect accusations that their arguments were technocratic, criticisms that were directed at speakers of the autonomous form in both 1965–66 and 1916. Speakers of the collective form were also less vulnerable to being critiqued as lacking authority to speak international law, because the authority to use collective international legal language was more diffuse than the authority to speak the autonomous form.

CONCLUSION

Examples of international law in an autonomous form were those where the requirement of legality was a criterion independent of other considerations. There were two features of legality in this autonomous form in the public debates. First, speakers separated the requirement of legality from other factors such as morality or alliance, and used an assessment of legality alone as the basis for their intervention in public debate. Autonomous forms of international legal language were more prominent in 2003 than in either 1965–66 or 1916, but they were used in all three periods. One reason for this appears to arise from the belief in 2003 that 'legality' in this technical sense can and should also control exercises of political power; beliefs that were evident too in both the Iraq Inquiry Report and the WTI Declaration described in Chapter 1. Second, legality as an autonomous justification was used by public, political and professional speakers and, when deployed by public and political speakers, it consisted of arguments that were coherent with the vocabulary and grammar of professional speakers of international law. In most cases, the political and public speakers who used international legal arguments in this autonomous way portrayed themselves as possessing whatever authority was needed to give a plausible opinion on international legality.

It was in the construction of competent arguments for the public debates that differences between the professional, political and public uses of international legal language emerged. Here, the intended audience for the contributions to the public debate – the wider public – seems to have been significant. The consistent use of international law as a part of the collective justifications of alliance or morality in 1965–66 and 1916 suggests that it was these languages that were more persuasive to those audiences. Competent speakers of international law in those debates characterised international law as supporting the aims of maintaining alliance relationships or as constituting moral obligations of the Australian state. By 2003, competent speakers of popular international legal language structured it as an autonomous measure of justification much more often than as a collective one. As a consequence, international legal language in the public debate of 2003 resembled more closely than before the competent arguments of professional international lawyers, although distance remained. The distinction between international law as an autonomous justification and international law as a collective justification can thus be cast as a characteristic of competence in participating in public debates.

An argument that international legal language has a long provenance in public debates does not necessarily make the public language of international legality a form of international law. Martti Koskenniemi, for example, has suggested that international legal arguments put forward by lay persons 'somehow fail as *legal* arguments'.[4] I argue, however, that the examples from Chapters 3, 4 and 5 illustrate uses of the vocabulary and grammar of international law with specific competences which, in combination with the dialogic nature of public debate and the role of the state in such debate, produce a popular form of international legality. This popular form of international law is of a different kind to that spoken by its professional users, but it nevertheless is international law. And, as with all languages, the public and political speakers of international law speak it with different levels of proficiency. In this sense, their uses can be analogised with non-native speakers of any language.[5] For example, just as non-native speakers of English speak a version of English that is recognised as such and understood by native speakers, so international legal language when spoken by public and political speakers can be considered to be a version of international law, with vocabulary, grammar and competences that nevertheless remain intelligible to professional international lawyers. Public and political speakers may have differing levels of ability in their 'second language' of international law – Prime Ministers, parliamentarians or domestic lawyers, for example, might be more able speakers of international law than trade union or religious leaders. In the same way that the use of English by non-native speakers does not undermine its identity as 'English', variations in fluency do not diminish a characterisation of international legal language in public debate as 'law'. Indeed, the multiple variants of English that are still recognised as English (American English, Australian English, Singaporean English and so on) suggest that there could be multiple variants of international legal language within international law.[6]

---

[4] Martti Koskenniemi, *From Apology to Utopia: The Structure of International Legal Argument* (Cambridge University Press, 2005) 566 (emphasis in original).

[5] I borrow the idea of the non-native speaker of international law from Anna Dolidze: Anna Dolidze, 'The Non-Native Speakers of International Law: The Case of Russia' (2015) *Baltic Yearbook of International Law* 77.

[6] Some possibilities for variations of international legal language include Anna Dolidze's work (ibid), as well as work on 'regional' and 'comparative' international laws: see, for example, Boris N Mamlyuk and Ugo Mattei, 'Comparative International Law' (2011) *Brooklyn Journal of International Law* 386; Teemu Ruskola, 'Where Is Asia? When Is Asia? Theorizing Comparative Law and International Law' (2010–11) 44 *UC Davis Law Review* 879; Urs Matthias Zachmann, 'Race and International Law in Japan's New Order in East Asia, 1938–1945' in Rotem Kowner and Walter Demel (eds.), *Race and Racism in Modern East Asia: Western and Eastern Constructions* (Brill, 2013) 453; Onuma Yasuaki, 'When was the Law of International Society Born? An Inquiry of the History of International Law from an Intercivilizational Perspective' (2000) 2 *Journal of the History*

6.1.3 Generalising from the Particular

All of the observations I have made so far arise from my examination in this book of three public debates in Australia. They are limited thus by the extent to which it is possible to generalise from the particular experience of a single state. I express my argument in general terms, however, because Australia is not unique in the ways that international law has been used in its public debates. Indeed, it is clear from all of the studies in Chapters 3, 4 and 5 that Australian governments and people have been consistently influenced by their counterparts in the US and the UK. The unflinching commitment of Australian governments to maintain alliance relationships with international partners and the shared tactics and languages of protest that were used in the 2003 and 1965–66 debates are two examples of the connections that Australians have maintained with the places beyond their borders.

If I have convinced readers about the existence of a popular form of international law in public debates in general, then it is clear that one study of one place can only begin to understand what this popular international law looks like and how it works. There is much more work to be done to develop a fuller picture of international law in public debates, including a need to understand its characteristics better and to explore the interactions between popular international law in public debates and the forms of popular international law generated by events such as peoples' tribunals. I hope that at least some readers can be persuaded to pursue further research into the features of popular international law.

6.2 Some Final Observations

One question that I have consistently been asked when discussing this book has been 'why?'. Why did I think that public and political speakers used international law? Why was there a shift from international law as a collective justification to international law as an autonomous justification? And what are the implications of taking seriously a popular international law? In writing what is primarily a descriptive project about the role of international law in public debate, I have not attempted to answer those questions. I briefly suggest some possibilities here though, at the end, as a way to think about the 'what next' of this book.

of International Law 1. For an introduction to the history of the English language, see Robert McCrum, Robert MacNeil and William Cran, *The Story of English* (Penguin Random House, 3rd revised ed., 2002).

6.2 SOME FINAL OBSERVATIONS

The collective international legal languages of class and morality in 1916 and 1965–66 and the autonomous language of legality in 2003 share one characteristic. In each case, the use of those languages transformed the claims of the people of a single nation into claims shared by the world in general. In 1916, the Industrial Workers of the World (IWW) made explicit arguments about the need for a class revolution around the world. In 1965–66, Australian speakers used the moral injustices of the Vietnam War, expressed for example via duplicating the text and tactics of US Vietnam War protests, to universalise the basis of their arguments against Australia's role in that war. And in 2003, the argument that the invasion of Iraq would be illegal relied on the collective standards of international law, the violation of which would be an offence not just against Australia or Iraq, but the world. It is possible that the shift to international law as an autonomous justification in popular international law allowed participants in public debate to demonstrate solidarity with people beyond national borders; a solidarity that was expressed in different ways in earlier public debates.

The shift from collective to autonomous forms of international legal language also seems to manifest what scholars have variously called the 'juridification of politics' or the fetishisation of law, a phenomenon of the late twentieth (and now early twenty-first) century.[7] Samuel Moyn, for example, has compared the US public debates over the 'War on Terror' with the debates over the Vietnam War to argue that the public debates on the 'War on Terror' evidenced a move from a generalised concern over the decision to go to war to concern about individual and criminal punishment for violations of the laws of war.[8] Moyn's identification of the criminal law as the way in which Americans debated their conduct of the War on Terror is consistent with other scholars' charting of international law's development of an orientation towards international criminal law in addressing war.[9]

---

[7] Gerry Simpson, '"Stop Calling it Aggression": War as Crime' (2008) 61 *Current Legal Problems* 191, 200. See also Gerry Simpson, *Law, War and Crime* (Polity Press, 2007), 132–58. On law as a fetish, see, for example, Christopher Tomlins and John Comaroff, '"Law As . . . ": Theory and Practice in Legal History' (2011) 1 *UC Irvine Law Review* 1039, 1060–72; Costas Douzinas, *Human Rights and Empire – The Political Philosophy of Cosmopolitanism* (Routledge, 2007) 216 (calling international law 'one of the great chimera of our time'); the essays collected in Nikolas M Rajkovic, Tanja Aalberts and Thomas Gammeltoft-Hansen, *The Power of Legality: Practices of International Law and their Politics* (Cambridge University Press, 2016).

[8] Samuel Moyn, 'From Antiwar Politics to Antitorture Politics' in Austin Sarat, Lawrence Douglas and Martha Merrill Umphrey (eds.), *Law and War* (Stanford University Press, 2014) 154, 156–57.

[9] See, for example, Simpson, *Law, War and Crime*, above n 7; Tor Krever, 'Dispensing Global Justice' (2014) *New Left Review* 85; Ruti Teitel, 'Humanity's Law: Rule of Law for

I have not asked the same questions that Moyn and others have, but there are resonances between Moyn's description of the narrowing of legal concerns in public debates and my observations about the shift from collective to autonomous justifications within these examples of popular international law.

Thinking of the shift from collective to autonomous justifications as a narrowing of concerns raises the question of what might have been lost from twenty-first-century public debates. The public debates of 1916 and 1965–66 highlight what public debates looked like when the collective forms of international legal language incorporated the ideas and vocabulary of class and of morality. During the 1916 debates, multiple conceptions of internationalism remained plausible, and the languages of international law were more expansive than they were in either 1965–66 or 2003. The collective language of class, in particular, kept the economic consequences of war at the forefront of public consciousness and briefly opened space for the radical syndicalist internationalism of the IWW to flourish.[10] In 1965–66, international law as a collective language of morality was prominent. Claims in the language of morality cast the UN *Charter* and treaty obligations as important not because they embodied legal obligations but because they represented larger commitments to humanity. In doing so, this collective form of international law seemed to minimise arguments about the authority of individual speakers to rely on international law. In 2003, the foregrounding of the question of legality allowed the Howard government to subordinate the questions about morality and the economic consequences of war that had been prominent in 1965–66 and 1916.

As I write this conclusion at the beginning of 2020, public debate seems to be incorporating again collective forms of international legal language. Australia's obstructionist position at the UN *Framework Convention on Climate Change* Conference of Parties meeting in Madrid in December 2019, for example, was described by some as having 'no legal basis',[11] employing the autonomous form of international law. Others, however, brought conceptions of morality back into international legal arguments, criticising Australia's climate position as having no

---

the New Global Politics' (2002) 35 *Cornell International Law Journal* 355; Immi Tallgren, 'The Sensibility and Sense of International Criminal Law' (2002) 13 *European Journal of International Law* 561.

[10] See text accompanying nn 127–55.

[11] Adam Morton, 'UN climate talks: Australia accused of "Cheating" and thwarting global deal', *The Guardian Online*, 16 December 2019 www.theguardian.com/environment/2019/dec/16/un-climate-talks-australia-accused-of-cheating-and-thwarting-global-deal.

6.2 SOME FINAL OBSERVATIONS

'scientific, moral or legal foundation',[12] and as a 'betrayal of trust which all countries signed up to at Paris'.[13] Concerns about class and inequality are also resurgent, with headlines such as 'World's richest 500 people saw their wealth jump 25 percent in 2019'[14] and 'Gilded Age 2.0: U.S. Income Inequality Increases to Pre-Great Depression Levels'[15] a regular feature of news reporting. The collective form of international legal language that incorporates conceptions of class is again becoming embedded in debates about international legal questions,[16] and concerns of the kind expressed by the IWW in 1916 seem certain to resume a place in public debates over international issues.

Writing at the beginning of 2020 about a popular international law also raises the possibility of a 'populist' rather than a 'popular' international law. If populist governments are understood as ones that aim to establish that they represent a mythical version of 'the people' in order to consolidate their power over that of competing elites,[17] then populism sits in tension with the popular international law that I argue exists. The popular international law

---

[12] Richie Merzian, quoted in Adam Morton, 'Australia's use of accounting loophole to meet Paris deal found to have no legal basis', *The Guardian Online*, 12 December 2019 www.theguardian.com/environment/2019/dec/12/australias-use-of-accounting-loophole-to-meet-paris-deal-found-to-have-no-legal-basis.

[13] Malte Meinshausen, quoted in Peter Hannam, 'Australia's "betrayal of trust" emissions plan to be tested in Madrid', *The Sydney Morning Herald Online*, 9 December 2019 www.smh.com.au/environment/climate-change/australia-s-betrayal-of-trust-emissions-plan-to-be-tested-in-madrid-20191208-p53hyv.html. For a brief outline of the Madrid meeting, see Kate Dooley, 'The Madrid climate talks failed spectacularly. Here's what went down', *The Conversation* (online 16 December 2019) https://theconversation.com/the-madrid-climate-talks-failed-spectacularly-heres-what-went-down-128921.

[14] Brooke Siepel, 'World's richest 500 people saw their wealth jump 25 percent in 2019', *Thehill.com* (online, 27 December 2019) https://thehill.com/policy/finance/476103-worlds-richest-500-people-saw-their-wealth-jump-25-percent-in-2019.

[15] Kevin Kelleher, 'Gilded Age 2.0: U.S. Income Inequality Increases to Pre-Great Depression Levels', *Fortune.com* (online, 13 February 2019) https://fortune.com/2019/02/13/us-income-inequality-bad-great-depression/.

[16] The multiple reports of Philip Alston, as UN Special Rapporteur on extreme poverty and human rights, are just one example of these debates. See, for example, Human Rights Council, *Visit to the United Kingdom of Great Britain and Northern Ireland – Report of the Special Rapporteur on extreme poverty and human rights*, 41st sess, Agenda Item 3, UN Doc A/HRC/41/39/Add.1 (adopted 23 April 2019). See also Jessica Whyte, *The Morals of the Market: Human Rights and the Rise of Neoliberalism* (Verso, 2019); Samuel Moyn, *Not Enough: Human Rights in an Unequal World* (Harvard University Press, 2018).

[17] See Heike Kreiger, 'Populist Governments and International Law' (2019) 30 *The European Journal of International Law* 971; Marcela Prieto Rudolphy, 'Populist Governments and International Law: A Reply to Heike Krieger' (2019) 30 *The European Journal of International Law* 997; Paul Blokker, 'Populist Governments and International Law' (2019) 30 *The European Journal of International Law* 1009.

that emerges in this book is constituted by the multiple conceptions of international law expressed by a diversity of voices in public debates. Chapters 3, 4 and 5 include many examples where public speakers have claimed the authority to speak international law in order to critique the policies and actions of their governments, rejecting an idea that there is a single 'people' whose interests are represented by a leader or government. A popular international law that is constituted by public and political speakers and that seeks to influence government actions conflicts with the notion that a government might be the only true representative of a 'people'. Indeed, the national and international solidarity between individuals and groups that popular international law seems to have enabled in 2003, 1965–66 and 1916, and the possibilities of different internationalisms that it raised in 1916, are potential antidotes to the authoritarian version of populist governments.[18]

In the polyphonic spirit of Herodotus, I have attempted in this book to open up understandings of the people who have spoken and who can speak the language of international law with authority. It seems only fitting then to give Herodotus the last word on how and why studying the contributions of all people matters:

> I shall proceed at once ... to describing the equal and the lesser cities. For the cities which were formerly great have most of them become insignificant; and such as are at present powerful, were weak in the olden time. I shall therefore discourse equally of both, convinced that human happiness never continues long in one stay.[19]

---

[18] For a slightly different version of this argument, see Christine Schwobel-Patel, 'Populism, International Law and the End of Keep Calm and Carry On Lawyering' (2018) 49 *Netherlands Yearbook of International Law* 97.

[19] Herodotus, *The Histories* (George Rawlinson trans, 1858–60), Book 1, http://classics.mit.edu/Herodotus/history.1.i.html.

BIBLIOGRAPHY

Primary Materials

Official Documents

Advancing the National Interest: Australia's Foreign and Trade Policy White Paper (Commonwealth of Australia, 2003)

Commonwealth, *Parliamentary Debates*, House of Representatives and Senate, 1915–1916, 1962–66, 1991, 2002–03, 2015

Flood, Philip, *Report of the Inquiry into Australian Intelligence Agencies* (Commonwealth of Australia, 2004)

Inspector General, United States Department of Defense, *Review of the Pre-Iraqi War Activities of the Office of the Under Secretary of Defense for Policy* (Report no. 07-INTEL-04, 9 February 2007) https://fas.org/irp/agency/dod/ig020907-decl.pdf

Media Releases of the Office of the Prime Minister of Australia, 2001–03 and 2015

National Security Council, *The National Security Strategy of the United States of America* (President of the United States of America, 2002)

New South Wales, *Parliamentary Debates*, Legislative Council, 1915

Pamphlets produced by the Australian Minister/Department for External Affairs, 1965–66

Parliamentary Joint Committee into ASIO, ASIS and DSD, *Intelligence on Iraq's Weapons of Mass Destruction* (Commonwealth of Australia, 2004)

The Report of the Iraq Inquiry: Report of a Committee of Privy Counsellors (6 July 2016) www.iraqinquiry.org.uk/

Speeches delivered by George W Bush, President of the United States, 2001–03

Speeches delivered by Dick Cheney, Vice-President of the United States, 2002–03

Speeches delivered by Alexander Downer, Foreign Minister of Australia, 2002–03

Speeches delivered by Harold Holt, Prime Minister of Australia, 1966

Speeches delivered by John Howard, Prime Minister of Australia, 2002–03

Speeches delivered by Billy Hughes, Prime Minister of Australia, 1915–16

Speeches delivered by Robert Menzies, Prime Minister of Australia, 1964–65

United States Senate Select Committee on Intelligence, *Report on the U.S. Intelligence Community's Prewar Intelligence Assessments on Iraq* (2004) https://fas.org/irp/congress/2004_rpt/ssci_iraq.pdf

United States Senate Select Committee on Intelligence, *Report of the Select Committee on Intelligence on Postwar Findings about Iraq's WMD Programs and Links to Terrorism and How They Compare With Prewar Assessments* (8 September 2006) www.intelligence.senate.gov/sites/default/files/publications/109331.pdf

Media Releases, Interviews and Pamphlets

Manifestos, variously pro- and anti-conscription, from 1916

Media interviews by the Australian Broadcasting Corporation, 1965–66 and 2002–03

Media releases from religious organisations and trade unions in Australia, 1965–66 and 2002–03

Pamphlets produced by JF Cairns, Communist Party of Australia, Liberal Party of Australia, 1965–66

Newspapers/Online News Services

ABC News (online)
The Advertiser (Adelaide)
The Age (Melbourne)
The Argus (Melbourne)
The Australian (Sydney)
Barrier Miner (Broken Hill)
The Bathurst Times (Bathurst)
The Brisbane Courier (Brisbane)
BBC News World Edition (online)
Border Watch (Mount Gambier)
The Canberra Times (Canberra)
The Catholic Press (Sydney)
The Conversation (online)
Chronicle and North Coast Advertiser (Queensland)
CNN (online)
Crikey (online)
Daily Herald (Adelaide)
Daily Telegraph (Launceston)
Direct Action (Sydney)
The Drum (online)

Examiner (Launceston)
Great Southern Star (Leongatha)
The Guardian (online)
Hamilton Spectator (Victoria)
Kyodo News (Tokyo)
Labor Call (Melbourne)
Mirror (online)
The Mirror of Australia (Sydney)
Mudgee Guardian and North-Western Representative (Mudgee)
The Murrumbidgee Irrigator (Leeton)
National Advocate (Bathurst)
New Matilda (online)
The New York Times (New York)
The Observer (online)
People (Sydney)
The Register (Adelaide)
Southern Cross (Adelaide)
Sunday Times (Sydney)
The Sydney Morning Herald (Sydney)
The Times (London)
Western Mail (Perth)
Worker (Brisbane)

Cases/Legislation/Treaties/International Materials

Commonwealth of Australia Constitution Act 1900 (Imp)
Defence Act 1903 (Cth)
Farey v Buvett (1916) 21 CLR 433
Human Rights Council, *Visit to the United Kingdom of Great Britain and Northern Ireland – Report of the Special Rapporteur on extreme poverty and human rights*, 41st sess, Agenda Item 3, UN Doc A/HRC/41/39/Add.1 (adopted 23 April 2019)
International Commission on Intervention and State Sovereignty, *The Responsibility to Protect* (International Development Research Centre, December 2001)
International Telegraphic Convention (1903) ATS 6
Iraq Liberation Act of 1998, PL 105–338, 112 STAT 3178, (1998)
Letter dated 23 September 2014 from the Permanent Representative of the United States of America to the United Nations addressed to the Secretary-General, S/2014/695, 23 September 2014
Letter dated 9 September 2015 from the Permanent Representative of Australia to the United Nations addressed to the President of the Security Council, S/2015/693, 9 September 2015

Military and Paramilitary Activities in and against Nicaragua (Nicaragua v United States) (Judgment) [1986] ICJ Rep 1
Military Service Referendum Act 1916 (Cth)
National Service Act 1964 (Cth)
SC Res 1441, UN SCOR, 57th sees, 4644th mtg, UN Doc S/RES/1441 (8 November 2002)
Statute of Westminster 1931 (Imp)
United Nations High Commissioner for Refugees, *Global Report 2008: Facing New Challenges* (Geneva, 2008)
Unlawful Associations Act 1916 (Cth)
War Precautions Act 1914–1916 (Cth)
Welsbach Light Co of Australasia v Commonwealth of Australia (1916) 22 CLR 268

Secondary Materials

Articles/Books/Reports

'A Giant of a Man, Gone but Never Forgotten' (2015) 40(1) *AEU SA Branch Journal* 10

Abadee, Nicole and Don Rothwell, 'The Howard Doctrine: Australia and Anticipatory Self-Defence against Terrorist Attacks' (2007) 26 *Australian Yearbook of International Law* 19

Aceves, William J, Everard Meade and Gershon Shafir (eds.), *Lessons and Legacies of the War on Terror: From Moral Panic to Permanent War* (Routledge, 2013)

'Agora: The Case of Iraq: International Law and Politics' (2011) 42 *Netherlands Yearbook of International Law* 69

Akande, Dapo, 'How and Why International Law Matters – Lessons from the UK's Iraq Inquiry', *EJIL: Talk! Blog of the European Journal of International Law* (Blog Post, 31 January 2010)

Alder, Michael C, *The Inherent Right of Self-Defence in International Law* (Springer, 2013) chapter 1

Alexander, Amanda, 'A Short History of International Humanitarian Law' (2015) 26 *European Journal of International Law* 109

Altwicker, Tilmann and Oliver Diggelmann, 'How is Progress Constructed in International Legal Scholarship?' (2014) 25 *European Journal of International Law* 425

Andersson, Stefan (ed.), *Revisiting the Vietnam War and International Law: Views and Interpretations of Richard Falk* (Cambridge University Press, 2017)

Anghie, Antony, *Imperialism, Sovereignty and the Making of International Law* (Cambridge University Press, 2007)

Anghie, Antony, 'Race, Self-Determination and Australian Empire' (2018) 19 *Melbourne Journal of International Law* 1

Anghie, Antony, 'Western Discourses of Sovereignty' in Julie Evans et al. (eds.), *Sovereignty: Frontiers of Possibility* (University of Hawai'i Press, 2013) 19

Aquinas, Thomas, 'Summa Theologica' in Larry May, Eric Rove and Steve Viner (eds.), *The Morality of War: Classical and Contemporary Readings* (Pearson Prentice Hall, 2006)

Armstrong, Pauline, *A History of the Save Our Sons Movement of Victoria: 1965-1973* (Master's Thesis, Monash University, 1991)

Arvidsson, Matilda and Miriam Bak McKenna, 'The Turn to History in International Law and the Sources Doctrine: Critical Approaches and Methodological Imaginaries' (2020) 33(1) *Leiden Journal of International Law* 37.

Ashby Wilson, Richard and Richard D Brown (eds.), *Humanitarianism and Suffering: The Mobilization of Empathy* (Cambridge University Press, 2009)

Austin, John L, *How to Do Things with Words* (Harvard University Press, 1962)

Bakhtin, Mikhail, *Problems of Dostoevsky's Poetics*, tr Caryl Emerson (University of Minnesota Press, 1984)

Barclay, Glen St J, *A Very Small Insurance Policy: The Politics of Australian Involvement in Vietnam 1954-1967* (University of Queensland Press, 1988)

Barnett, Michael and Thomas G Weiss, *Humanitarianism Contested: Where Angels Fear to Tread* (Routledge, 2013)

Barnett, Michael and Thomas G Weiss (eds.), *Humanitarianism in Question: Politics, Power, Ethics* (Cornell University Press, 2008)

Barrett, John, *Falling In: Australians and 'Boy Conscription', 1911-1915* (Hale & Iremonger, 1979)

Beaulac, Stephane, *The Power of Language in the Making of International Law: The Word Sovereignty in Bodin and Vattel and the Myth of Westphalia* (Brill, 2004)

Beaumont, Joan, *Broken Nation: Australians in the Great War* (Allen & Unwin, 2013)

Beaumont, Joan, *Going to War 1914-18: The View from the Australian Parliament* (Strategic and Defence Studies Centre, ANU College of Asia and the Pacific, Australian National University, 2014)

Beaumont, Joan, '"Unitedly We Have Fought": Imperial Loyalty and the Australian War Effort' (2014) 90 *International Affairs* 397

Beazley, Kim C, 'Federal Labor and the Vietnam Commitment' in Peter King (ed.), *Australia's Vietnam: Australia in the Second Indo-China War* (Allen & Unwin, 1983) 36

Becker Lorca, Arnulf, 'Eurocentrism in the History of International Law' in Bardo Fassbender and Anne Peters (eds.), *The Oxford Handbook of the History of International Law* (Oxford University Press, 2012) 1034

Becker Lorca, Arnulf, *Mestizo International Law: A Global Intellectual History 1842–1933* (Cambridge University Press, 2014)

Beckett, Jason, 'Rebel without a Cause? Martti Koskenniemi and the Critical Legal Project' (2006) 7 *German Law Journal* 1045

Bedford, Ian, 'The Industrial Workers of the World in Australia' (1967) 13 *Labour History* 40

Bellamy, Alex J, 'International Law and the War with Iraq' (2003) 4 *Melbourne Journal of International Law* 497

Bellamy, Alex J, *Just Wars: From Cicero to Iraq* (Polity Press, 2006)

Bellinger, John, 'The Chilcot Inquiry and the Legal Basis for the Iraq War', Lawfare (Blog Post, 11 July 2016)

Benton, Lauren and Lisa Ford, *Rage for Order: The British Empire and the Origins of International Law* (Harvard University Press, 2016)

Berman, Harold J, *Law and Language: Effective Symbols of Community* (Cambridge University Press, 2013)

Berman, Nathaniel, 'A Perilous Ambivalence: Nationalist Desire, Legal Autonomy, and the Limits of the Interwar Framework' (1992) 33 *Harvard International Law Journal* 353

Berman, Nathaniel, '"But the Alternative is Despair": European Nationalism and the Modernist Renewal of International Law' (1992–93) 106 *Harvard Law Review* 1792

Berman, Nathaniel, 'Legitimacy through Defiance: From Goa to Iraq' (2005) 23 *Wisconsin International Law Journal* 93

Berman, Nathaniel, *Passion and Ambivalence: Colonialism, Nationalism and International Law* (Martinus Nijhoff, 2012)

Bianchi, Andrea, Daniel Peat and Matthew Windsor (eds.), *Interpretation in International Law* (Oxford University Press, 2015)

Black, Christine, Shaun McVeigh and Richard Johnstone, 'Of the South' (2007) 16 *Griffith Law Review* 299

Blair, Tony, *A Journey: My Political Life* (Alfred A Knopf, 2010)

Blokker, Paul, 'Populist Governments and International Law' (2019) 30 *The European Journal of International Law* 1009

Bolton, Geoffrey, *Paul Hasluck: A Life* (UWA Publishing, 2015)

Bongiorno, Frank, 'The Price of Nostalgia: Menzies, the "Liberal" Tradition and Australian Foreign Policy' (2005) 51 *Australian Journal of Politics and History* 400

Borgen, Christopher J, 'Language of Law and the Practice of Politics: Great Powers and the Rhetoric of Self-Determination in the Cases of Kosovo and South Ossetia' (2009) 10 *The Chicago Journal of International Law* 1

Borowiak, Craig, 'The World Tribunal on Iraq: Citizens' Tribunals and the Struggle for Accountability' (2008) 30(2) *New Political Science* 161–86, 177

Boulden, Jane, 'The Security Council and Terrorism' in Vaughan Lowe, Adam Roberts and Jennifer Welsh (eds.), *United Nations Security Council and*

War: The Evolution of Thought and Practice Since 1945 (Oxford University Press, 2008) 608

Boyle, James, 'Ideals and Things: International Legal Scholarship and the Prison-House of Language' (1985) 26 *Harvard Journal of International Law* 327

Brett, Judith, *Robert Menzies' Forgotten People* (Melbourne University Press, 2007)

Brownlie, Ian, *International Law and the Use of Force by States* (Oxford University Press, 1963)

Brunnee, Jutta and Stephen J Toope, 'Slouching towards New "Just" Wars: The Hegemon after September 11th' (2004) 18 *International Relations* 405

Burgis, Michelle L, *Boundaries of Discourse in the International Court of Justice: Mapping Arguments in Arab Territorial Disputes* (Brill, 2009)

Burgis-Kasthala, Michelle Leanne, 'Over-Stating Palestine's UN Membership Bid? An Ethnographic Study on the Narratives of Statehood' (2014) 25 *European Journal of International Law* 677

Burgmann, Verity, 'Cosmopolitanism and the Labour Movement' (2015) 34 *Social Alternatives* 39

Burgmann, Verity, *Revolutionary Industrial Unionism: The Industrial Workers of the World in Australia* (Cambridge University Press, 1995)

Bush, George W, *Decision Points* (Broadway Paperbacks, 2010)

Byrnes, Andrew, '"The Law Was Warful": The Iraq War and the Role of International Lawyers in the Domestic Reception of International Law' in Hilary Charlesworth et al. (eds.), *The Fluid State: International Law and National Legal Systems* (Federation Press, 2005) 229

Byrnes, Andrew and Gabrielle Simm, 'International Peoples' Tribunals: Their Nature, Practice and Significance' in Andrew Byrnes and Gabrielle Simm (eds.), *Peoples' Tribunals and International Law* (Cambridge University Press, 2017) 11

Byrnes, Andrew and Gabrielle Simm, 'Reflections on the Past and Future of International Peoples' Tribunals' in Andrew Byrnes and Gabrielle Simm (eds.), *Peoples' Tribunals and International Law* (Cambridge University Press, 2017) 259

Cain, Frank, *The Wobblies at War: A History of the IWW and the Great War in Australia* (Spectrum Publications, 1993)

Cairns, JF, *Eagle and the Lotus: Western Intervention in Vietnam 1847–1968* (Lansdowne Press, 1969)

Cairns, JF, *Vietnam: Is it Truth We Want?* (Victorian Branch of the Australian Labor Party, 1965)

Campbell, Bill and Chris Moraitis, 'Memorandum of Advice to the Commonwealth Government on the Use of Force against Iraq', reproduced in (2003) 4 *Melbourne Journal of International Law* 178

Carne, Greg, 'Neither Principled nor Pragmatic? International Law, International Terrorism and the Howard Government' (2008) 27 *Australian Year Book of International Law* 11

Carty, Anthony, 'Language Games of International Law: Koskenniemi as the Discipline's Wittgenstein' (2012) 13 *Melbourne Journal of International Law* 859

Cass, Deborah Z, 'Navigating the Newstream: Recent Critical Scholarship in International Law' (1996) 65 *Nordic Journal of International Law* 341

Caulfield, Michael, *The Vietnam Years: From the Jungle to the Australian Suburbs* (Hachette Australia, 2007)

Chakrabarty, Dipesh, *Provincializing Europe: Postcolonial Thought and Historical Difference* (Princeton University Press, 2000)

Chapdelaine-Feliciati, Clara, 'The Sense, Meaning and Significance of the Twin International Covenants on Political and Economic Rights' (2013) 196 *Semiotica* 325

Charlesworth, Hilary, 'International Law: A Discipline of Crisis' (2002) 65 *Modern Law Review* 377

Charlesworth, Hilary, 'Saddam Hussein: My Part in his Downfall' (2005) 23(1) *Wisconsin International Law Journal* 127

Charlesworth, Hilary and Gillian Triggs, 'Australia and the International Protection of Human Rights' in Donald R Rothwell and Emily Crawford (eds.), *International Law in Australia* (Thomson Reuters, 3rd ed., 2017)

Charlesworth, Hilary, et al., 'Deep Anxieties: Australia and the International Legal Order' (2003) 25 *Sydney Law Review* 423

Charlesworth, Hilary, et al., *No Country Is an Island: Australia and International Law* (UNSW Press, 2006)

Chemerinsky, Erwin, 'In Defence of Judicial Review: The Perils of Popular Constitutionalism' (2004) *University of Illinois Law Review* 673

Cheney, Dick, *In My Time: A Personal and Political Memoir* (Threshold Editions, 2011)

Chesterman, Simon, *Just War or Just Peace: Humanitarian Intervention and International Law* (Oxford University Press, 2002)

Chiam, Madelaine, 'International Human Rights Treaties and Institutions in the Protection of Human Rights in Australia' in Matthew Groves, Janina Boughey and Dan Meagher (eds.), *The Legal Protection of Rights in Australia* (Hart, 2019) 229

Chiam, Madelaine, 'International Law in Australia (3rd ed) Book Review' (2018) 35 *Australian Yearbook of International Law* 228

Chiam, Madelaine, 'Tasmanian Dams and Australia's Relationship with International Law' (2015) 24 *Griffith Law Review* 89

Chiam, Madelaine, 'Tom Barker's "To Arms!" Poster: Internationalism and Resistance in First World War Australia' (2017) 5(1) *London Review of International Law* 125

Chiam, Madelaine and Anna Hood, 'Nuclear Humanitarianism' (2019) 24 *Journal of Conflict and Security Law* 473

Childe, Vere Gordon, *How Labour Governs: A Study of Workers' Representation in Australia* (first published 1923, published online by Sydney University Library, 1998)

Chimni, Bhupinder S, 'Globalization, Humanitarianism and the Erosion of Refugee Protection' (2000) 13(3) *Journal of Refugee Studies* 243

Chimni, Bhupinder S, 'Prolegomena to a Class Approach to International Law' (2010) 21 *European Journal of International Law* 57

Chinkin, Christine, 'Peoples' Tribunals: Legitimate or Rough Justice' (2006) 24 *Windsor Year Book of Access to Justice* 201, 216-17

Chomsky, Noam, *Current Issues in Linguistic Theory* (Mouton, 6th ed., 1975)

Chow, Pok Yin S, 'Culture as Collective Memories: An Emerging Concept in International Law and Discourse on Cultural Rights' (2014) 14 *Human Rights Law Review* 611

Clark, Manning, *A History of Australia, Volume 6: 'The Old Dead Tree and the Young Tree Green' 1916-1935* (Melbourne University Press, 1991)

Clarke, Richard A, *Against all Enemies: Inside America's War on Terror* (Free Press, 2004)

Coates, Benjamin Allen, *Legalist Empire: International Law and American Foreign Relations in the Early Twentieth Century* (Oxford University Press, 2016)

Cochrane, Peter, 'At War at Home: Australian Attitudes during the Vietnam Years' in Gregory Pemberton (ed.), *Vietnam Remembered* (Weldon, 1990) 165

Cockayne, James and David M Malone, 'The Security Council and the 1991 and 2003 Wars in Iraq' in Vaughan Lowe, Adam Roberts and Jennifer Welsh (eds.), *United Nations Security Council and War: The Evolution of Thought and Practice Since 1945* (Oxford University Press, 2008) 384

Conley, John M and William M O'Barr, *Just Words: Law, Language and Power* (University of Chicago Press, 2nd ed., 2005)

Conley, John M and William M O'Barr, *Rules versus Relationships: The Ethnography of Legal Discourse* (University of Chicago Press, 1990)

Constable, Marianne, *Just Silences: The Limits and Possibilities of Modern Law* (Princeton University Press, 2005)

Cordes-Holland, River, 'The National Interest or Good International Citizenship? Australia and Its Approach to International and Public Climate Law' in Kim Rubenstein and Brad Jessup (eds.), *Environmental Discourses in Public and International Law* (Cambridge University Press, 2012) 286

Cotterrell, Roger, 'The Concept of Legal Culture' in David Nelken (ed.), *Comparing Legal Cultures* (Routledge, 1997)

Cotterrell, Roger, *Law, Culture and Society: Legal Ideas in the Mirror of Social Theory* (Routledge, 2006)

Cover, Robert M, 'The Supreme Court, 1982 Term: Foreword' (1983-84) 97 *Harvard Law Review* 4

Cover, Robert, 'Violence and the Word' (1985-86) 95 *Yale Law Journal* 1601

Coverdale, John F, 'An Introduction to the Just War Tradition' (2004) 16 *Pace International Law Review* 221

Craven, Matthew, 'Introduction: International Law and its Histories' in Matthew Craven et al. (eds.), *Time, History and International Law* (Brill, 2007) 1

Craven, Matthew, et al., 'We Are Teachers of International Law' (2004) 17(2) *Leiden Journal of International Law* 363

Crawford, James, 'International Law as a Discipline and a Profession' (2012) 106 *American Society of International Law Proceedings* 471

Crawford, James R, *Brownlie's Principles of Public International Law* (Oxford University Press, 8th ed., 2012)

Çubukçu, Ayça, *For the Love of Humanity: The World Tribunal on Iraq* (University of Pennsylvania Press, 2018)

Curthoys, Ann, 'The Anti-War Movements' in Jeffrey Grey and Jeff Doyle (eds.), *Vietnam: War, Myth and Memory: Comparative Perspectives on Australia's War in Vietnam* (Allen & Unwin, 1992) 81

Curthoys, Ann, 'Mobilising Dissent: The Later Stages of Protest' in Gregory Pemberton (ed.), *Vietnam Remembered* (Weldon, 1990) 138

Curthoys, Ann, 'White, British and European: Historicising Identity in Settler Societies' in Jane Carey and Claire McLisky (eds.), *Creating White Australia* (Sydney University Press, 2009) 3

Curthoys, Ann and John Docker, *Is History Fiction?* (UNSW Press, 2010)

Curthoys, Ann and Marilyn Lake, *Connected Worlds: History in Transnational Perspective* (ANU Press, 2005)

Curtis, Jonathan, 'To the Last Man: Australia's Entry to War in 1914' (Research Paper, Parliamentary Library, Parliament of Australia, 31 July 2014)

D'Aspremont, Jean, 'Critical Histories of International Law and the Repression of Disciplinary Imagination' (2019) 7 *London Review of International Law* 89

D'Aspremont, Jean, *Epistemic Forces in International Law: Foundational Doctrines and Techniques of International Legal Argumentation* (Elgar, 2015)

D'Aspremont, Jean, 'Wording in International Law' (2012) 25(3) *Leiden Journal of International Law* 575

Darlington, Ralph, 'Re-Evaluating Syndicalist Opposition to the First World War' (2012) 53 *Labour History* 517

de Carvalho, Evandro Menezes, *Semiotics of International Law: Trade and Translation*, tr Luciana Carvalho Fonseca (Springer, 2011)

De, Rohit, *A People's Constitution: The Everyday Life of Law in the Indian Republic* (Princeton University Press, 2018)

Dehm, Sara, 'Accusing "Europe". Articulations of Migrant Justice and a Popular International Law' in Andrew Byrnes and Gabrielle Simm (eds.), *Peoples' Tribunals and International Law* (Cambridge University Press, 2017) 157

Dennis, Peter and Jeffrey Grey, *Emergency and Confrontation: Australian Military Operations in Malaya and Borneo 1950–1966* (Allen & Unwin and Australian War Memorial, 1996)

Dennis, Peter, et al., *The Oxford Companion to Australian Military History* (Oxford University Press, 2009)

Desautels-Stein, Justin, 'Back in Style' (2014) 25 *Law and Critique* 141

Desautels-Stein, Justin, 'International Legal Structuralism: A Primer' (2016) 8 *International Theory* 201

Desautels-Stein, Justin, *The Jurisprudence of Style: A Structuralist History of American Pragmatism and Liberal Legal Thought* (Cambridge University Press, 2018)

Dinstein, Yoram, *War, Aggression and Self-Defence* (Cambridge University Press, 5th ed., 2011)

Dolgopol, Tina, 'The Judgment of the Tokyo Women's Tribunal' (2003) 28 *Alternative Law Journal* 242

Dolidze, Anna, 'The Non-Native Speakers of International Law: The Case of Russia' (2015) 15 *Baltic Yearbook of International Law* 77

Donnelly, Tom, 'Making Popular Constitutionalism Work' (2012) 1 *Wisconsin Law Review* 159

Duffy, Helen, *The 'War on Terror' and the Framework of International Law* (Cambridge University Press, 2015)

Dyrenfurth, Nick, '"Conscription Is Not Abhorrent to Laborites and Socialists": Revisiting the Australian Labour Movement's Attitude towards Military Conscription during World War I' (2012) 103 *Labour History* 145

Edwards, Peter, *A Nation at War: Australian Politics, Society and Diplomacy during the Vietnam War 1965-75* (Allen & Unwin and Australian War Memorial, 1997)

Edwards, Peter, *Australia and the Vietnam War* (NewSouth Books, 2014)

Edwards, Peter, *Crises and Commitments: The Politics and Diplomacy of Australia's Involvement in Southeast Asian Conflicts 1948-1965* (Allen & Unwin and Australian War Memorial, 1992)

Ellsberg, Daniel, *Secrets: A Memoir of Vietnam and the Pentagon Papers* (Viking, 2003)

Emden, Christian J and David Midgley, 'Beyond Habermas? From the Bourgeois Public Sphere to Global Publics' in Christian J Emden and David Midgley (eds.), *Beyond Habermas: Democracy, Knowledge and the Public Sphere* (Berghahn Books, 2012) 1

Errington, Wayne and Peter Van Onselen, *John Winston Howard: The Definitive Biography* (Melbourne University Press, 2008)

Eslava, Luis, *Local Space, Global Life: The Everyday Operation of International Law and Development* (Cambridge University Press, 2015)

Ewick, Patricia and Susan S Silbey, *The Common Place of Law: Stories from Everyday Lives* (University of Chicago Press, 1998)

Falk, Richard, *The Costs of War: International Law, the UN and World Order after Iraq* (Taylor & Francis, 2012)

Falk, Richard (ed.), *The Vietnam War and International Law* (American Society of International Law, republished Princeton University Press, 2015) vol 1–4

Farrell, Frank, 'Socialism, Internationalism and the Australian Labour Movement' (1985) 15 *Labour/Le Travail* 125

Fasolt, Constantin, *The Limits of History* (Chicago University Press, 2004)

Fassbender, Bardo and Anne Peters (eds.), *The Oxford Handbook of the History of International Law* (Oxford University Press, 2012)

Findlay, PT, *Protest Politics and Psychological Warfare: The Communist Role in the Anti-Vietnam War and Anti-Conscription Movement in Australia* (The Hawthorn Press, 1968)

Firestone, Bernard J, 'Failed Mediation: U Thant, the Johnson Administration, and the Vietnam War' (2013) 37 *Diplomatic History* 1060

Fitzgerald, John, 'Who Cares What They Think? John Winston Howard, William Morris Hughes and the Pragmatic Vision of Australian National Sovereignty' in A Broinowski (ed.), *Double Vision: Asian Accounts of Australia* (ANU E-Press, 2010) 15

Fitzhardinge, LF, *The Little Digger 1914–52: William Morris Hughes, A Political Biography* (Angus & Robertson, 1979) vol 2

Foucault, Michel, *The Birth of Biopolitics: Lectures at the College de France 1978–1979* tr G Burchell (Palgrave Macmillan, 2008)

Foucault, Michel, 'Nietzsche, Genealogy, History' in Paul Rabinow (ed.), *The Foucault Reader* (Pantheon Books, 1984) 76

Frame, Tom, *The Life and Death of Harold Holt* (Allen & Unwin, 2005)

Fraser, Malcolm, *Dangerous Allies* (Melbourne University Press, 2014)

Fraser, Nancy, 'Rethinking the Public Sphere: A Contribution to the Critique of Actually Existing Democracy' (1990) 25/26 *Social Text* 56

Fraser, Nancy, 'Transnationalizing the Public Sphere: On the Legitimacy and Efficacy of Public Opinion in a Post-Westphalian World' European Institute for Progressive Cultural Policies (Article, March 2007) https://eipcp.net/transversal/0605/fraser/en.html

Freeman, Michael and Fiona Smith (eds.), *Law and Language* (Oxford University Press, 2013)

Freudenberg, Graham, 'The Australian Labor Party and Vietnam' (1979) 33 *The Australian Outlook* 157

Friedman, Lawrence, *The Legal System: A Social Science Perspective* (Russell Sage Foundation, 1975)

Friedman, Lawrence M, 'The Concept of Legal Culture: A Reply' in David Nelken (ed.), *Comparing Legal Cultures* (Routledge, 1997) 33

Friedman, Lawrence M, 'The Concept of the Self in Legal Culture' (1990) 38 *Cleveland State Law Review* 517

Friedman, Lawrence M, *The Republic of Choice: Law, Authority, and Culture* (Harvard University Press, 1990)

Friedman, Lawrence M, *Total Justice: What Americans Want from the Legal System and Why* (Russell Sage Foundation, 1985)

Fry, EC, *Tom Barker and the IWW: Oral History* (Australian Society for the Study of Labour History and Industrial Workers of the World, 1965/1999)

Gaita, Raimond, 'Radical Critique, Scepticism and Commonsense' (1991) 29 *Royal Institute of Philosophy Supplement* 157

Gammage, Bill, *The Broken Years: Australian Soldiers in the Great War* (Penguin, 1974)

Garland, David, 'What is a "History of the Present"? On Foucault's Genealogies and their Critical Preconditions' (2014) 16 *Punishment & Society* 365

Garran, Robert, *True Believer: John Howard, George Bush and the American Alliance* (Allen & Unwin, 2004)

Garwood-Gowers, Andrew, 'Pre-Emptive Self-Defence: A Necessary Development or the Road to International Anarchy' (2004) 23 *Australian Year Book of International Law* 51

Gevers, Christopher, 'To Seek with Beauty to set the World Right: Cold War International Law and the Radical "Imaginative Geography" of Pan-Africanism' in Matthew Craven, Sundhya Pahuja and Gerry Simpson (eds.), *International Law and the Cold War* (Cambridge University Press, 2020)

Getachew, Adom, *Worldmaking after Empire: The Rise and Fall of Self-Determination* (Princeton University Press, 2019).

Gleeson, Kathleen, *Australia's 'War on Terror' Discourse* (Routledge, 2014)

Goodrich, Peter, *Languages of Law: From Logics of Memory to Nomadic Masks* (Weidenfeld & Nicholson, 1990)

Goodrich, Peter, 'Law and Language: An Historical and Critical Introduction' (1984) 11 *Journal of Law and Society* 173

Goodrich, Peter, *Reading the Law: A Critical Introduction to Legal Method and Techniques* (Blackwell, 1986)

Goot, Murray and Rodney Tiffen, 'Public Opinion and the Politics of the Polls' in Peter King (ed.), *Australia's Vietnam: Australia in the Second Indo-China War* (Allen & Unwin, 1983) 129

Gordon, Geoff, 'Legal Equality and Innate Cosmopolitanism in Contemporary Discourses of International Law' (2012) 43 *Netherlands Yearbook of International Law* 183

Gordon, Richard and Warren Osmond, 'An Overview of the Australian New Left' in Richard Gordon (ed.), *The Australian New Left: Critical Essays and Strategy* (William Heinemann, 1970) 3

Gordon, Robert W and Morton J Horowitz (eds.), *Law, Society, and History: Themes in the Legal Sociology and Legal History of Lawrence W Friedman* (Cambridge University Press, 2011)

Green, Peter, 'The Great Marathon Man' (online, 15 May 2008) 55(8) *The New York Review of Books*, 33

Gungwu, Wang, 'In Memoriam: Professor C.P. Fitzgerald 1902–1992' (1993) 29 *The Australian Journal of Chinese Affairs* 161

Guyatt, Chris, 'The Anti-Conscription Movement' in Roy Forward and Bob Reece (eds.), *Conscription in Australia* (University of Queensland Press, 1968) 178

Habermas, Jurgen, *Between Facts and Norms: Contributions to a Discourse Theory of Law and Democracy* (MIT Press, 1998)

Habermas, Jurgen, *The Structural Transformation of the Public Sphere: An Inquiry into a Category of Bourgeois Society*, tr Thomas Burger and Frederick Lawrence (MIT Press, 1991)

Hagan, James, *The ACTU: A Short History on the Occasion of the 50th Anniversary 1927–1977* (Reed, 1977)

Hakimi, Monica, 'Defensive Force against Non-State Actors: The State of Play' (2015) 91 *International Law Studies* 1

Hamel-Green, Michael E, 'The Resisters: A History of the Anti-Conscription Movement 1964–72' in Peter King (ed.), *Australia's Vietnam: Australia in the Second Indo-China War* (Allen & Unwin, 1983) 100

Haque, Adil Ahmad, *Law and Morality at War* (Oxford University Press, 2017)

Harris-Hogan, Shandon, 'Remembering the Bali Bombings Ten Years On', The Conversation (online, 12 October 2012)

Hasluck, Paul, *Sir Robert Menzies* (Melbourne University Press, 1980)

Hathaway, Oona, 'What the Chilcot Report Teaches Us About National Security Lawyering', *Just Security* (Forum Post, 11 July 2016)

Hauser, Gerard A, *Vernacular Voices: The Rhetoric of Publics and Public Spheres* (University of South Carolina Press, 1999)

Hearn, Mark, 'Bound with the Empire: Narratives of Race, Nation and Empire in the Australian Labor Party's Defence Policy 1901–21' (2013) 32 *War & Society* 95

Hehir, A and R Murray (eds.), *Libya, the Responsibility to Protect and the Future of Humanitarian Intervention* (Palgrave Macmillan, 2013)

Helmke, Belinda, *Under Attack: Challenges to the Rules Governing the International Use of Force* (Ashgate, 2013)

Henry, Adam, 'Keating: The Man who Discovered Asia?' (2006) 5 *ISAA Review* 21

Hernandez, Gleider I, 'The Responsibility of the International Legal Academic: Situating the Grammarian within the "Invisible College"' in Jean D'Aspremont et al. (eds.), *International Law as a Profession* (Cambridge University Press, 2017) 160

Herodotus, *The Histories*, tr George Rawlinson, Book 4 (*The Internet Classics Archive*) http://classics.mit.edu/Herodotus/history.html

Hirst, JB, 'Australian Defence and Conscription: A Re-Assessment Part I' (1993) 25 *Australian Historical Studies* 608

Holland, Jack, 'Howard's War on Terror: A Conceivable, Communicable and Coercive Foreign Policy Discourse' (2010) 45 *Australian Journal of Political Science* 643

Holland, Jack, *Selling the War on Terror: Foreign Policy Discourses after 9/11* (Taylor and Francis, 2012)

Holland, Jack and Matt McDonald, 'Australian Identity, Interventionism and the "War on Terror"' in Asaf Siniver (ed.), *International Terrorism Post 9/11: Comparative Dynamics and Responses* (Routledge, 2010) 184

Holloway, EJ, *The Australian Victory Over Conscription in 1916-17* (Anti-Conscription Jubilee Committee Melbourne, 1966)

Howard, John, *Lazarus Rising: A Personal and Political Autobiography* (HarperCollins, revised ed., 2013)

Howard, John, *The Menzies Era: The Years that Shaped Modern Australia* (Harper Collins, 2014)

Hull, Isabel V, *A Scrap of Paper: Breaking and Making International Law during the Great War* (Cornell University Press, 2014)

Hunter, Ian, 'Global Justice and Regional Metaphysics: On the Critical History of the Law of Nature and Nations' in Shaunnagh Dorsett and Ian Hunter (eds.), *Law and Politics in British Postcolonial Thought: Transpositions of Empire* (Palgrave MacMillan, 2010) 11

Inglis, KS, 'Conscription in Peace and War, 1911-1945' in Roy Forward and Bob Reece (eds.), *Conscription in Australia* (University of Queensland Press, 1968) 22

Isakhan, Benjamin (ed.), *The Legacy of Iraq: From the 2003 War to the 'Islamic State'* (Cambridge University Press, 2015)

Jackman, Christine, *Inside Kevin07: The Plan, the People, the Prize* (Melbourne University Press, 2008)

Jackson, Richard, *Writing the War on Terrorism: Language, Politics and Counter-Terrorism* (University of Manchester Press, 2005)

Janis, Mark, *America and the Law of Nations 1776-1939* (Oxford University Press, 2010)

Jauncey, LC, *The Story of Conscription in Australia* (MacMillan of Australia, re-issue, 1968)

Johns, Fleur, Richard Joyce and Sundhya Pahuja (eds.), *Events: The Force of International Law* (Routledge, 2010)

Jordens, Ann Mari, 'Conscription and Dissent: The Genesis of Anti War Protest' in Gregory Pemberton (ed.), *Vietnam Remembered* (Weldon, 1990) 60

Joske, Percy, *Sir Robert Menzies 1894-1978: A New, Informal Memoir* (Angus & Robertson, 1978)

Jouannet, Emmanuelle T and Anne Peters, 'The Journal of the History of International Law: A Forum for New Research' (2014) 16 *Journal of the History of International Law* 1

Jury of Conscience, 'Declaration of Jury of Conscience World Tribunal on Iraq: Istanbul 23-27 June 2005' (2005) 81 (1) *Feminist Review* 95-102

Kaplan, Robert D, 'A Historian for Our Time' (Jan/Feb 2007) *The Atlantic Monthly* 78

Kennedy, David, *A World of Struggle: How Power, Law, and Expertise Shape Global Political Economy* (Princeton University Press, 2016)

Kennedy, David, 'Challenging Expert Rule: The Politics of Global Governance' (2005) 27 *Sydney Law Review* 5

Kennedy, David, *International Legal Structures* (Nomos, 1987)

Kennedy, David, 'The Last Treatise: Project and Person (Reflections on Martti Koskenniemi's From Apology to Utopia)' (2006) 7 *German Law Journal* 982

Kennedy, David, 'The Move to Institutions' (1987) 8 *Cardozo Law Review* 841

Kennedy, David, *Of War and Law* (Princeton University Press, 2006)

Kennedy, David, 'Theses about International Law Discourse' (1980) 23 *German Yearbook of International Law* 353

Kennedy, David, 'The Twentieth-Century Discipline of International Law in the United States' in Austin Sarat, Bryant Garth and Robert A Kagan (eds.), *Looking Back at Law's Century* (Cornell University Press, 2002) 386

Kennedy, David, 'When Renewal Repeats: Thinking against the Box' (1999–2000) 32 *New York Journal of International Law and Politics* 335

Kidwai, MHM, 'International Personality and the British Dominions: Evolution and Accomplishment' (1975–76) 9 *University of Queensland Law Journal* 76

Kildea, Jeff, 'Australian Catholics and Conscription in the Great War' (2002) 26 *The Journal of Religious History* 298

Kildea, Jeff, *Tearing the Fabric: Sectarianism in Australia 1910–1925* (Citadel Books, 2002)

Knop, Karen, 'The Tokyo Women's Tribunal and the Turn to Fiction' in Fleur Johns, Richard Joyce and Sundhya Pahuja (eds.), *Events: The Force of International Law* (Routledge, 2010) 145

Knox, Robert, 'Marxist Approaches to International Law' *Oxford Bibliographies in International Law Online*, 28 March 2018

Knox, Robert, 'Marxist Approaches to International Law' in Anne Orford and Florian Hoffman (eds.), *The Oxford Handbook of the Theory of International Law* (Oxford University Press, 2016) 306

Korhonen, Outi, *International Law Situated: An Analysis of the Lawyer's Stance towards Culture, History and Community* (Kluwer law International, 2000)

Korhonen, Outi, 'New International Law: Silences, Defence or Deliverance?' (1996) 7 *European Journal of International Law* 1

Koskenniemi, Martti, *From Apology to Utopia* (Cambridge University Press, 2nd ed., 2006)

Koskenniemi, Martti, *From Apology to Utopia: The Structure of International Legal Argument* (Cambridge University Press, reissue, 2005)

Koskenniemi, Martti, *The Gentle Civilizer of Nations: The Rise and Fall of International Law 1870–1960* (Cambridge University Press, 2001)

Koskenniemi, Martti, 'Histories of International Law: Dealing with Eurocentrism' (2011) 19 *Rechtsgeschichte*

Koskenniemi, Martti, 'Histories of International Law: Significance and Problems for a Critical View' (2013) 27 *Temple International and Comparative Law Journal* 215

Koskenniemi, Martti, 'A History of International Law Histories' in Bardo Fassbender and Anne Peter (eds.), *The Oxford Handbook of the History of International Law* (Oxford University Press, 2012)

Koskenniemi, Martti, *The Politics of International Law* (Hart, 2011)

Koskenniemi, Martti, 'What Should International Lawyers Learn from Karl Marx?' (2004) *Leiden Journal of International Law* 229

Kramer, Larry D, 'The Supreme Court, 2000 Term: Foreword' (2001) 115 *Harvard Law Review* 4

Kramer, Larry D, 'Undercover Anti-Populism' (2005) 73(4) *Fordham Law Review* 1343–44

Kreiger, Heike, 'Populist Governments and International Law' (2019) 30 *The European Journal of International Law* 971

Krever, Tor, 'Dispensing Global Justice' (2014) *New Left Review* 85

Krever, Tor, 'Remembering the Russell Tribunal' (2017) 5 *London Review of International Law* 483

Kritsiotis, Dino, 'Arguments of Mass Confusion' (2004) 15 *European Journal of International Law* 233

Kritsiotis, Dino, 'The Power of International Law as Language' (1997–98) 34 *California Western Law Review* 397

Kuhn, Rick, 'The Australian Left, Nationalism and the Vietnam War' (1997) 72 *Labour History* 163

Lack, John, 'Class or Nation? Worker Loyalties in Melbourne during the Great War' (2015) 86 *Victorian Historical Journal* 141

Lake, Marilyn, *A Divided Society: Tasmania during World War I* (Melbourne University Press, 1975)

Lake, Marilyn, 'British World or New World? Anglo-Saxonism and Australian Engagement with America' (2013) 10 *History Australia* 36

Lake, Marilyn, 'From Mississippi to Melbourne via Natal: The Invention of the Literacy Test as a Technology of Racial Exclusion' in Ann Curthoys and Marilyn Lake (eds.), *Connected Worlds: History in Transnational Perspective* (ANU Press, 2005) 209

Lake, Marilyn and Henry Reynolds, *Drawing the Global Colour Line: White Men's Countries and the International Challenge of Racial Equality* (Cambridge University Press, 2008)

Langley, Greg, *A Decade of Dissent: Vietnam and the Conflict on the Australian Home Front* (Allen & Unwin, 1992)

Lavelle, Ashley, 'Labor and Vietnam: A Reappraisal' (2006) 90 *Labor History* 119

Lee, Peter, *Blair's Just War: Iraq and the Illusion of Morality* (Palgrave Macmillan, 2012)

Lee, Thomas H, 'The Just War Tradition and Natural Law: A Discussion' (2005) 28 *Fordham International Law Journal* 756

Lesaffer, Randall, 'Too Much History: From War as Sanction to the Sanctioning of War' in Marc Weller (ed.), *The Oxford Handbook of the Use of Force in International Law* (Oxford University Press, 2015) 35

Levi, Margaret, 'The Institution of Conscription' (Spring 1996) 20 *Social Science History* 133

Lewis, Malcolm M, 'The International Status of the British Self-Governing Dominions' (1922–23) 3 *British Yearbook of International Law* 21

Limqueco, Peter and Peter Weiss (eds.), *Prevent the Crime of Silence: Reports from the Sessions of the International War Crimes Tribunal Founded by Bertrand Russell* (Allen Lane, 1971)

Linderfalk, Ulf, 'The Functionality of Conceptual Terms in International Law and International Legal Discourse' (2013/14) 6 *European Journal of Legal Studies* 27

Linderfalk, Ulf, 'The Post-9/11 Discourse Revisited: The Self-Image of the International Legal Scientific Discipline' (2010) 2 *Gottingen Journal of International Law* 893

Liste, Philip, 'Articulating the Nexus of Politics and Law: War in Iraq and the Practice within Two Legal Systems' (2008) 2 *International Political Sociology* 38

Liste, Philip, '"Public" International Law? Democracy and Discourses of Legal Reality' (2011) 42 *Netherlands Yearbook of International Law* 177

Lowe, Vaughan, 'The Iraq Crisis: What Now?' (2003) 52 *International and Comparative Law Quarterly* 85

Macintyre, Stuart, *A Concise History of Australia* (Cambridge University Press, 1999) 160

Main, JM, *Conscription: The Australian Debate, 1901–70* (Cassell Australia, 1970)

Mamdani, Mahmood, *Good Muslim, Bad Muslim: America, the Cold War and the Roots of Terror* (Doubleday, 2005)

Mamlyuk, Boris N and Ugo Mattei, 'Comparative International Law' (2011) *Brooklyn Journal of International Law* 386

Marks, Russell, '"1968" in Australia: The Student Movement and the New Left' in Piccini, Smith and Worley (eds.), *The Far Left in Australia since 1945* (Routledge, 2018) 134

Marks, Russell, 'Towards an Intellectual History of the Australian New Left: Some Definitional Problems' (2009) 34 *Melbourne Journal of Politics* 82

Marks, Susan, (ed.), *International Law on the Left: Re-Examining Marxist Legacies* (Cambridge University Press, 2008)

Marr, David and Marian Wilkinson, *Dark Victory: How a Government Lied Its Way to Political Triumph* (Allen & Unwin, 2004)

Martin, AW and Robert Menzies, *A Life, Volume 1 1894–1943* (Melbourne University Press, 1993)

Martin, AW and Robert Menzies, *A Life, Volume 2 1944–1978* (Melbourne University Press, 1999)

Mathew, Pene, 'Resolution 1371: A Call to Pre-Empt Asylum Seekers' (or 'Osama, the Asylum Seeker') in Jane McAdam (ed.), *Forced Migration, Human Rights and Security* (Hart Publishing, 2008) 21

May, Christopher, *The Rule of Law as the Common Sense of Global Politics* (Edward Elgar, 2014)

Mazower, Mark, *Governing the World: The History of an Idea* (Penguin Press, 2012)

Mazower, Mark, *No Enchanted Palace: The End of Empire and the Ideological Origins of the United Nations* (Princeton University Press, 2013)

McAdam, Jane and Kate Purcell, 'Refugee Protection in the Howard Years: Obstructing the Right to Seek Asylum' (2008) 27 *Australian Year Book of International Law* 87

MacDonald, Michael, *Overreach: Delusions of Regime Change in Iraq* (Harvard University Press, 2014)

McCrum, Robert, Robert MacNeil and William Cran, *The Story of English* (Penguin Random House, 3rd revised ed., 2002)

McGraw, David, 'The Howard Government's Foreign Policy: Really Realist?' (2008) 43 *Australian Journal of Political Science* 465

McKernan, Michael, *Australian Churches at War: Attitudes and Activities of the Major Churches 1914–18* (Catholic Theological Faculty, 1980)

McKillen, Elizabeth, *Making the World Safe for Workers: Labor, the Left and Wilsonian Internationalism* (University of Illinois Press, 2013)

McKinley, BJ, 'The Conscription Referenda and the Labor Movement in Geelong' (1968) 14 *Labour History* 59

McLean, David, 'From British Colony to American Satellite? Australia and the USA during the Cold War' (2006) 52 *Australian Journal of Politics and History* 64

McQuilton, John, 'Doing the "Back Block Boys Some Good": The Exemption Court Hearings in North-Eastern Victoria, 1916' (2000) 115 *Australian Historical Studies* 237

Meaney, Neville, *A History of Australian Defence and Foreign Policy, 1901–23. Volume 1, The Search for Security in the Pacific, 1901–14* (Sydney University Press, 2009)

Meaney, Neville, *A History of Australian Defence and Foreign Policy, 1901–23, Volume 2, Australia and World Crisis, 1914–1923* (Sydney University Press, 2009)

Meaney, Neville, 'Britishness and Australian Identity: The Problem of Nationalism in Australian History and Historiography' (2001) 32 *Australian Historical Studies* 76

Meaney, Neville, 'The Problem of Nationalism and Transnationalism in Australian History: A Reply to Marilyn Lake and Christopher Waters' (2015) 12 *History Australia* 209

Meaney, Neville, *The Search for Security in the Pacific 1901-14* (Sydney University Press, 1976)

Merry, Sally Engle, *Getting Justice and Getting Even: Legal Consciousness among Working-Class Americans* (University of Chicago Press, 1990)

Merry, Sally Engle, *Human Rights and Gender Violence: Translating International Law into Local Justice* (University of Chicago Press, 2006)

Mertz, Elizabeth, 'Language, Law and Social Meanings: Linguistic/Anthropological Contributions to the Study of Law' (1992) 26(2) *Law & Society Review* 413

Mieville, China, *Between Equal Rights: A Marxist Theory of International Law* (Brill, 2005)

Minow, Martha, Michael Ryan and Austin Sarat (eds.), *Narrative, Violence and the Law: The Essays of Robert Cover* (University of Michigan Press, 1983)

Mori, Tadashi, *Origins of the Right of Self-Defence in International Law: From the Caroline Incident to the United Nations Charter* (Brill/Nijhoff, 2018) 25-40

Moses, John A, 'Australian Anglican Leaders and the Great War 1914-18: The "Prussian Menace", Conscription and National Solidarity' (2001) 25 *The Journal of Religious History* 306

Mowbray, Jacqueline, *Linguistic Justice: International Law and Language Policy* (Oxford University Press, 2012)

Moyn, Samuel, 'From Antiwar Politics to Antitorture Politics' in Austin Sarat, Lawrence Douglas and Martha Merrill Umphrey (eds.), *Law and War* (Stanford University Press, 2014) 154

Moyn, Samuel, *Not Enough: Human Rights in an Unequal World* (Harvard University Press, 2018)

Mulholland, Marc, '"Marxists of Strict Observance?" The Second International, National Defence, and the Question of War' (2015) 58 *Historical Journal* 615

Murav, Harriet, 'Narrative and Rhetoric' in Austin Sarat, Matthew Anderson and Cathrine O Frank (eds.), *Law and the Humanities: An Introduction* (Cambridge University Press, 2009) 377

Murphy, DJ, 'Religion, Race and Conscription in World War I' (1974) 20 *Australian Journal of Politics and History* 155

Murphy, John, *Harvest of Fear: A History of Australia's Vietnam War* (Allen & Unwin, 1993)

Murphy, Kate, '"In the Backblocks of Capitalism": Australian Student Activism in the Global 1960s' (2015) 46 *Australian Historical Studies* 252

Neff, Stephen C, *War and the Law of Nations: A General History* (Cambridge University Press, 2005)

Noone, Val, *Disturbing the War: Melbourne Catholics and Vietnam* (Spectrum, 1993)

Novak, Michael, 'A Just War: Was the War in Iraq Just?' (2004) 9 *Nexus, A Journal of Opinion* 11

O'Connell, DP, 'The Evolution of Australia's International Personality' in DP O'Connell (ed.), *International Law in Australia* (Lawbook, 1965) 1

O'Connell, Mary Ellen, 'Peace and War' in Bardo Fassbender and Anne Peters (eds.), *The Oxford Handbook of the History of International Law* (Oxford University Press, 2012) 272

O'Driscoll, Cian, 'Re-Negotiating the Just War: The Invasion of Iraq and Punitive War' (2006) 19 *Cambridge Review of International Affairs* 405

O'Farrell, Patrick, 'Foreword' in LC Jauncey (ed.), *The Story of Conscription in Australia* (MacMillan of Australia, re-issue, 1968) xiii

Oppenheim, Lassa, *International Law: A Treatise* (Longmans, 1912)

Orford, Anne, 'A Journal of the Voyage from Apology to Utopia' (2006) 7 *German Law Journal* 993

Orford, Anne, *International Authority and the Responsibility to Protect* (Cambridge University Press, 2011)

Orford, Anne, 'On International Legal Method' (2013) 1 *London Review of International Law* 166

Orford, Anne, *Reading Humanitarian Intervention: Human Rights and the Use of Force in International Law* (Cambridge University Press, 2003)

Orford, Anne, 'The Past as Law or as History? The Relevance of Imperialism for Modern International Law', *International Law and Justice Working Papers* 2012/2, New York University School of Law

Painter, Genevieve, 'A Letter from the Haudenosaunee Confederacy to King George V: Writing and Reading Jurisdictions in International Legal History' (2017) *London Review of International Law* 7

Parfitt, Rose, 'The Anti-Neutral Suit: International Legal Futurists, 1914–2017' (2017) 5 *London Review of International Law* 87

Parfitt, Rose, *The Process of International Legal Reproduction: Subjectivity, Historiography, Law, Violence* (Cambridge University Press, 2019)

Payne, Trish, *War and Words: The Australian Press and the Vietnam War* (Melbourne University Press, 2007)

Pedersen, Susan, *The Guardians: The League of Nations and the Crisis of Empire* (Oxford University Press, 2015)

Peevers, Charlotte, 'Media Spectacles of Legal Accountability in the Reporting of an Official History' (2018) 87 *The British Yearbook of International Law* 231

Peevers, Charlotte, *The Politics of Justifying Force: The Suez Crisis, the Iraq War and International Law* (Oxford University Press, 2013)

Pemberton, Gregory, *All the Way: Australia's Road to Vietnam* (Allen & Unwin, 1987)

Pether, Penelope, 'Language' in Austin Sarat, Matthew Anderson and Cathrine O Frank (eds.), *Law and the Humanities: An Introduction* (Cambridge University Press, 2009) 315

Piccini, Jon, *Transnational Protest, Australia and the 1960s* (Palgrave McMillan, 2016)

Piccini, Jon, Evan Smith and Matthew Worley (eds.), *The Far Left In Australia since 1945* (Routledge, 2018)

Porter, Elisabeth, 'No Just War: Political Reflections on Australian Churches' Condemnation of the Iraq War' (2006) 52 *Australian Journal of Politics and History* 471

Porter, Robert, *Paul Hasluck: A Political Biography* (UWA Press, 1993)

Purcell, Kate, 'On the Uses and Advantages of Genealogy for International Law' (2019) *Leiden Journal of International Law* 1

Rajagopal, Balakrishnan, 'Martti Koskenniemi's From Apology to Utopia: A Reflection' (2006) 7 *German Law Journal* 1089

Rajah, Jothie, *Authoritarian Rule of Law: Legislation, Discourse and Legitimacy in Singapore* (Cambridge University Press, 2012)

Rajkovic, Nikolas M, Tanja Aalberts and Thomas Gammeltoft-Hansen, *The Power of Legality: Practices of International Law and their Politics* (Cambridge University Press, 2016)

Rasulov, Akbar, '"The Nameless Rapture of the Struggle": Towards a Marxist Class-Theoretic Approach to International Law' (2008) 19 *Finnish Yearbook of International Law* 243

Regan, Richard J, *Just War: Principles and Cases* (Catholic University of America Press, 2nd ed., 2013)

Reichman, Ravit, 'Narrative and Rhetoric' in Austin Sarat, Matthew Anderson and Cathrine O Frank (eds.), *Law and the Humanities: An Introduction* (Cambridge University Press, 2009) 377

Reisman, Michael and Andrew Armstrong, 'The Past and Future of the Claim of Preemptive Self-Defense' (2006) *Yale Law School Faculty Scholarship Series* 957

Roberts, Jennifer T, *Herodotus: A Very Short Introduction* (Oxford University Press, 2011)

Roberts-Wray, Sir Kenneth, *Commonwealth and Colonial Law* (Stevens & Sons, 1966)

Robertson, Alec, 'CPA in the Anti-War Movement' (Oct–Nov 1970) *Australian Left Review* 39

Rothwell, Donald R and Emily Crawford (eds.), *International Law in Australia* (Thomson Reuters, 2017)

Rudolphy, Marcela Prieto, 'Populist Governments and International Law: A Reply to Heike Krieger (2019) 30 *The European Journal of International Law* 997

Ruskola, Teemu, 'Where is Asia? When is Asia? Theorizing Comparative Law and International Law' (2010–11) 44 *UC Davis Law Review* 879

Russell, Lani, 'Today the Students, Tomorrow the Workers! Radical Student Politics and the Australian Labour Movement 1960–72' (PhD Thesis, University of Technology Sydney, 1999)

Sammut, Jeremy, 'The Long Demise of the White Australia Policy' (November 2005) 49(11) *Quadrant* 34

Sands, Philippe, 'A Grand and Disastrous Deceit' (online, 28 July 2016) 38(15) *London Review of Books* 9

Sands, Philippe, *Lawless World: American and the Making and Breaking of Global Rules* (Allen Lane, 2005)

Santamaria, BA, *Daniel Mannix: The Quality of Leadership* (Melbourne University Press, 1984)

Sarat, Austin, Matthew Anderson and Cathrine O Frank (eds.), *Law and the Humanities: An Introduction* (Cambridge University Press, 2014)

Saunders, Malcolm, 'The ALP's Response to the Anti-Vietnam War Movement: 1965–73' (1983) 44 *Labour History* 75

Saunders, Malcolm, '"Law and Order" and the Anti-Vietnam War Movement: 1965–72' (1982) 28 *Australian Journal of Politics and History* 367

Saunders, Malcolm J, 'The Trade Unions in Australia and Opposition to Vietnam and Conscription: 1965–73' (1982) 43 *Labour History* 64

Saunders, Malcolm, 'The Vietnam Moratorium Movement in Australia 1969–1973' (PhD Thesis, Flinders University, 1977)

Saunders, Malcolm and Ralph Summy, 'One Hundred Years of an Australian Peace Movement, 1885–1984: Part I: From the Sudan Campaign to the Outbreak of the Second World War' (1984) 10 *Peace & Change* 39

Saunders, Malcolm and Ralph Summy, 'One Hundred Years of an Australian Peace Movement, 1885–1984: Part II: From the Second World War to Vietnam and Beyond' (1984) 10 *Peace & Change* 57

Schmidt, Christopher W, 'Conceptions of Law in the Civil Rights Movement' (2011) 1(3) *UC Irvine Law Review* 641

Schwobel-Patel, Christine, 'Populism, International Law and the End of Keep Calm and Carry On Lawyering' (2018) 49 *Netherlands Yearbook of International Law* 97

Scobbie, Iain, 'Towards the Elimination of International Law: Some Radical Scepticism about Sceptical Radicalism' (1990) 61 *British Yearbook of International Law* 339

Scott, Ernest, *Official History of Australia in the War of 1914–18: Australia during the War* (Angus and Robertson, 1936) vol 11

Scott, Shirley V, 'The Political Life of Public International Lawyers: Granting the Imprimatur' (2007) 21 *International Relations* 411

Scott, Shirley V and Olivia Ambler, 'Does Legality Really Matter? Accounting for the Decline in US Foreign Policy Legitimacy following the 2003 Invasion of Iraq' (2007) 13 *European Journal of International Relations* 67

Shamir, Ronen and Dana Weiss, 'Semiotics of Indicators: The Case of Corporate Human Rights Responsibility' in Kevin Davis et al. (eds.), *Governance by Indicators: Global Power through Quantification and Rankings* (Oxford University Press, 2012)

Sifris, Ronli, 'Operation Iraqi Freedom: United States v Iraq' (2003) 4 *Melbourne Journal of International Law* 521

Silbey, Susan S, 'Legal Culture and Cultures of Legality' in John R Hall, Laura Grindstaff and Ming-Cheng Lo (eds.), *Handbook of Cultural Sociology* (Routledge, 2010) 473

Simpson, Gerry, *Great Powers and Outlaw States: Unequal Sovereigns in the International Legal Order* (Cambridge University Press, 2004)

Simpson, Gerry, *Law, War and Crime* (Polity Press, 2007)

Simpson, Gerry, '"Stop Calling it Aggression": War as Crime (2008) 61(1) *Current Legal Problems* 191

Simpson, Gerry, 'The War in Iraq and International Law' (2005) 6 *Melbourne Journal of International Law* 167

Simpson, Gerry, 'Warriors, Humanitarians, Lawyers: The Howard Government and the Use of Force' (2008) 27 *Australian Yearbook of International Law* 143

Skinner, Quentin, 'Meaning and Understanding in the History of Ideas' (1969) 8 *History and Theory* 3

Skouteris, Thomas, *The Notion of Progress in International Law Discourse* (TMC Asser Press, 2010)

Sluga, Glenda, *Internationalism in the Age of Nationalism* (University of Pennsylvania Press, 2013)

Smart, Judith, 'The Right to Speak and the Right to Be Heard: The Popular Disruption of Conscriptionist Meetings in Melbourne 1916' (1989) 23 *Australian Historical Studies* 203

Smith, Fiona, 'Power, Rules and the WTO' (2013) 53 *Boston College Law Review* 1063

Sökmen, Müge Gürsoy (ed.), *World Tribunal on Iraq: Making the Case against War* (Olive Branch Press, 2008)

Stanley, Laura and Phillip Deery, 'The Menzies Government, the American Alliance and the Cuban Missile Crisis' (2013) *Australian Journal of Politics and History* 178

Stephens, Tim, 'International Courts and Sustainable Development: Using Old Tools to Shape a New Discourse' in Kim Rubenstein and Brad Jessup (eds.), *Environmental Discourses in Public and International Law* (Cambridge University Press, 2012) 195

Stock, Jenny Tilby, 'Farmers and the Rural Vote in South Australia in World War I: The 1916 Conscription Referendum' (1985) 21 *Historical Studies* 391

Storr, Cait, *International Status in the Shadow of Empire: Nauru and the Histories of International Law* (Cambridge University Press, 2020)

Storr, Cait, '"Imperium in Imperio": Sub-Imperialism and the Formation of Australia as a Subject of International Law' (2018) 19 *Melbourne Journal of International Law* 335

Strangio, Paul, *Keeper of the Faith: A Biography of Jim Cairns* (Melbourne University Press, 2002)

Strawson, John, 'Provoking International Law: War and Regime Change in Iraq' in Fleur Johns, Richard Joyce and Sundhya Pahuja (eds.), *Events: The Force of International Law* (Routledge, 2010) 246

Summy, Ralph V, 'A Reply to Fred Wells' in Roy Forward and Bob Reece (eds.), *Conscription in Australia* (University of Queensland Press, 1968) 200

Summy, Ralph, 'Militancy and the Australian Peace Movement 1960–67' (1970) 5 *Australian Journal of Political Science* 148

Sunstein, Cass R, 'If People Would Be Outraged by Their Rulings, Should Judges Care?' (2007) 60 *Stanford Law Review* 155

Suskind, Ron, *The Price of Loyalty: George W Bush, the White House, and the Education of Paul O'Neill* (Simon & Schuster, 2004)

Sweeney, Joseph C, 'The Just War Ethic in International Law' (2004) 27 *Fordham International Law Journal* 1865

Teitel, Ruti, 'Humanity's Law: Rule of Law for the New Global Politics' (2002) 35 *Cornell International Law Journal* 355

Tallgren, Immi, 'The Sensibility and Sense of International Criminal Law' (2002) 13 *European Journal of International Law* 561

Terracini, Paul, *John Stoward Moyes and the Social Gospel: A Study in Christian Social Engagement* (Xlibris AU, 2015)

Terracini, Paul, 'Moyes, Menzies, and the Vietnam War: New Insights into the Public Correspondence between the Prime Minister and the Bishops' (2012) 36 *Journal of Religious History* 70

Thomas, Rosalind, 'Introduction' in Robert B Strassler (ed.), *The Landmark Herodotus: The Histories* (First Anchor Books, 2009) ix

Thorpe, Wayne, 'The European Syndicalists and War, 1914–1918' (2001) 10 *Contemporary European History* 1

Thucydides, *History of the Peloponnesian War*, tr Rex Warner (Penguin Classics, 1974)

Tiefenbrun, Susan, *Decoding International Law* (Oxford University Press, 2010)

Tiersma, Peter, *Legal Language* (University of Chicago Press, 1999)

Tiffen, Rodney, 'The War the Media Lost: Australian News Coverage of Vietnam' in Gregory Pemberton (ed.), *Vietnam Remembered* (Weldon, 1990) 110

Tomlins, Christopher and John Comaroff, '"Law As . . . ": Theory and Practice in Legal History' (2011) 1 *UC Irvine Law Review* 1039

Toope, Stephen J, 'Public Commitment to International Law: Canadian and British Media Perspectives on the Use of Force' in Christopher PM Waters (ed.), *British and Canadian Perspectives on International Law* (Brill, 2006) 17

Tuck, Richard, 'History of Political Thought' in Peter Burke (ed.), *New Perspectives on Historical Writing* (Pennsylvania State University Press, 2001) 218

Twomey, Anne, 'International Law and the Executive' in Brian R Opeskin and Donald R Rothwell (eds.), *International Law and Australian Federalism* (Melbourne University Press, 1997) 69

Turner, Ian, *Sydney's Burning* (Alpha Books, 1967)
Vaypan, Grigory, 'Choosing among the Shades of Nuance: The Discourse of Proportionality in International Law' (2015) 15 *Global Jurist* 237
Venzke, Ingo, *How Interpretation Makes International Law: On Semantic Change and Normative Twists* (Oxford University Press, 2012)
Walker, Bertha, *How to Defeat Conscription: A Story of the 1916 and 1917 Campaigns in Victoria* (Anti-Conscription Jubilee Committee Melbourne, 1968) 10
Wallensteen, Peter and Patrick Johansson, 'Security Council Decisions in Perspective' in David Malone (ed.), *The UN Security Council: From the Cold War to the 21st Century* (Lynne Rienne, 2004) 17
Walzer, Michael, *Just and Unjust Wars: A Moral Argument with Historical Illustrations* (Basic Books, 5th ed., 2015)
Ward, Stuart, *Australia and the British Embrace: The Demise of the Imperial Ideal* (Melbourne University Press, 2001)
Waters, Christopher, 'A Reply to Neville Meaney' (2015) 12 *History Australia* 232
Waters, Christopher, 'Nationalism, Britishness and Australian History: The Meaney Thesis Revisited' (2013) 10 *History Australia* 12
Watt, Alan, *Vietnam: An Australian Analysis* (FW Cheshire, 1968)
Weeks, Albert L, *The Choice of War: The Iraq War and the Just War Tradition* (Praeger Security International, 2010)
Weller, Mark (ed.), *The Oxford Handbook of the Use of Force in International Law* (Oxford University Press, 2015)
Wells, Fred, 'A Comment on Mr Guyatt's Chapter' in Roy Forward and Bob Reece (eds.), *Conscription in Australia* (University of Queensland Press, 1968) 191
Werner, Wouter G, 'The Curious Career of Lawfare' (2010) 43 *Case Western Reserve Journal of International Law* 61
White, Craig M, *Iraq: The Moral Reckoning: Applying Just War Theory to the 2003 War Decision* (Lexington Book, 2010)
White, James Boyd, *The Legal Imagination: Studies in the Nature of Legal Thought and Expression* (Little Brown and Co, abridged ed, 1973)
Whyte, Jessica, *The Morals of the Market: Human Rights and the Rise of Neoliberalism* (Verso, 2019)
Wilf, Steven, *Law's Imagined Republic: Popular Politics and Criminal Justice in Revolutionary America* (Cambridge University Press, 2010)
Wilkie, Andrew, *Axis of Deceit: The Extraordinary Story of an Australian Whistleblower* (Black Inc Agenda, 2nd ed., 2010)
Williams, George, 'A Decade of Australian Anti-Terror Laws' (2011) 35 *Melbourne University Law Review* 1136
Williams, Paul D, 'Holt, Johnson and the 1966 Federal Election: A Question of Causality' (2001) 47 *Australian Journal of Politics and History* 366
Wilson, Richard Ashby and Richard D Brown (eds.), *Humanitarianism and Suffering: The Mobilization of Empathy* (Cambridge University Press, 2009)

Windschuttle, Keith, *The White Australia Policy* (Macleay Press, 2004)

Withers, Glenn, 'The 1916–17 Conscription Referenda: A Cliometric Re-Appraisal' (1982) 20 *Historical Studies* 36

Witt, John Fabian, *Lincoln's Code: The Laws of War in American History* (Free Press, 2012)

Woodward, Bob, *Plan of Attack: The Definitive Account of the Decision to Invade Iraq* (Simon & Schuster, 2004)

Woodard, Garry, *Asian Alternatives: Australia's Vietnam Decision and Lessons on Going to War* (Melbourne University Press, 2004)

Yasuaki, Onuma, 'When was the Law of International Society Born? An Inquiry of the History of International Law from an Intercivilizational Perspective' (2000) 2 *Journal of the History of International Law* 1

York, Barry, 'The Australian Anti-Vietnam Movement, 1965–73' (1983) 15 *Melbourne Journal of Politics* 24

Yost, Charles W, 'The United Nations: Crisis of Confidence and Will' (1966) 45 *Foreign Affairs* 19

Zachmann, Urs Matthias, 'Race and International Law in Japan's New Order in East Asia, 1938–1945' in Rotem Kowner and Walter Demel (eds.), *Race and Racism in Modern East Asia: Western and Eastern Constructions* (Brill, 2013) 453

Zifcak, Spencer, 'The Responsibility to Protect after Libya and Syria' (2012) 13 *Melbourne Journal of International Law* 59

Zines, Leslie, 'The Growth of Australian Nationhood and Its Effect on the Powers of the Commonwealth' in Leslie Zines (ed.), *Commentaries on the Australian Constitution* (Butterworths, 1977) 1

Websites

Australian Dictionary of Biography http://adb.anu.edu.au/
Australian War Memorial www.awm.gov.au/
Australians for War Powers Reform www.warpowersreform.org.au/
Iraq Body Count www.iraqbodycount.org/
Just Security www.justsecurity.org/
Lawfare www.lawfareblog.com/
National Archives of Australia, *Australia's Prime Ministers* http://primeministers.naa.gov.au/
Newspoll www.theaustralian.com.au/national-affairs/newspoll
John Menadue: Pearls and Irritations https://johnmenadue.com/blog/?p=4440

INDEX

accountability
  peoples' tribunals, 21
aggression
  Iraq War, 8, 61
  Vietnam War, 101–2, 108, 110, 112, 118, 122, 124, 126, 177
alliance policy
  ANZUS Treaty. *see* ANZUS Treaty
  Iraq War debates (2003)
    Australian Council of Trade Unions (ACTU), 83
    collective justification for war, 15, 81–84
    foreign policy agenda, 44, 47–50, 81–84, 86
  Vietnam War debates (1965–66), 95–96, 110–11, 113–14, 128–30, 132–33, 180
ANZUS Treaty
  Iraq War, 83–84
  Vietnam War, 111, 112–16
  see also alliance policy
Asquith, Herbert Henry (UK Prime Minister), 140, 141
Association for International Co-operation and Disarmament (AICD), 100, 123
asylum seekers
  Tampa affair, 46–47
Australia, New Zealand and United States Collective Security Treaty. *see* ANZUS Treaty
Australian Council of Trade Unions (ACTU), 81, 85, 86, 99
  humanitarian consequences of war argument, 71–77, 87
  pre-emptive self-defence argument, 71–77
  US–Australian alliance, 83

Australian Education Union (AEU)
  Iraq War debates (2003), 43, 62–64
  see also Durbridge, Rob (federal secretary of Australian Education Union)
Australian nationhood, 12–13, 17
Australia's international status
  Dominion law, 138–41
  lack of, 149–50, 151
  limited foreign affairs power, 140
  support for Britain's war effort, 141
  see also Australia's relationship with the British Empire
Australia's relationship with the British Empire, 138, 139, 149, 170, 173
  Hughes' Manifesto for Conscription, 160–62
  Mannix on conscription, 162–64
autonomous justification for war, 3, 15, 91, 131, 175, 177
  collective justifications for war compared, 85–86
  legality requirement, 15–16, 41–42, 43, 57, 64, 70, 85, 149, 152, 170, 177–78, 181
  shift from collective justification, 181–82

Bali terrorist attacks, 51
Barker, Tom (Industrial Workers of the World (IWW)), 165–70, 172–73
bishops' objections to the Vietnam War
  adherence to Geneva Accords, 109, 130
  exchange of letters with Menzies, 108–12
  international legal language, use of, 109–10

INDEX

US commitment to refrain use of force, 109
see also religious groups
Blair, Tony (UK Prime Minister), 4, 8, 63
   Camp David summit, 57
   just war, 79
Blix, Hans, 52
Bush, George W (US President), 8, 43
   Australian alignment with, 47–50, 86
   Camp David summit, 57
   just war, 79

Cairns, Jim (MP for the Labor Party), 93, 99, 120
   legal justification for intervention in Vietnam, 116, 117–18, 121
   moratorium movement, 107
   treaty obligations under SEATO, 116, 118–19, 122, 130, 132
Calwell, Arthur (Labor Party leader), 97, 99, 104, 105, 113
Cambodia, 96
Catholic Bishops of Australia
   Iraq War debates (2003), 43, 77, 78–81
   see also religious groups
Charter of the United Nations (UN Charter), 12, 135
   Iraq War, 51
      prohibition on the use of force (Art. 2(4)), 41
      recognition of a state's 'inherent' right to self-defence (Art. 51), 41, 73
      regulation of use of force, 133
      Vietnam War, 16, 89, 107, 110, 112, 125, 133, 182
      conflict of obligations, 117
Chilcot, John
   Iraq Inquiry Report, 2016 (UK), 3–6
civil liberties debate
   conscription, 157–60
   freedom debate, 159–60
   World War I debates (1916), 17, 138, 149, 157–60, 164, 170–71

class, 138, 175
   language of class
      'equality-of-sacrifice' argument, 165–70, 172
      First World War I debate (1916), 165–70
collective justification for war
   aggression, 15
   autonomous justifications for war compared, 86
   humanitarianism, 15, 72, 74–77
   see also humanitarian consequences of war
   international law as a standard of morality, 15
   see also international law as a standard of morality; morality
   just war doctrine, 15
   see also just war
   language, 15
   see also language of international law; language of morality
   self-defence, 15, 84
      pre-emptive self-defence argument, 72–74
      see also pre-emptive self-defence; self-defence argument
   shift to autonomous justification, 181–82
   support for an alliance, 15, 81–84
colonial nationalism, 17, 139, 142, 149, 151, 156, 164, 168, 171, 172
   see also White Australia
competent international legal argument
   First World War I debates (1916), 171
   Iraq War debates (2003), 3, 85
      Durbridge's January 2003 speech, 62–64
   language of international law, 2, 15–16, 25, 33–34, 36, 178–79
   Vietnam War debates (1965–66), 131
conscription, 92
   civil liberties debate, 157–60
   equality of sacrifice, 171

conscription (cont.)
  First World War I debates, 135–36
  No-Conscription Council of New South Wales, 153–57
  opposition to, 144–46
  religious groups, 144–45
  Universal Service League, 137, 144
  Vietnam War, 92, 96–97, 106
  White Australia Anti-Conscription Manifesto, 153–57, 170
conscription referendums, 137, 143–47, 152
Cook, Joseph (Australian Prime Minister), 141
Crean, Simon (leader of Australian Labor Party), 59–60
crimes against humanity, 127
  Iraq War as, 7–8
  Vietnam War, 126

Defence Act 1903 (Cth), 135, 142–44, 150, 152, 156
'domino theory', 96, 107
Downer, Alexander (Australian Minister for Foreign Affairs), 43, 85
  September 2002 speech, 47, 49, 57, 71, 76, 82, 85
  international law as a standard, 61
  Iraq's failure to comply with Security Council resolutions, 59
  Iraqi involvement with international terrorism, 59
  language of international law, 59
  legality, 60
Durbridge, Rob (federal secretary of Australian Education Union), 175
  January 2003 speech, 86
  humanitarian consequences of war, 62–64
  pre-emptive self-defence, 63
  role of the UN, 62
  see also Australian Education Union (AEU)

duty to empire. see Australia's relationship with the British Empire

Eurocentrism of international law, 11, 13

fetishisation of law, 181
First World War. see World War I debates (1916)
Fisher, Andrew (Australian Prime Minister), 141
foregrounding of legal expertise
  Iraq War debates (2003), 64–71, 86
  Vietnam War debates (1965–66), 132

Geneva Accords (1954), 90, 109, 110, 117, 122, 123–24, 130
Gorton, John (Australian Prime Minister), 92, 107

Hague Peace Conference (1899), 135
Hague Peace Conference (1907), 135
Hasluck, Paul (Australian Minister for External Affairs), 92, 96, 118–19, 120, 132
Herodotus, 9–10, 73, 184
Hill, Robert (Australian Defence Minister), 47, 50, 57, 82, 83
Holt, Harold (Australian Prime Minister), 93, 95, 102–3, 116, 128, 131, 132
home defence and overseas service distinguished, 142–43, 150, 152
Howard, John (Australian Prime Minister), 43, 44, 85, 132, 175, 182
  ABC television interview (18 March 2003), 64–71
  accountability, lack of, 55–56
  Address to the Nation (20 March 2003), 55, 81–84
  foreign policy agenda, 44
    elimination of outside threats, 44
    US–Australian alliance, 44, 47–50, 81–84, 86

Hughes, William Morris (Australian
    Prime Minister), 137, 141,
    158, 175
  Manifesto for Conscription, 160–62
  White Australia regime, 155–57
humanitarian consequences of war,
    44, 85
  Iraq War debates (2003)
    just war debate, 77–81
    pre-emption debate, 71–77

Immigration Restriction Act 1901
    (Cth), 153
imperialism, 129–30
Indonesia, 95, 96, 97
Industrial Workers of the World
    (IWW), 182
  Barker
    equality-of-sacrifice argument,
      165–70
'insurance policy', 96, 107
international law as a legal standard of
    humanity, 9, 16, 121, 124
international law as a standard of
    morality, 121, 132
  aggression and self-defence, 123–26
  collective justification for war, 15
  immorality and illegality in the
    means and methods, 126–28
  self-determination as a moral
    obligation, 121–22
international law as the 'law of
    nations', 136
international law, nature of, 1
international legal history, 36–40
international solidarity, 44, 86, 130,
    132–33, 181, 184
interpretation of UNSC resolutions, 52
Iraq War, 52–54, 84, 119
Iraq Inquiry (UK, 2016)
  criticisms, 5
  formalist view of international
    law, 5–6
  legality of the war, 3–6
  monologic nature, 10
Iraq War debates (2003), 16
  alliance policy, 15, 44, 47–50, 81–84,
    86, 180

Australian Education Union (AEU),
    43, 62–64
Australian Government support, 43
competence of public speakers,
    62–64
context, 42–44
foregrounding of legal expertise,
    64–71, 86
just war, 77–81
legal language and legality, 57–62
legality of the use of force, 1
moral legitimacy of pre-emptive self
    defence, 78
just war, 78
pre-emptive self-defence, 49, 63–64,
    71–77, 84
public and political speakers' use of
    legal language, 64–71
religious debate, 43, 77, 78–81
weapons of mass destruction debate,
    48–50

Johnson, Lyndon (US President), 104,
    112, 123–24, 125
juridification of politics, 181
jury of conscience
  Iraq War, 7
jus ad bellum, 127
jus in bello, 126–28, 134
just war, 15, 73, 74, 85–86, 125
  humanitarianism, 44, 78–80, 177
  Iraq War debates (2003), 77–81
  moral legitimacy of pre-emptive
    self defence, 78
  legality in the use of force, 80–81
  Vietnam War, 124–26

language of international law, 2, 15,
    25–26, 175
  competent international legal
    argument, 34
  duty to the British Empire, 164
    Hughes, 160–62
    Mannix, 162–64
  external discourse and internal
    determinations of
    governments, 29
  grammar of international law, 27–28

INDEX

language of international law (cont.)
  Iraq War debates (2003), 85
    conflagration of 'law' and 'legality', 65
    Downer's September 2002 speech, 57–62
    foregrounding of legal expertise, 65
    public and political speakers use of legal language, 64–71
  structuralism, 26–27, 33–36
  Vietnam War debates (1965–66), 131–33
  World War I debates (1916), 136
language of morality, 182
intervention in a civil war, 122
Laos, 94–95
law and politics, tensions between, 8
law as a 'quibble', 138, 149–52
law of nations, 139
  Dominion law, 138–41
League of Nations, 12, 35, 136, 148, 169, 172
legal advice
  legality of Iraq War, 53
    Blair Government, 4, 5
    Howard Government, 53, 65, 66–69, 119
  see also legality of war; professional expertise
legal cultures
  external and internal, 31–32
legality of war
  Iraq Inquiry Report, 2016 (UK), 3–6
  Iraq War, 41–42, 182
  pre-WWI, 134, 148, 149
  World War I debate (1916)
    Australia's lack of international legal status, 149–50
    government's power to conscript, 150–51
  see also legal advice

Malaysia, 95, 96, 97
Mannix, Daniel (Catholic Archbishop of Melbourne), 138, 145, 175
  conscription, 162–64
  see also religious groups

Menzies, Robert (Australian Prime Minister), 92, 94, 95–102, 132, 175
  alliance policy, 128–29
  exchange of letters with Anglican bishops, 108–12
  justifications for intervention in Vietnam, 112–13, 131
  legality of Vietnam War, 115–16
  speech (29 April 1965), 112
  speech (4 May 1965), 112–13
morality
  international law as a standard of morality, 121, 132
  aggression and self-defence, 123–26
  collective justification for war, 15
  immorality and illegality in the means and methods, 126–28
  self-determination as a moral obligation, 121–22
  moral legitimacy of pre-emptive self defence, 78
  morality or religion as justifications for war
    Iraq invasion, 65, 78, 80–81, 87–88
    Vietnam War, 109–10
  see also just war
moratorium movement, 92, 93, 107
Moyes, Rev. John, 108, 125, 130
My Lai massacre, 127
9/11 terrorist attacks, impact of, 45

Nixon, Richard (US President), 92
No-Conscription Council of New South Wales, 154–57

O'Brien, Kerry (ABC TV), 64–71, 82, 85, 87, 175, 176

peoples' tribunals, 7, 20
  accountability aim, 21
  criticisms, 21–22
  de-centralisation of state, 21
  galvanising popular opinion, 21, 180
Political Labor Council (PLC), 175
  Anti-Conscription Manifesto, 157–58

politicians
  use of international law in public debate, 2, 18, 30, 32–33
popular constitutionalism, 19–22
popular international law, 14, 19–22, 174
  autonomous language of legality, 177–78
  collective language of legality, 177
  speakers of international legal language, 174–77
popular law, 19
pre-emptive self-defence, 44
  Iraq War debates (2003), 49, 63–64, 71–77, 84
  moral legitimacy, 78
  see also self-defence argument
professional expertise, 119
  rejection of, 6, 9
  see also legal advice
public debate, concept and role, 23
  argument and persuasion, 23–24
  emergence and evolution in relation to international law, 1–3
  role of the state, 24

racial discrimination, 12, 45, 153–54, 155
religious groups
  Iraq War debates (2003), 45
    Catholic Bishops of Australia, 43, 78–81, 87
    just war arguments, 77–81, 87
  use of international law in public debate, 2, 18
  Vietnam War debates (1965–66), 124–26
  see also bishops' objections to the Vietnam War; Catholic Bishops of Australia; Mannix, Daniel (Catholic Archbishop of Melbourne); Ryan, Tighe (editor of *The Catholic Press*)
right to self-determination, 108, 110, 117, 121, 122, 124, 129
  Vietnam War debates (1965–66), 121–22

Russell Tribunals, 20
Ryan, Tighe (editor of *The Catholic Press*), 138, 150, 163
  see also religious groups

SEATO Treaty, 119. see South East Asian Treaty Organization obligations
Security Council Resolution 1441, 4, 5, 51, 52, 53, 68, 119
  see also interpretation of UNSC resolutions; United Nations Security Council
Security Council Resolution 678, 53, 66, 68
  see also interpretation of UNSC resolutions; United Nations Security Council
Security Council Resolution 687, 53, 66, 68
  see also interpretation of UNSC resolutions; United Nations Security Council
self-defence argument, 15, 41
  Vietnam War, 89, 121–22, 123, 124, 177
  see also pre-emptive self-defence
self-determination. see right to self-determination
South East Asian Treaty Organization obligations
  Vietnam War, 90, 95, 111, 112–16, 118–20
sovereignty, 45
  Australian, 45
  Vietnam. see right to self-determination
speakers of international legal language, 174
  political speakers, 32–33, 64–71
  popular international law, 174–77
  professional international lawyers, 30–32
  public speakers, 32–33, 62–71
Straw, Jack (UK Foreign Secretary), 4, 58
structuralism, 26–27, 33–35, 39

Tampa affair, 46
Thailand, 95, 96
Thucydides, 9–10
trade unions
   Iraq War debates (2003), 43
      Australian Education Union, 43
   use of international law in public debate, 2, 18
   see also Australian Council of Trade Unions (ACTU); Australian Education Union (AEU); Durbridge, Rob (federal secretary of Australian Education Union)
types of narrative, 9–11

UN Charter. see Charter of the United Nations (UN Charter)
United Nations Security Council
   Iraq War
      Australian undermining of Security Council authority, 51–54
      interpretation of resolutions, 52–54, 84, 119
      UK undermining of Security Council authority, 4
      Resolution 678, 53, 66, 68
      Resolution 687, 53, 66, 68
      Resolution 1441, 4, 5, 51, 52, 53, 68
   tensions with People's Republic of China, 90
   tensions with USSR, 90
   Vietnam War, 91
   see also interpretation of UNSC resolutions
Universal Service League (USL), 137, 144, 150
   'legal quibble', 150–52
use of force
   pre-WWI international law, 148
   regulation of, 89–90
users of international law in public debate, 2, 24,
see also trade unions; religious groups politicians; religious groups; trade unions

Vietnam Action Campaign (VAC), 100
Vietnam War debates (1965–66), 16–17, 89
   alliance policy, 95–96
   anti-war groups, 104–6
   Bishops' pamphlet, 103
   conduct of US forces, 126–28
   conscription, 92, 96–97, 106
   context, 94–107
   genocide and crimes against humanity, 126
   Holt, Harold (Australian Prime Minister), 102–3
   infantry commitment, 112–16
   invitation from South Vietnam, 112, 116
   language, 91
   Menzies, Robert (Australian Prime Minister), 95–102
   moral and religious aspects of conflict, 110
   public reaction of Australia's military commitment, 98–102, 105–7
   right to self-determination, 110
   SEATO pamphlet, 103, 118–19, 120, 131
   Viet Nam Questions and Answers, 103, 121–22, 126, 131
vocabulary and grammar of international law. see language of international law

war on terror, 42, 181–82
Watt, Alan (Diplomat and former head of DEA), 118–19
weapons of mass destruction debate (Iraq), 43, 47, 48–50, 54, 56–57, 58–59, 71, 72, 80, 82, 84
White Australia, 17, 138, 159, 160, 166, 170–71
   No-Conscription Council of New South Wales, 153–57
   see also colonial nationalism
Whitlam, Gough (Leader of the Labor Party), 106, 107, 114–16, 120
World Tribunal on Iraq (WTI), 3, 7–9
   polyphonic nature, 10
World War I debates (1916), 17

2003 and 1965 debates compared, 134–36, 148–49, 170, 176–77
civil liberties debate, 157–60
conscription debate
    First World War I debates, 135–36
    opposition to, 144–46
    religious groups, 144–45
    Universal Service League, 137, 144

Vietnam War, 92, 96–97, 106
White Australia Anti-Conscription Manifesto, 153–57
language of class, 165
'equality-of-sacrifice' argument, 165–70, 172

Printed in the United States
by Baker & Taylor Publisher Services